Clothing

COMFORT AND FUNCTION

FIBER SCIENCE SERIES

Series Editor

L. REBENFELD

Textile Research Institute
Princeton, New Jersey

ESSENTIAL FIBER CHEMISTRY
by M. Carter

CLOTHING: COMFORT AND FUNCTION
by Lyman Fourt and Norman R. S. Hollies

STRUCTURE AND PROPERTIES OF TEXTILE FIBERS
by L. Rebenfeld

Other Volumes in Preparation

Clothing

COMFORT AND FUNCTION

LYMAN FOURT and NORMAN R. S. HOLLIES

GILLETTE RESEARCH INSTITUTE, INC.
HARRIS RESEARCH LABORATORIES DIVISION
ROCKVILLE, MARYLAND

MARCEL DEKKER, INC., New York   1970

MARCEL DEKKER, INC., 95 Madison Avenue, New York, New York 10016

Library of Congress Catalog Card Number 70-134699
ISBN 0-8247-1214-5

PRINTED IN THE UNITED STATES OF AMERICA

PREFACE

This book attempts to bring out a unified view of clothing and its function. In the preparation we have been aided by discussions with Dr. Stephen J. Kennedy and Mr. Louis I. Weiner of the U.S. Army Natick Laboratories and Dr. Ralph Goldman of the U. S. Army Research Institute of Environmental Medicine at Natick. Each of them has aided in supplying reference material and copies of reports. Earlier discussions with the late Dr. Alan Woodcock, and others of the Laboratories at Natick, and with members of the National Academy of Sciences, National Research Council QM Advisory Committees on Textiles and on Biophysics of Clothing, over an extended period, have been the foundation of this work. One of the authors, Lyman Fourt, owes a debt of memory and inspiration to Dr. E. F. DuBois, who was his host at the Russell Sage Laboratory at Cornell for trials of "Artificial Sweating Man No. 10 (or higher)." We also remember, gratefully, discussions with many workers, especially the late Mrs. Margaret Ionides Cochran and the late Dr., then Major, Paul Siple, in the OQMG in Tempo Building A in Washington. Both authors are indebted over the whole period of their work in clothing and textiles to Dr. Kennedy and Dr. Milton Harris.

We have drawn heavily on Government reports from studies at the U.S. Army Natick Laboratories, at the old Climatic Research Laboratory, Lawrence, Massachusetts, at Wright Field, at Fort Knox, at the Naval Medical Research Institute, the U.S. Army Institute for Environmental Medicine, and at Canadian and British installations and other Commonwealth agencies. Wherever possible, we have cited the published papers resulting from such Government reports; however, we have not always found corresponding papers. The AD numbers of U.S. Government reports are given when we could find them, to aid in securing copies, but the serious student of the older literature will probably need to go to one of the longer-established centers to consult reports in the library or in laboratory files. We have also attempted to cover the published literature of all countries, using searches made for us in "Textile Technology Digest" by the Institute of Textile Technology, Charlottesville, Virginia, and our own searches in Index Medicus and the Abstracts of the Textile Institute, as well as the files of this laboratory covering work since 1941.

In addition, we are indebted to the U.S. Army Natick Laboratories for support of part of this work.

We wish to thank many publishers of journals and books for permission to quote copyright material. New quotations are acknowledged at each point of use.

Lyman Fourt

Norman R. S. Hollies

FOREWORD

Since the publication of the classic volume "The Physiology of Heat Regulation and the Science of Clothing" by Newburgh, much new work has been done which has added considerably to basic knowledge of the comfort and function of clothing. The preparation of this monograph has been undertaken in order to bring together a summary of recent work on comfort, particularly work conducted or sponsored by the U.S. Army Natick Laboratories, as well as to review other reports and papers on comfort in clothing which have been published during this period. It is felt that further progress in this area will be greatly assisted by making available to all research people in this field a unified review of the present state of knowledge in the science of clothing.

Illustrative of new knowledge gained since the publication of Newburgh has been the development of relatively simple procedures for characterizing the ability of clothing systems to pass evaporative (latent) heat. The use of these new measures together with the conventional clothing insulation unit (Clo) provide a unique means for characterizing clothing comfort in terms which facilitate the prediction of comfort in simulated and actual field situations. For the development of these procedures we are especially indebted to the late Dr. Alan H. Woodcock of the U.S. Army Research Institute of Environmental Medicine.

The issuance of this monograph provides an opportunity to acknowledge important contributions to the science of clothing made by many individuals. Among the great number to whom we are indebted are: the late Dr. Paul A. Siple of the Army Research Office; Dr. Harwood S. Belding of the University of Pittsburgh, formerly Research Director of the Army Climatic Research Laboratories; Dr. Steven M. Horvath of the University of California, Chairman of the National Research Council Committee on Biophysics of Clothing; Dr. E. T. Renbourn formerly with the Army Personnel Research Establishment, Ministry of Defense in England; and Dr. Ralph F. Goldman and Mr. John R. Breckenridge of the Military Ergonomics Laboratory of the U.S. Army Research Institute of Environmental Medicine.

It is sincerely hoped that the publication of this monograph will stimulate additional investigations and studies which will contribute to the understanding of the basic requirements for making significant improvements in the comfort and performance of clothing for the benefit of soldiers and civilians alike.

STEPHEN J. KENNEDY
Director, Clothing and Personal
Life Support Equipment Laboratory
U.S. Army Natick Laboratories
Natick, Massachusetts

CONTENTS

Clothing

COMFORT AND FUNCTION

Chapter 1

FACTORS INVOLVED

IN THE STUDY OF CLOTHING

I. THE BALANCE NEEDED FOR COMFORT

DuBois [123] and Burton [75] have indicated the details of a familiar concept, that the well being of a man depends upon the balance between his energy production and the exchange of energy with the environment. This energy balance must be maintained within the limits of tolerance for heating or cooling of the body. This concept of balance between body and environment is modified by the intervention of clothing, which from one point of view is a part of the environment, but from another can be regarded as an extension and modification of the body itself. In cold and temperate climates, and in warm climates when clothing is worn, the temperature of the clothing, especially its inner layers, rises or falls with the underlying skin. Clothing is selected and adjusted by conscious intent to secure comfort or at least as much protection from adverse environment as possible.

Kennedy et al. [258] have discussed three interrelated elements in the soldier's clothing system: the material properties, the clothing design, and the mind and body of the man. That discussion leads to the thought that the clothing, the body and its physiology, and the environment are like the three legs which are necessary for the stability of a stool. Indeed, the unclothed man could not survive long by just his physiological resources in many of the environments of earth in which large populations flourish. The discussion will emphasize the point that clothing interacts with the physiology of the body, and that the functions of clothing are essential to man in all but exceptional and limited environments.

II. SCOPE OF PRESENT STUDY

Emphasis in this study is given to the interactions of clothing with the heat balance of the body, including both that part of heat exchange which is determined by temperature differences ("sensible" heat) and the large portion of the total energy exchange of the body which is governed by vapor pressure or water vapor concentration differences ("latent" heat). The discussion on heat and moisture relations in clothing (Chapter 4) will show the reasons for handling these two main types of energy exchange as a combined interaction system, not two separate or parallel ones. A given kilocalorie of energy may travel part of the way from skin to environment by evaporation at the skin, but the water vapor may condense in the clothing causing the energy to travel the rest of the way as "sensible" heat. Only when the skin is relatively cool, with minimal sweating, do purely thermal difference considerations govern. These cool conditions are among the most important conditions for which clothing is worn; hence, the historic emphasis on purely thermal properties of clothing. Fortunately, the capacity of the body's sweat glands to provide evaporative cooling is so large that man can cope, even in relative discomfort, with a wide range of warm environments and excess amounts of clothing.

Besides the interaction of clothing with the body, the protective function of the clothing against sun, wind, and rain, wet foliage, and immersion in water will be considered. Protection against fire, flame, industrial heat as in steel mills and glass works, and even the heat pulses of nuclear explosions will be included since these are all conditions in which clothing of not too extraordinary character can provide appreciable protection. We shall not deal with the heating or cooling of clothing by auxiliary power, although this is the means of greatly extending man's functional range. In fact, we concentrate the discussion upon clothing that a soldier or a sailor can wear and be mobile for his duties, upon clothing a civilian can wear to go about his daily life, or an explorer or hunter or farmer can take with him in the field.

Excluded from this discussion are all direct considerations of strength, durability, abrasion resistance, or wear-life of clothing—and almost all considerations of style and fashion. Styles of clothing of other peoples, times, and places, however, are instructive for suggestions of alternatives of design to accomplish function. Some examples of suggestions from the study of historic and local styles are brought out in Chapter 3, clothing considered as a structured assemblage of materials, and at other points. Almost completely disregarded are considerations of appearance, such as "well pressed" or "unwrinkled" or "smooth." Some of the factors underlying these enter indirectly in the consideration of surface characteristics of fabrics in Chapter 6 and in connection with the difficulties of obtaining similar fabrics from different fibers, which is one of the major problems in assessing differences between fibers (Chapter 7). This discussion of clothing is from the point of view of utility and function, not from the point of view of appearance or current or historic or ethnic style.

Other areas which are excluded comprise the whole question of skin irritation or dermatitis which (fortunately, not often) may be caused by fibers, dyes, or finishes, although frictional contact with the skin and drag of wet fabric against the skin are included. Excluded also is the question of germicidal or antimildew or antimoth finishes, or protection of the fiber against deterioration by ultraviolet light. The cleaning of fabrics and their sterilization to prevent transmission of disease is also largely excluded although some aspects of clothing sanitation and personal hygiene require attention in the course of tests in which particular garments need to be worn by different test subjects. Suitable methods depend upon the article and the questions being tested; the health aspects of tests by wearing the clothing are discussed in Chapter 5.

III. BROADER ASPECTS OF COMFORT

A. Quiet Comfort and Comfort while Working

Much of civilian life away from work, most office work, and much other work seeks the "quiet comfort" or "resting comfort" condition. Winslow et al. [458] in 1939 and Gagge et al. [168] in 1967 distinguish between "comfort" or "pleasantness" and "thermal neutrality," but find that both scales of subjective ratings center at nearly the same conditions. They have shown that the minimum of discomfort votes or the maximum of comfort ratings for unclothed subjects, and the point of neutrality for thermal sensation, come at air temperatures in the range of 28 to 30°C (82 to 86°F)

> . . . where there is an absence of temperature regulatory effort by sweating, vasoconstriction and vasodilation. The sense of discomfort increases more rapidly for ambient temperatures below 28°C than for those above 28°, while thermal sensation increases rapidly each side of a neutral ambient temperature. Discomfort, on the other hand, correlates best with lowering

average skin temperature towards cold and with increased
sweating towards hot environments . . . .

The conclusions . . . apply only to those steady-state and
transient conditions when one goes from the comfortable to
the uncomfortable, from the neutral to the cold, and from the
neutral to the warm, and when there is progressive discomfort
caused by either cold or heat. When the transients are re-
versed, or when one goes from the uncomfortable to the comfortable, from hot to neutral or cold, from cold to neutral or
warm, man's sensory response no longer follows the simple
pattern outlined above. [168]

The observations of Winslow et al. and Gagge et al. refer to men sitting
at rest, without clothing. Clothing shifts the range of comfort or pleasantness toward the cool side, as does exercise. Exercise in the heat produces
extensive sweating; light clothing will become wet (on the inner surface, if
water repellent) and evaporation will increase, tending to restore thermal
balance and avoid continual warming or storage of energy in the body. The
working man or the man playing tennis or handball is more comfortable
sweating—the criteria for the exercising subject are different from quiet
comfort and are still being investigated by physiologists and psychologists
[245, 407]. Gagge et al. [169] have determined a neutral point or comfort
zone in exercise extending up to 65% skin wettedness. The point for the
present is that the concept of quiet or resting comfort, with certain skin
temperatures, absence of body cooling or warming, absence of sweating,
and cyclic vasomotor regulation (especially in the arms and hands, legs
and feet, fingers and toes), without general vasodilation or constriction is
too limited for the general study of desirable clothing conditions for
military use or for men at physical work or active sport.
    Another advantage of a functional approach to comfort is that we can
deal with clothing for real life, not just for "polite" or "on display" life.
As Thorstein Veblen [432] noted, among the social functions of clothing
are "conspicuous display" or "conspicuous waste" and the unspoken
declaration that the wearer does not have to do physical work. Indeed,
much "Sunday best" would be uncomfortably warm or restraining if one
had to work in it; the first thing a motorist who gets a flat and has to
change a wheel does is to take off his coat, roll up his sleeves, and loosen
his tie. Few men wear their suit coats in their own homes, or even in their

offices except to go to see the boss. The quiet comfort ideal is closely tied to ceremonial rather than functional clothing, and while its requirements can be measured by the methods we discuss, it is by definition noncritical.

B. Noncritical or Critical Conditions

In addition, civilian life and to a large extent industrial work avoid the extremes of environment. Sport, exploration, and military duty seek to push man's effectiveness as far as possible into extremes of performance or difficult terrestrial environments or even into space. Fire-fighting presents some of the same extreme high temperature hazards as space ship re-entry or protection against thermal effects of nuclear weapons. To extend man's effectiveness against hostile environments is the general goal, so that our considerations will go beyond quiet comfort and beyond working comfort to the limits of effectiveness. Often one benefit of clothing such as protection against insects by insect-bite-proof clothing, or by screens and mosquito nets, has a cost, for example, decreased cooling by evaporation and convection; the net worth must be assessed in terms of overall effectiveness in the whole situation. Effective work can be done with considerably more tolerance of sweating than of malaria or infected leech bites.

The variability of ordinary clothing for a given place and weather reflects the wide latitude of noncritical conditions. The need to carry heavy, bulky clothing with one when it is cold emphasizes the need for the best possible design and choice of materials under critical winter or arctic conditions. Under critical conditions there may be no "comfort" in any sense: The merit of clothing variations can then be judged in terms of "tolerance time," which for experimental work should be set below "survival time" but should, ideally, be a significant indicator or comparison of survival possibilities. The very fact of discomfort may increase survival; it can act as a stimulus to behavioral adjustment, as by lighting a fire or constructing a shelter.

IV. NONTHERMAL COMPONENTS OF COMFORT

We all know that thermal balance is not the whole story, even for quiet comfort. The ego-assurance of being suitably dressed, neat, clean, and "respectable" even if poor in money, or of being in *haut mode, le denier cri,* or of conspicuous consumption, if more affluent, with all the range between is an important component of self-confidence and being at ease.

A soldier who is being married wears his Class A, or "dress," uniform so that all may see that this is clothing of which he is indeed proud.

Factors which are more physical include surface finish and surface character (Chapters 2, 6), flexibility and drape [99]; all the shear and buckling properties related to motion in the plane of the fabric [28-30, 110, 311], and to "tailorability" and ease of fit to the complexly curved surfaces of the body; all the seam characteristics and design features (darts, gores, orientation with respect to warp or bias) which *make* clothing; all the adjustments for size and peculiarities of the individual, to secure good fit.

Other physical properties also influence comfort. The electrostatic characteristics of fibers, and the mutual electric interaction of fabrics and the skin may play a larger role that we know [202, 255, 274]. The water holding capacity of fabrics is extremely important and the related properties of thickness and compressibility. The harshness or softness is primarily determined by fiber size and size range and distribution, secondarily by twist, and in a tertiary way by finishing processes such as spot welding or cementing by finishes added outside the fiber, or stiffening by polymers polymerized within the fiber. Other factors influencing comfort include softeners, "scroop" agents, or antislip finishes such as colloidal silica which increase fiber-to-fiber friction, mechanical finishing including singeing to remove surface fiber, shearing, pressing and setting, or napping or sanding or yarn bulking to increase freedom of surface fibers. Measurement of these features is discussed in part in Chapter 6; the bodily sensation or recognition is discussed in part (contact effects) in Chapter 2.

It seems likely that most of the reported differences in "comfort" between fibers, such as those between nylon and wool or nylon and cotton, which defy explanation in terms of thermal or moisture effects (although such explanations have been suggested as major factors by many) [25, 27, 298, 299], arise in fact from the nonthermal, contact sensation aspects of comfort. The nonhygroscopic character of many man-made fibers is often cited as the reason for reported deficiencies in comfort; this is part of the "accepted wisdom" of textiles, but there is little positive, direct evidence that lack of moisture adsorption is directly involved. Chapter 7 will give examples of different fibers or blends put through "identical" industrial textile processing, but with quite different yarns and fabrics emerging. Cassie [90, 91, 93, 94] has suggested that some unique relations of the elastic moduli of wool account for its unique position in the world's regard as a fiber for clothing: This may help, but advances in making and using man-made fibers suggest that the uniqueness of wool may be more historical than permanent. The fact is that optimum structures, finishes, and uses have to be found for each fiber and each blend with significant differences of composition; that the differences between optimum structures, or between the structures obtained by what were intended to be uniform processes, are easily recognizable. The body has great sensitivity to differences; it is easy to dislike some part of novel experiences and to describe this as discomfort. The multifactor studies of Mehrtens and McAllister [300], Hoffman [45, 215, 216], and Brand [63] are the most promising leads to untangle this web and increase understanding of customer reaction and acceptance of the different fibers. Further developments can be expected. Major producers of synthetic fibers have a great stake in this; the bulk of published work comes from the duPont Company [63, 215, 216, 274, 300] to whom all students of the relations of fiber properties to the aesthetic and subjective factors of consumer acceptance must be grateful. Additional information has appeared under the sponsorship of the U.S. Army Quartermaster [16] and the Textile Institute [418], as well as other papers from time to time.

V. QUANTITIES AND UNITS FOR DESCRIPTION OF THE TRIAD; ENVIRONMENT, CLOTHING, AND MAN*

While everyone is familiar with the general variations of the environment with weather, season, locality, and time of day, and is equally familiar with clothing for a wide variety of purposes, as well as the varied levels of our own activity, from rest to exhausting work, it will be useful in our discussion to become more analytical and to standardize the vocabulary, to assign more definite meanings to words which may be used in different ways in different contexts, and to begin or renew a familiarization with the quantitative units in which the elements of the triad are measured. We shall use metric units, including Centigrade temperature, the kilogram calorie (1000 g water 1°C), and the practical electrical unit of power or rate of doing work (W), as primary units, with English system or engineering equivalents in parentheses, i.e., 37°C (98°F) or 1 m (40 in.), usually, as here, with rounded values (recognizable by having only one or, at most, two significant figures) unless equal precision is needed in each system. The degree of accuracy possible even for averages in most clothing or physiological tests of practicable scale is seldom better than (or even up to)

---

*Since this discussion was prepared, a committee report [167] on "Proposed Standard Symbols for Thermal Physiology" has been published.

two significant figures, although differences, as of temperature, may need to be stated with this precision. Tables of four-figure and of rounded-off, two-figure, conversion factors are given in the Appendix.

One arbitrary nonmetric unit, the Clo unit of thermal insulation for either air layers or fabric, is used as a primary unit for discussion. This exception is made because of the wide use of Clo units for practical discussion of military clothing by U.S. and Canadian physiologists. As Burton [77] has reported, the Clo unit, because of its instant understandability, is an invaluable help in exposition to nonspecialists such as Generals, Admirals, Congressional or Parliamentary Committees. The Clo unit was intended [166] to be thought of in familiar terms, as the thermal insulation in a business suit as worn in Philadelphia, New Haven, or Toronto, or a soldier's wool uniform for cool weather, or the added insulation given by a substantial top coat. It must be noted that these familiar approximate equivalents are not the definition itself, which is precisely stated in physical terms as $0.18°C$ m² hr/kg cal and is not subject to revision by collection of statistics [78].

Since the Clo unit, although a physical unit, is arbitrary or practical, a corresponding metric physical unit, the thermal ohm (T-Ω) is also given. One T-Ω equals 6.45 Clo, or one Clo is 0.155 T-Ω. The T-Ω dimensions are $°C$ m²/W [317]; the T-Ω can be considered as the thermal resistance which requires a temperature difference, in $°C$, to cause heat energy to go through it at the rate of 1 W for each square meter. Like the Clo, the T-Ω is a unit of area resistivity, just as a "weight" of a fabric is conventionally weight per unit area. One can have Clo/unit thickness, or T-Ω/unit thickness, but unless this is specified, one understands "per square meter of fabric or clothing with thickness as-is." The T-Ω has direct advantages in specifying the amount of electric heating needed, and since any physical, physiological, or engineering unit of power or energy transfer rate can readily be converted to watts, the T-Ω has been chosen as the single metric unit for thermal insulation in this discussion. The T-Ω unit is an old suggestion, advocated before World War I in Smithsonian Institute publications. Randolph [338] employed the T-Ω in 1912. Nelms [317] used the same unit in 1964 apparently without reference to the older work (although referring to the Tog unit) and has designated the T-Ω as the "Res" unit. We believe T-Ω is more self-explanatory and favor precedent. The T-Ω is a tenfold greater thermal insulation than the unit, the "Tog," proposed by Peirce and Rees [330] as a practical unit for clothing. One Tog is 0.645 Clo and is approximately the insulation of light summer clothing. Thus, in effect, we are giving our clothing insulations in Clo units and in 10-Tog units.

The definitions related to environment, clothing, and man which follow are introductory; discussions in depth can be found in the detailed presentations and in the reference cited in the text. In the discussion of the means for specifying and quantitatively describing each of the elements of the triad (environment, clothing, man) which follows, we attempt to identify the general scope of pertinent measurements, but specify at this point only a minimum number of quantities, a minimum sufficient for much useful quantitative work, by no means exhausting the possibilities of measurement or description for any of the triad.

Typical methods for determining quantities are usually but not always mentioned; no detail of method and precautions to avoid errors is attempted; this will be done more thoroughly in Chapter 6 except where some details of procedure are required for an "operational definition." References are given to current general sources; details and precautions pertinent to work with human subjects, clothing, and fabrics are presented in Chapters 2, 5, and 6.

A. Quantities and Units for Description of the Environment

At least four quantities must be specified to give a general description of the environment: (1) temperature; (2) relative humidity or moisture content of the air; (3) air movement—rate, direction, and variability or turbulence; and (4) radiant heat from the sun or other sources of thermal radiation. There are still other factors, such as whether the men are indoors or outdoors or whether there is mist, rain, drip from trees, or wetting by contact with brush or foliage, snow, or spray from waves. These are special cases of the four main quantities to be discussed, and call for description in words to set the picture. One combined measurement of radiation and convection by some form of globe thermometer may also be useful.

These measurements are needed in following the flow of energy from the body to the environment or the reverse: They will cover energy transfer by each of the four main routes: conduction, convection, radiation, and evaporation. Table 1-1 gives an overall view of the four routes and the factors of environment, clothing, and the body which make up a minimum set for a complete energy balance.

For all the routes, considerations of individual body areas, each with its own characteristic covering and temperatures, will be required to get the best determination of heat balance, although useful estimates can be obtained by measurements of temperature at a limited number of points (Chapter 5).

Table 1-1. Routes of Energy Transfer and Factors Involved

Route	Environmental factors	Clothing or intermediate factors	Body factors
Conduction	Temperature difference	Thermal resistance of the material or air layers	Surface temperature
Convection	Air temperature Air movement	Wind penetration, including arrangement (neck, cuffs, etc.) to close out wind	Proportion exposed or clothed; surface temperature
Radiation	Temperature of each surface and of sky; solid angle taken up by each surface; emissivity of each surface	Emissivity, surface temperature	Proportion exposed or covered; surface temperatures
Evaporation	Vapor pressure in air or temperature and relative humidity	Resistance to vapor diffusion, or permeability index; area of clothing which is wet	Surface temperature and area which is wet

Temperature or difference of temperature: This is the most important and most familiar quantity. For air or walls, this means the "dry bulb" temperature; at the skin or in the clothing, if moisture is present, the measured temperature may be affected by evaporation, but is taken as the indication of an originally dry sensor, such as a thermocouple, left at the spot until it comes into steady state with local moisture and temperature relations. The sensor should itself produce minimum disturbance to the flow of heat or moisture.

Units for temperature or temperature difference: the Centigrade degree (for up-to-date precision one can say Celsius [409] but the distinction lies at the very limit of precision for clothing or physiology). Each degree C is 9/5 the span of a Fahrenheit degree ($1.8°F$). A few comparisons are tabulated, some rounded to nearest whole degrees.

	°C	°F	Notes
Boiling water (sea level)	100	212	Exactly
Normal (fever thermometer)	37	98.6	Exactly
Freezing water, melting ice	0	32	Exactly
"Zero weather"	–18	0	
Coincidence	–40	–40	Exactly
Absolute zero	–273 (Kelvin)	–460 (Rankine)	

The unusually arbitrary nature of the Fahrenheit scale outweighs the advantages of its familiarity to English speaking people, who are its only users.

Atmospheric Pressure: The unit of measure is atmospheres, referred to 760 mm Hg or 14.7 psi as unity. This is 29.92 in. of mercury at $0°C$, or 1013 millibars, units used in Weather Bureau reports. For water vapor pressure, we also use mm Hg, using the shorter term Torr (1 Torr = 1 mm Hg). This will be reduced to Standard Temperature and Pressure (STP), $0°C$ and whole pressure equal to one atmosphere at sea level, when required. Often "raw data" measurements or differences at prevailing pressure and temperature are sufficient for discussion, but the data for reduction to STP should be provided.

Vapor Pressure and Relative Humidity (R.H.): R.H. is vapor pressure at prevailing temperature, divided by saturation vapor pressure of water at the same temperature, as percent. Vapor pressure tends to vary much less through the day than relative humidity. To the extent that moisture content is constant in the air near the ground, the R.H. goes down or up as the temperature rises or falls. While R.H. is one of the most important environmental factors for the adsorbed water content of clothing and does influence rate of evaporation of sweat from the skin, sweat can still evaporate into air which has 100% R.H., if the temperature of the air is below skin temperature. Evaporation from the skin is proportional to the difference between saturation vapor pressure at skin temperature and vapor pressure in the air. Air at 100% R.H. at 25°C (77°F) is at only 66% R.H. when raised to 32°C (89.6°F), a representative skin temperature. The saturation vapor pressure at 32°C is 35.7 Torr; at 25°C, 23.7 Torr. Evaporation at the skin is indeed slower into 25°C air at 100% than into drier (50% R.H.) air at that temperature; the vapor pressure differences are 12.0 and 18.9 Torr, respectively; the drier air will evaporate water from the skin at one and one-half times the rate for the saturated air, other factors being equal.

In this discussion, the vapor pressure of water from sweat has been considered to be the same as that of pure water; it is, of course, slightly lower because there is a solute content as secreted, and this concentration increases as evaporation continues. However, the error is not large and can be neglected in comparison with the much larger other uncertainties. Its size can be estimated; the solute content as secreted varies with location on the body, the length of time sweating has been going on, and the rate of sweating. According to Kuno [268], a representative value is about 0.1 M NaCl; the depression of vapor pressure at skin temperature is, therefore, between 0.1 and 0.2 Torr. If the sweat on the surface of the skin becomes more concentrated by evaporation there is really no problem, because effective evaporative cooling is taking place.

Additional factors are that if clothing is worn, the air which is held near the skin, even though raised in temperature, becomes saturated at the new temperature and retards evaporation to the limit set by diffusion on the free side. Clothing impedes the convection of warm air away from the skin. Water vapor can escape at a lesser rate by diffusing through this retained air layer and through the clothing. In so doing it will encounter cooler outer layers of clothing as it diffuses away from the warmest spot, the skin. If the air nearest the skin is saturated, there will be condensation in the clothing which will warm the clothing itself, reducing the temperature gradient near the skin, and thus retarding the alternative direct thermal route for escape of energy. Thus, as a further unpleasant feature of high atmospheric humidity, the clothing becomes warmer and wetter by condensation of water vapor (a sort of within-clothing steam heat) as well as by any blotting or wicking of liquid sweat directly from the skin.

The R.H. may be calculated from dry and wet bulb temperatures, dry bulb temperature and dew point, or dry bulb and vapor pressure, or dry bulb and water content, if any of these paired measurements are available, or can be separately indicated by the lengthening or contraction of a polymeric fiber or film, including human hair or nylon fiber hygrometers [3]. A method based on moisture adsorption by swatches is discussed in Chapter 5 in connection with measuring the R.H. inside clothing.

Air Movement: Wind can be measured in linear units per unit time, as cm/sec, ft/min, or miles/hr. Wind outdoors is gusty, varying from zero speed to twice the average or more. Records of velocity and direction can be obtained, but an average equivalent rate is usually sufficient. The jet of air from a fan, or the current in a wind tunnel, is usually more steady, and more constant in direction but will contain much or little turbulence depending upon the precautions taken [327]. Description of the turbulence or smoothness by visualization with smoke (for greatest simplicity, as from a cigarette) is helpful. More elaborate methods using smoke are given in the book "Wind Tunnel Technique" by Pankhurst and Holder [327] which should be studied in any laboratory concerned with directed and controlled air movement. A more general description of turbulence can be given in terms of the Reynolds number,

$$N_R = DV/S = DV \rho\, g/\eta \qquad (1\text{-}1)$$

where D is characteristic diameter (such as a man's shoulder width) in cm; V is average velocity in cm/sec; S is kinematic viscosity in Stokes; ρ is density in g/cm^3 ($0.0012\ g/cm^3$ for dry air at $20°C$); η is viscosity in poise, dyn sec/cm^2 (180×10^{-6} poise for dry air at $20°C$); g is acceleration of gravity; and N_R is dimensionless and has similar numerical values for any system of consistent units such as is used above.

The values of N_R give one a general idea of the prevalence of laminar flow or of turbulence; if below 2000, the stream will almost certainly be laminar; local turbulence can be set up, but will be damped out; above N_R values of 3000 to 4000, general turbulence is almost certain except near a surface, where there will be laminar and transitional layers.

Two examples illustrate the use of N_R, setting up the equation as $V = 2000\eta D\rho g$. (a) If the characteristic dimension for a man is 40 cm, any air speed above 4×10^{-3} cm/sec, i.e., almost any air speed, will produce turbulence. (b) If the characteristic diameter of the holes in a fabric is 0.01 cm, and 1/6 of the area is holes, then air flows up to 3 cm/sec through the holes, or 1 ft^3/ft^2/min through the fabric will be laminar.

Schlieren optical methods are powerful tools for showing local flow and vapor or heat transfer conditions, as discussed in Chapter 6. It should be kept in mind that with "still" indoor air there will usually be large scale, slow moving convection cells, currents along the walls, and convection currents along surfaces of test subjects where there is heat or vapor transfer; while "calm" outdoor air is seldom below 225 cm/sec (5 miles/hr) in general motion. Whether tests are indoors or outdoors and the control of air movement, if indoors, or the general weather and wind (and sunshine-cloudiness) if outdoors, should always be noted in reporting test results. In some cases a thermal anemometer (hot wire or other heated element) can be used to measure equivalent steady air flow in terms of equivalent cooling power [327]. Measurements of wind speed and temperature have been combined by Siple [101, 386] into "Wind Chill" values useful to describe some aspects of cold environments, within the limitations discussed by Burton [87].

Sun or Thermal Radiation: Outdoor tests need to note the time of year, the time of day, and the latitude to specify the solar radiation—also the degree of overcast or haze, and the character of the terrain, snow covered, marshy, green, shady, or bare. These characteristics can be used to estimate albedo, the general diffuse reflectivity in the visible region or the corresponding infrared (9 μ peak, long wave) albedo.

Indoor tests need to specify the nature of surrounding surfaces, whether nonemissive (metallic) or freely emitting infrared (most others). The effective cleanness of metal surfaces needs to be assured. Measurements with a radiometer [197, 410] can assure this; more radiation will be received at any given wall temperature from nonmetallic or contaminated metallic surfaces than from bright, clean aluminum surfaces. Aluminum paints or aluminum ("silver") textile finishes are an intermediate case. The emissivity should be checked, for a 50-100°C source, and checked during the course of the tests, since wear and contamination are very likely to produce changes.

The basic measurements needed for thermal radiation effects are the temperatures of the clothing surface or of the exposed skin [410]; the temperatures of the surroundings, including for outdoors the radiation-equivalent temperature of the sky or clouds; for each surface, the fractional emission, or the fractional reflectivity (either is unity minus the other in accord with Kirchhoff's law) [199, 437]. A broad wavelength band such as that of the radiation from a surface at 50°C or higher, to say 100°, is appropriate, unless one is dealing with very high temperature sources, or with sunlight, for which the measure is the albedo, the percent diffuse reflectance for white light.

Globe Thermometer for Combined Temperature, Radiation, and Convection: Use of the blackened, 15 cm (or 15.2 cm = 6 in.) diameter globe thermometer (Vernon) [470] as an indicator of combined radiation and convection conditions has been advocated for environmental studies. The original globe thermometer is an arbitrarily chosen member of a family of instruments which give integrated indications of changes in

radiation and wind effect. Correlation can be shown to the integrated response of the human subject to sun (or in general, thermal radiation) and
to wind. Such an instrument used in the course of outdoor experiments
will help in comparisons from day to day, but is less needed for indoor
tests where conditions can be controlled and specified. Equivalence (for
the instrument, not necessarily for man) of different combinations of wall
and air can be verified. Various alternatives and modifications, such as
Woodcock's proposal to use a light gray painted globe, 50% reflective in
the visible range [470], have been made to improve the correlation with
sunshine. Whatever type of globe thermometer or integrator is used, it
should be clearly described or referenced to a good description.

B. Quantities and Units to Describe Clothing

As will be developed further, clothing can be described either in terms
of what it does (Chapter 2) or of its structure and composition (Chapter 3). The most general functional properties are (1) thermal insulation
(resistance to passage of heat); (2) resistance to evaporation; and (3) resistance to penetration by wind, and the most general structural properties
are: (1) thickness from skin to exterior; (2) weight; and (3) surface area.
Other more specific structural properties are defined at point of use in
specific discussions.

Thermal insulation: The Clo unit has already been discussed (Sect. 5)
as an exception to the primary use of the metric system. It is worth
emphasizing three points: (1) that the Clo or the T-Ω is a resistance unit,
so that the total thermal insulation of a clothing assembly can be added up,
layer by layer; (2) that every layer must be accounted for, including air
layers between fabric layers and the film layer between the outer surface,
either skin or cloth, and the general environment; and (3) that the heat
flow is governed by an Ohm's law type of relation, in which flow is proportional to potential (temperature difference) divided by resistance. The
resistance is a direct property of the clothing system and is relatively independent of the boundary conditions. While flow rates can be used and
are useful for adding up flow through parallel routes of different resistance
(and often different boundary conditions), the flow depends on the
boundary conditions. While both Clo values and vapor resistance values
have temperature coefficients, these are small compared with the direct
effect of temperature as a boundary condition, or its effect on saturation
vapor pressure. Vapor resistance is usually determined near 21°C and so
presents no problems in comparisons. However, temperature as high as

100°C may be used on the hot side in tests of fabric insulation, or as low as –40°C outside in tests on men. The chief (2/3 or larger) part of the thermal transmission is through air, for which the thermal conductivity changes 0.3% per °C [270]. The temperature coefficient for fiber materials themselves is not established, but that for similar organic compounds is less than for air. Calculating for air alone, Table 1-2 shows some apparent or relative Clo values for material which has 1 Clo at the defining temperature range. In general, the temperature coefficient causes a favorable or conservative error when the clothing is to be used for protection against the cold and underestimates the thermal burden in conditions warmer than those of the test. In the ranges shown, the error due to temperature coefficient is not larger than 10%.

Table 1-2. Variation of Insulation with Temperature

°C Hot side	°C Cold side	°C Average	Difference of average °C	Apparent Clo value[a]
100	20	60	+33	0.90
50	20	36	+ 8	0.98
33	21	27	0	1.00
32	0	16	–11	1.03
28	–18(0°F)	5	–22	1.07
28	–40	–6	–33	1.10

[a]Apparent Clo value of material which has 1 Clo thermal resistance under the defining conditions.

Three types of measurements of Clo are possible and should be distinguished from each other in discussion:

(1) *Thermal resistance, from thickness.*

$$Clo = 1.6 \times \text{(thickness in cm)}$$
$$= 4 \times \text{(thickness in in.)}$$

Include air spaces up to 5 mm or 0.2 in. Maximum insulation for some materials may approach 2 Clo/cm but the factors above are representative of good clothing.

(2) *Thermal resistance, physically measured.* Using a thermal manikin or a portion of such a model dressed in properly fitted clothing maintained at a constant temperature difference between manikin surface and ambient:

$$\text{Clo} = 0.155°\text{C m}^2/\text{W}$$
$$= 0.18°\text{C m}^2 \text{ hr/kg cal}$$

Fabric layer resistance can be measured physically by flat plate methods as discussed in Chapter 6. Clothing thermal resistance will differ from the sum of fabric resistance, by virtue of air space and thickness differences, and curvature. The fit of the clothing must be normal in looseness or tightness and in adjustment and manner of wear to permit comparison with other methods.

(3) *Thermal resistance, physiologically measured.*

$$\text{Clo} = 0.18°\text{C m}^2 \text{ hr/kg cal}$$

when the heat losses by insensible perspiration and respiration are accounted for, and the kg cal/m² hr metabolism is determined by oxygen consumption, with allowance for external work and storage by body heating or cooling. Physiological measurements will agree more closely with physical measurements, the less the body cooling or heating, and the better the information on diet, which is involved in energy estimate from O_2 use. Body movement and sweating should be minimized for direct comparison with physical measurement, but can be varied for their own interest. Physiological measurements are the only means of estimating the effect of bodily motion, of sweating, and of clothing arrangement by the wearer. Mechanical models are not developed which can simulate body movement, while arbitrary wetting can give only limit conditions, not the sequence for clothing as it becomes wet by sweat. Details and references are given in Chapter 5.

Resistance to Evaporation: Simple and reliable methods for this measurement in terms of equivalent thickness of still air have been developed [151, 422, 444] and are described critically in Chapter 6. Methods for determining i_m, the permeability index [462] are also discussed in Chapters 2 and 6. The permeability index, i_m, is a dimensionless ratio ranging from zero, no permeability to water vapor, to unity. Since i_m is defined [462] as

$$i_m = \frac{\text{ratio} \dfrac{\text{resistance of material to passage of heat}}{\text{resistance of material to passage of vapor}}}{\text{ratio} \dfrac{\text{resistance of air to passage of heat}}{\text{resistance of air to passage of vapor}}}$$

knowledge of thermal resistance of material, or of vapor resistance, each capable of being independently determined, gives one method to determine i_m; such results can be compared with direct determination of i_m as a check on correct understanding and description of a clothing system, as discussed further in Chapter 2.

Resistance to Wind Penetration: No satisfactory generally accepted method has been developed, although several starts have been made [322, 324, 323] as discussed in Chapters 2 and 5. It is usual to rank individual fabrics or assemblies from greatest wind resistance to least in the order of air permeability from least air permeability to greatest. Methods are discussed in Chapter 6. This gives only a rank order. The interaction of fabric thickness with wind penetration is largely unknown.

Thickness of Clothing (as distinguished from fabric thickness): For fabric, it can be measured under specified pressure or tension as outlined in Chapter 6, but for clothing it should be measured as worn, on a properly fitted man or manikin. While manikins have been made representing medians and known points in the ranges of human size, the quickest economical route to a laboratory manikin of proper size may be to make a "dress form" of a representative individual. The thickness to be measured is the radial thickness from outside the skin; this can be obtained (the method appears to have originated with Cochran and Siple) [104, 187, 278] by a tape measure applied without squeezing the clothing, and applied at the same level as each layer is removed. The measured periphery is considered as a circle, to calculate the radius.

Clothing Weight (obtained after adjustment of moisture content, or as-is, depending on the interest): To prevent moisture changes, weighings can be made in closed containers (tin cans with tight lids or plastic sacks). For greater precision, changes in barometric pressure between days or during the day can be noted to separate changes in buoyancy of air from changes in moisture content. This correction is, however, small compared with variations in amount of sweat secreted or evaporated in different tests. For clothing of average density 1.3 (wool), the correction for each kilogram of clothing is only 0.0013 g for each Torr difference of barometric pressure.

Clothing Surface Area: An approximation for the total clothing area is to take the underlying "DuBois" body area from height and weight [122, 383]. Herrington suggests adding 0.13 m² to DuBois body area for each kilogram of clothing [209] and outlines a more elaborate procedure based on lateral silhouette and its correlation with body area. The chief merit of this suggestion is simplicity in a matter which is certainly not precise in practice because the area varies with lying, sitting, standing, and any major change of stance.

C. Quantities and Units for Description of Man and His Activity or Heat Production

Individual men differ widely in weight, in height, and in bodily build as has been analyzed by Sheldon [385] and in muscular development and degree of physical fitness or training. Some measures of the effect of physical training [402] indicate gains such as 60% in maximum rate of work on a treadmill after training. Hence it is important to arrange a series of tests to balance out training and learning effects.

Fortunately, the number of the "measures of man" which are necessary for the study of clothing is relatively small. The metabolic rate for a given period is primary; it is the measure of heat production, the "money" in which the cost of all activity can be measured. The DuBois surface area, the temperature of each main element of body surface (or selected surface points, as discussed by Teichner [415]), and the average skin temperature are required. The interior temperature, measured in the rectum, is weighted 2 to 1 against average surface temperature in determining body cooling or warming [209]. The signals to the central nervous system for physiological changes have been shown by Benzinger [40, 41] to be indicated by temperatures measured on the ear drum. Whole body weight and its changes are essential to follow evaporation. Vasoconstriction or the relaxation and dilation of surface blood vessels are important indications of bodily state, correlated with surface temperature. The steady or cyclic state of vasodilation and blood flow to the arms, hands, and fingers, indicated by a continuous or frequent check of finger temperature, is also instructive, especially in and near the zone of quiet comfort [116]. Heart rate is also a quickly responsive indicator of stress upon the body. Many other physical, physiological, or biochemical measurements can be and have been made, which contribute to clothing studies but a good start can be made with just seven: (1) metabolism; (2) evaporation; (3) surface temperature; (4) rectal temperatures to obtain the body heat content, whether increasing or decreasing; (5) tympanic membrane temperature, for correlation with central nervous system conditions; (6) DuBois surface area of the subject; and (7) heart rate.

Various modes of combining these measurements, or of utilizing the rate of change in such measurements, or the crossing of critical levels, have been much discussed by physiologists and students of clothing and students of exercise or stress, without complete satisfaction. A discussion with respect to testing of clothing will be undertaken in Section 7.

Activity or Metabolism: Physiologists usually use the kg cal/m² hr. Fifty of these correspond approximately to the metabolism of a man under quiet but alert conditions (sitting, in Table 1-3) and have been termed 1 Met [166]. Watts for the whole man are roughly twice the metabolism in kg cal/m² hr, as will be discussed further in the section on "Reference Man." Various activities are described by Table 1-3 (the basic data are from Forbes in Newburgh's book [143]). It should be noted that variation from individual to individual is large, especially for the heavier grades of work, even with training, although training does lower the metabolic cost. Forbes indicates variations of ±10% between individuals, and for a given individual with his state of training.

A more extensive set of data for activities and progression is given by Spector [401] from which selections are given in Table 1-4 in terms of the whole man. Goldman and Iampietro [180] have shown that added load and body weight are equivalent in energy cost for progression, within wide ranges. Forbes [143] states that in addition to the effect of its weight, clothing adds to the metabolic cost of walking or running, by less than 5% for street clothing, and by approximately 10% for arctic clothing. The cost varies greatly with fit.

Evaporation: This is determined by weight change. Details are discussed in Chapter 2 and in Chapter 5, Sect. III. A. 3. Sweat secreted is also determined by weighing; not all may be evaporated, so the clothes and the man must each be weighed. Weight is measured in the usual way, in kg. Scales sensitive to at least 5 g are desirable for evaporative loss studies, but the total, on the order of 70 kg, presents problems in rapid and precise weighing. Precision on weight change is more valuable than absolute values of total weight. Water added by drinking, or lost as urine, must be accounted for in following weight change, and the temperature noted, for complete heat balance.

Surface Temperature: The average of temperature measurements in each of a number of areas is weighed in terms of the fraction of body area represented. As many as 20 separate measurements have been averaged [200], while correlations and comparisons with a 10-point system have indicated that for many purposes, one measurement, on the medial thigh, can be representative of the average of the whole [415].

Table 1-3. General Levels of Activity[a]

Condition or activity (young man, average rather than peak training)	Total metabolism (including basal)	
	$\frac{\text{kg cal}}{\text{m}^2 \text{ hr}}$	Watts for "Reference Man"
Sleeping, post digestive	36	72
Lying quietly, post digestive	40	80
(Average for day, including digestion)		
Sitting	50	100
Standing	60	120
Strolling, 1½ mph	90	180
Level walk, 3 mph	155	310
Level run, 10 mph	500	1000
Sprint (cannot be sustained for an hour, only for a few seconds)	(2000)	(4000)
Light activity	60-100	120-200
Work, light	100-180	200-360
Work, moderate	180-280	360-560
Work, heavy	280-380	560-760
Work, exhausting	over 380	over 760

[a]Reprinted from Ref. [143] by courtesy of W. B. Saunders, Co.

In the cold, measurements of toe and finger temperatures are useful checks on reported sensations and precautions against freezing.

Rectal Temperature: Measured as an indicator of core temperature, rectal temperature changes are combined with changes in surface temperature to give an estimate of body cooling (loss of heat) or warming. A curved probe bearing a thermocouple or thermistor, inserted 8 cm, is recommended [472]. The fact that rectal temperature depends on the technique of measurement, and is only a relatively convenient indicator of deep body temperature, not a measure of average deep body temperature, is emphasized by Burton [88]. A weighing of 1 for average surface temperature, and 2 for core temperature has been used [209].

Area: The whole surface of a man is not effective for dissipating energy by radiation. Opposing surfaces block each other under the arms or between the legs. The total area, often called the DuBois area, is measured by

Table 1-4. Energy Cost of Various Activities[a]

	kg cal/hr	Increase over basal, %
Driving car	168	139
Driving motorcycle	204	191
Shoveling, 8 kg load, 1 m lift, 12/min	450	541
Coal mining, loading	426	507
Walking, horizontal, 9 kg clothing and apparatus,		
Hard surface road, 5.5 km/hr	330	370
Grass covered road, 5.6 km/hr	390	456
Plowed field, 5.3 km/hr	480	584
Walking, hard snow, 6 km/hr	714	917
Walking, hard snow, 9.1 km/hr	966	1277
Walking, soft snow, 20 kg load, 2.9 km/hr	1242	1669
Walking, snow shoes, soft snow, 4 km/hr	828	1080
Walking, 20 kg load, 1.6 km/hr	210	199
Walking, 20 kg load, 3.2 km/hr	270	285
Walking, 20 kg load, 4.8 km/hr	360	413
Walking, 20 kg load, 6.4 km/hr	540	669
Running, 20 kg load, 8.0 km/hr	846	1105

[a]Data are from Tables 315 and 316 of Spector [401], reprinted by courtesy of W. B. Saunders, Co.

height-weight formulas or by more elaborate means. The metric unit, m^2, is used. Precision much greater than 0.1 m^2 is not usual, although areas may be stated to two decimal places. The area for radiation depends on the posture, from 0.50 (curled up) to 0.80 times the whole area. A good figure for sitting, or for the "mummy" position, is 0.7-0.75 [198, 383].

VI. ENVIRONMENTAL RANGES AND CORRESPONDING CLOTHING

A great deal of systematic work on clothing and climate was accomplished in the U.S. and Canada during World War II to know and be prepared for the clothing needs in locations and climates anywhere in the world. This has continued with efforts at service unification (one type of uniform and equipment for U.S. Army, Navy, Marines, and Air Force, instead of four, wherever possible), simplified logistics, and a fit-together, global uniform concept with basic units for the temperate zone to which items could be added for the colder, or subtracted for the warmer, zones, so that tropical gear could be close to U.S. summer equipment, and polar gear added to the U.S. winter uniform. The older work of World War II is summarized in the book edited by Newburgh [320].

In England, systematic and organized study of climate-clothing-man relations has combined new experimental work with review and re-interpretation of the knowledge derived from a new look at three centuries of imperial and colonial experience. E. T. Renbourn of the Clothing, Equipment and Physiological Research Establishment, Farnsborough, has presented fascinating historical studies, illustrated by contemporary photographs or drawings (some from the Indian Mutiny of 1857) [347] and field reports for all continents [344-346, 348, 350].

Commonwealth and Tripartite (and NATO) conferences on "Clothing and General Stores," in which the U.S. Quartermaster group have also participated as observers or contributors, have been held periodically, involving such groups as the Clothing, Equipment and Physiological Research Establishment (U.K.), the Canadian Defense Research Laboratories, and their opposite numbers in Australia, Pakistan, India, and other Commonwealth countries.

Work in this same tradition continues: for example, studies of acclimatization from cool and humid in England to hot and arid in Aden [128] and in Israel [370]; for mountain conditions in Pakistan [6], and for polar conditions by many nations in Antarctica. Good general discussions of Antarctic conditions are presented by Siple [389] and by Henry [207], and technical reports can be located through Aerospace Medicine and Biology, NASA SP 7011, which covers both the report and general literature. In Russia, Canada, and Alaska, large populations—compared with as recently as 1940—are coming to live in the Arctic on permafrost in cities, not isolated settlements [135]. The Arctic Institute and other groups under private, national, or United Nations auspices have nurtured advances in living in every type of environment. United Nations organizations and national efforts are stimulating development and better health through adaptation to environment in the developing countries. In general, these agencies are concerned only in small part with clothing, but are excellent sources of climatic and geographic and ethnological and ecological information.

The most thorough and detailed studies of clothing requirements for the world's environments have probably been those of the U.S. Army

Quartermaster Corps. These have resulted in a "World Guide for Field Clothing Requirements" [403], and more detailed studies of special regions such as "Clothing Almanacs" and "Climatic Handbooks." The Clothing Almanacs give clothing requirements month by month with regard for altitude and other factors, based on detailed study of the climate and weather. Examples are: the United States [12] or South East Asia [13]. The Climatic Handbooks describe the weather and terrain of accessible western hemisphere localities which can be used as examples of important climatic types and terrains. Selected examples are: Yuma, Arizona (desert) [249]; Fort Sherman and Fort Gulick, Canal Zone (wet tropics) [448]; Fort Greely, Alaska and Fort Churchill, Canada (dry cold) [201]; and for temperate conditions, Fort Lee, Virginia [360], an important Quartermaster Center for field and engineering testing of clothing and home of the famous "Combat Course" for wear-testing of clothing resistance to abrasion in use. It is interesting to compare the depth of detail now available to the information available in World War II when heavy dependence was wisely put on "men who had been there" and on such records as could be hastily assembled. The information had become fairly well systematized by the time Wulsin, Siple, and others contributed summaries to Newburgh's compilation [320].

The Weather Bureau has compiled and published summaries of long term records for particular localities: for example, the Climatic Handbook for Washington, D.C. [477], which was published in 1949, covered 75 years. Such compilations available in the files of the Weather Bureau permit finding the probable frequency of particular weather combinations, and how many days such combinations can be expected to persist.

These studies can be summarized in a relatively small number of climatic combinations as set out in Table 1-5, which gives the temperature ranges used in the Quartermaster Clothing Almanacs [12]. Table 1-6 is a summary of a discussion by Siple [387] based on the layer principle. Table 1-7 illustrates the climatic zone concepts by means of some specific locations. All of these groupings are based on four directions of departure from temperate: hot-dry, hot-wet, cold-wet, and cold-dry.

It is important to realize that extremes of temperature and humidity, although often considered singly, do not often come simultaneously. Thus, high temperatures (above 35°C, 95°F) are not associated with the highest relative humidities, but usually with rather dry conditions. High relative humidities usually are registered from midnight till after the sun is up—the period of winter fog—because that is the period when the air near the ground is cool, and with rather moderate daytime temperatures,

Table 1-5. Classification of U.S. Climatic Zones[a]

| | Average temperature of | | | |
| | Coldest month | | Warmest month | |
	°F	°C	°F	°C
I Tropical	Above 68	20	Above 68	20
II Semitropical	50-68	10-20	Above 68	20
III Warm Temperate	32-50	0-10	Above 68	20
IV Mild Temperate	Below 32	0-10	50-68	10-20
V Cool Temperate	Below 32	0	Above 68	20
VI Cold Temperate	14-32	–10-0	50-68	10-20
VII Arctic	Below 14	–10	Below 68	20

[a]Data from Clothing Almanac 21: United States [12].

27-32°F. Even the most humid jungles are seldom high in dry bulb temperature. Tables of climatic extremes have been compiled [390].

A useful set of references covering a wider range includes travel guides and especially such publications as "Exploration Medicine" by Edholm and Bacharach [127]. In general, a tactical commander might prefer to have "country boys" from parts of the country which have cold winters, to any other recruits, but the often nonverbalized skills of outdoor living can be put in words and planned practical training exercises so that they can be taught to and learned by all who have the desire or need to be outdoorsmen. Special books on microclimate, such as Geiger's "The Climate near the Ground" [172] are helpful for understanding the environmental side. Older books, such as those of Huntington on "Civilization and Climate" [243], contain more of New England self-satisfaction and self-congratulation than factual data acceptable to a United Nations Committee, but such books do begin the exploration of the question of the relation of the "Energy of Nations" [295], or national character, to the environment, and (rather incidentally) to the clothing and housing suitable for the various localities and their seasons. The whole question of permanent tropical domicile of families of temperate zone— mainly European—origin has been discussed by D. H. K. Lee [276]. It is natural for each of us to bring family, tribal, or national feelings to the problem of man and locality; the fact probably is that wherever "natives" can live,

Table 1-6. Classification of Climates[a]

By clothing required for warmth[b]	By temperature and moisture	By regions and seasons
Less than a complete layer	Hot, humid	Tropical and sub-tropical; temperate, summer; deep mines
One layer (by day), more may be needed at night	Hot, dry	Desert; temperate, summer
Two layers		Temperate, fall and spring, mild winter
Three layers	Cold, dry Cold, wet	Temperate, cold winter; oceanic influence, fog, sun often clouded over
Four layers	Cold, dry	Subpolar, winter; polar, summer
Activity needed for balance with any practicable clothing; shelter needed for rest	Extreme cold dry	Polar winter

[a]Adapted from a discussion by Siple [387].

[b]There is a gradation from light to heavy in each layer so that there is overlap.

anyone can live, and that people with developed technology and a wide and deep educational base can live better—even in areas (and climates) presently not considered habitable.

VII. PHYSIOLOGICAL INDICATORS OF COMFORT OR STRESS

The search for objective indications of comfort or safe endurance has been based on the general concept of heat balance; that one should be comfortable in a thermally neutral condition, neither gaining nor losing body heat

Table 1-7. Global Areas for Field Clothing Requirements[a]

Area	Description	Example
1	Warm or hot all year	Panama Canal Zone
2	Warm or hot summers, mild winters	Gulf Coast of U.S.
3	Mild all year	Coastal Southern California to 35°N; e.g., Los Angeles, Pasadena
4	Warm to hot summers, cool to cold winters	Arkansas, Tennessee, southern Kentucky
5	Mild to warm summers, cool to cold winters	California coast and central valley north of 35°N; e.g., San Francisco, Sacramento
6	Mild or warm summers, cold winters	Utah through Pennsylvania; Connecticut, Massachusetts, Rhode Island
7	Mild summers, cool to cold winters	Vancouver, Nova Scotia, Newfoundland
8	Mild or warm summers, very cold winters	North Dakota, northern New York, Vermont, New Hampshire, Maine
9	Cool summers, extremely cold winters	Interior Alaska, Yukon, Hudson Bay, Labrador, Greenland, Antarctica

[a]Based on mean daily minimum temperatures and daily and monthly extremes of temperature; also on precipitation and duration of seasons. From "World Guide to Field Clothing Requirements," by Sprague and Ross [403].

content, and with "normal" skin temperature in all areas. As shown in Chapter 7, this approach has proven rather incapable, in practice, of differentiating between various types of fibers made into similar garments. Either there really is no difference in comfort between nylon and cotton, where much "accepted opinion" reports a difference (albeit usually without any quantitative objective evidence), or the right quantities to measure have not been found. Reliable subjective comparisons can be obtained as will be explained in Chapter 7. To some extent, the cyclic change of circulation to the extremities is an indication of temperature regulation in the neutral zone by vasomotor control mechanisms. Flow in the finger is an indicator of such vasomotor control [74]. The temperature of other areas of the body does not yield much information on the boundaries of the comfort state.

While not sensitive indicators of comfort, heart rate, sweating rate, and deep body and skin temperatures do give useful information about stress by either heat or cold. Safety limits in each direction should be observed, as discussed in Chapter 5, so that tests can be terminated without risk to the subjects. There have been numerous proposals for combining indications from temperatures at selected locations, sweat rates, heart rates, variations of temperature with environment or work, and amount of sweat secreted in certain periods, as well as blood lactic acid content or catecholamine content, in indices of stress. These factors are also used together to indicate adaptation or acclimatization to heat or cold. No one of these seems to have wide acceptance; each has value in special circumstances, and one or more, hopefully appropriate to the test situation, should be observed and recorded. Much effort has gone into telemetry so that observations can be taken on men in the open, but observation at intervals (15-30 min) is still a useful procedure.

VIII. FACTORS FOR MENTAL ARITHMETIC
IN CLOTHING PROBLEMS

It is a great advantage of the "Clo" and "Met" units [166] for clothing insulation and metabolic activity that they lend themselves to mental arithmetic in terms readily understood by persons not technically trained in either physics or physiology. This convenience can be extended by using some additional approximations. To emphasize that these constants are not for any "standard" agreed upon by some standardizing group, we describe the man characterized by this group of mental arithmetic values as "Reference Man" and the properties of his clothing as "Reference Clothing." These are not properties of average man (or some specified group such as U.S. soldiers), but are representative of the central group in that they lie well toward the center of the normal range. The convenience as a representative case for mental arithmetic is the chief merit of these figures. For actual men, the range of variation should be divided into groups which can be fitted with similar clothing by their tailoring measurements and body type as has been discussed for winter or arctic clothing by Winston and Kennedy [460].

A. Reference Man: 1 Met = 100 W, Area = 1.7 m²

The Met unit is on a square meter basis. The energy production of a whole man, at the rate of 1 Met, is his area in square meters $\times$ 50 kg cal/m² hr or times 50 $\times$ 1.16 W/m². For the convenience value, 1 Met corresponds to 100 W; this calls for a man of area 1.72 m², or, rounded, 1.7 m² (area cannot readily be estimated to greater precision than ±0.05 m²).

It is frequently stated that an average young American male, i.e., a typical soldier, has 1.8 m² effective area, so that if we take 1 Met = 100 W for "Reference Man" we would have a small American, or perhaps a large Oriental or city dweller in either Europe or America, according to Spector's compilation on national and ethnic groups [400]. Much physiological data is in kg cal/m² hr; this can be approximated into watts for "Reference Man" by multiplying by 2.

B. Dry and Evaporative Heat Loss, Cool Side

Some of the energy loss from a man, even in the cold, is by insensible perspiration through the skin, and by evaporation of water in the respiratory passages, and by warming the air which is breathed. Burton calculated [81] that only 2.35 kg cal/hr were required to warm air from 20 to 37°C, for the respiration of a resting man. This and the much larger evaporation, both respiratory and through the skin, can be lumped together at 25% of the metabolism, for approximation in cool temperatures, with no frank sweating. With definite sweat secretion, as well as for exercise in the cold while wearing clothing, special account should be taken of evaporation, by means of weight change.

C. Skin Temperature; Evaporation Relations

The range of skin temperatures during active sweating is narrow; one temperature can be used for mental arithmetic on evaporative cooling. Burton [79] has advocated using 0.6 kg cal as the cooling produced by evaporating 1 g of water at skin temperature, instead of 0.58 as listed in "Steam Tables" for this range. The larger value is more accurate because it includes the energy absorbed in mixing with the general atmosphere. Hardy [197] gives a complete discussion, but this point has often not been recognized. It is in fact small compared with other uncertainties in physiological measurements, especially the uncertainty regarding the efficiency of evaporation in the clothing for cooling the body. The value 0.6 kg cal/g is convenient for mental arithmetic, assuming 100% efficiency. At 34°C, the saturation vapor pressure is 40 Torr, another convenient value.

Burton [79] indicates a useful approximation: to take the evaporative cooling (kg cal/m² hr) as 5 times the vapor pressure difference in Torr (mm Hg) from skin to general environment divided by the resistance from skin to air, measured in centimeters of still air. In addition, Burton points out that while 1 Clo is the thermal insulation of an ordinary business suit, 1 cm of air is, quite approximately, its vapor resistance, so that for some purposes Clo values and centimeter air values can be equated.

For many purposes, the evaporative resistance in centimeters of still air may be taken as twice the clothing thickness (2 to 4 times fabric thickness). For closer equality of thermal and vapor resistance, the factor would of course be 1.6.

D. Reference Clothing: 1 cm = 1.6 Clo

The tape-measure method of determining clothing thickness, and of estimating Clo value by the increase of thickness using a factor of 1.6 cm/Clo or 4 Clo/in., has been mentioned. The originators of this method counted air spaces up to 0.2 in. (5 mm) and converted by the rule: 1 in. = 4 Clo. Burton has found, considering the initial slope of the line of Clo units against thickness of air space, that the practical maximum insulation of air space layers in tests with rather simple equipment appeared to be 4.7 Clo/in. [84]. Monego et al. [307] have reported measurements on polyurethane foam layers that extend to 5.20 Clo/in., so the possibility of insulation values in the range 5 Clo/in. is real for flat sheets of material. However, 5 Clo/in. or 2 Clo/cm, convenient as it would be for the metric system, is probably not possible in real clothing because of the curvature effects and the convection in vertical air spaces, as discussed by Burton. Therefore, the conservative estimate, 4 Clo/in. or 1.6 Clo/cm, should be used. This is equivalent to 0.25 T-Ω/cm or 0.62 T-Ω/in., to two significant figures.

Chapter 2

CLOTHING CONSIDERED AS A

SYSTEM INTERACTING WITH THE BODY

I. CLOTHING AS A QUASIPHYSIOLOGICAL SYSTEM

Just as the several physiological functions of the body can be analyzed and described as systems, such as the digestive system or the nervous system, we can consider clothing as a quasiphysiological system, an extension of the body which interacts with the body. Smuts' [391] concept of "holism," that a whole is more than the sum of its parts, that it is the parts in a definite structural arrangement and with mutual activities that constitutes the whole, is a guide to thinking about the functioning of clothing while worn on the body. It is important to realize that the clothing is not just a passive cover for the skin, but that it interacts with and modifies the heat regulating function of the skin and has effects which are modified by body movement. Some of this interaction is automatic, derived from the physical properties of the clothing materials and their spacing around the body; the larger scale interactions, however, arise from conscious choice of amount and kind of clothing, and mode of wearing, especially how the clothing is closed up or left open and loose.

II. CLOTHING AS AIR OR MODIFIED AIR

We need to think of fabrics as mixtures of air and fiber, in which the fiber dominates by weight and visibility, but the air dominates by volume. Table 2-1 shows a range of representative fabrics with weight (per unit area), thickness, and fractional volume of fiber. The pressure at which

31

Table 2-1. Fiber Volume in Fabrics

Fiber, fabrics	Fiber volume %	Weight (oz/yd²)	(g/m²)	Pressure (g/cm²)	Thick-ness (mm)	Refer-ence
Cotton						
Sateen, increasing	21	10.6	360	0.7	1.12	[54]
pressure	28			7.0	0.81	
	38			70	0.61	
Knit undershirt	13	4.2	142	7.0	0.71	[151]
Balloon cloth	25	2.0	67.6	7.0	0.17	
Herringbone twill	27	8.1	274	7.0	0.66	
L19 Shirley cloth	41	7.4	250	7.0	0.41	
J. P. Stevens 1650	48	7.9	267	7.0	0.38	
Warp knit	12	4.3	145	3.5	0.81	[445]
Flannelette	10	4.6	155	3.5	0.99	
Chambray	24	5.5	186	3.5	0.51	
Plain	32	4.5	152	3.5	0.31	
Wool						
Serge, 16 oz.	25	10.4	351	7.0	0.96	[151]
Shirting, increasing	10	14.2	480	0.7	3.94	
pressure	11			7.0	3.33	[54]
	15			70	2.39	
2/2 twill	19	10.0	338	3.5	1.35	[445]
Melton	24	21.9	740	3.5	2.5	
Nylon, filament						
3 oz. twill	40	3.1	9.61	7.0	0.20	[151]
Similar, calendered	60	3.2	10.31	7.0	0.15	

the thickness was measured is also shown. In use, the pressure on fabrics varies, and the thickness is also influenced by the effects of tension. It is the thicker and more voluminous fabrics which are more hairy on the surfaces and more compressible in internal structure, while the measured thickness of thin or firm fabrics varies much less with conditions of measurement. The pressures used in Table 2-1 are all relatively high compared with most conditions of use, so that the calculated fiber volumes are correspondingly high estimates.

Table 2-1 includes examples of the most tightly woven cotton fabrics, but even they do not rise as high as 50% fiber volume; with wool fabrics, one is seldom above 20 to 30%; with filament yarn fabrics in twill weave, one can weave to higher fiber volumes than for the hairier staple yarns which are spun from short fibers, but even so, to go above 50% fiber volume requires weaving at the limit. Flattening of thermoplastic fibers by calendering can also increase the volume occupied by fiber. The table illustrates the fact that only exceptional fabrics depart from the range characteristic of most apparel fabrics for which the space between the surfaces is from 60 to 90% air.

Fabrics, no matter how gossamer, have thickness and add to the resistance to transfer of heat and moisture, more because this thickness is largely composed of air than because it contains fiber. Women report that even a sheer nylon stocking gives perceptible protection against cold and that added warmth is noticeable in summer. Clothing fabrics range in thickness from about 2 mils to 200 (1000 mils = 1 in.) (50 microns (μ) to 5 mm) per layer, although some sweaters, pile fabrics, overcoatings, and blankets and materials used in sleeping bags are thicker.

A. The Limit Case: The Air Film as Clothing

Even in the limiting case, no clothing, the surface of the body is not in immediate contact with the general environment. This contact is mediated through a personal atmosphere, the film layer next to the surface of the skin. This film layer is the result of the frictional drag between moving air and any surface. The skin by its surface roughness or hairiness certainly affects the thickness of this layer; however, hair is a major influence only on the head; the controlling factor for the thickness of the film layer is the wind speed in the environment or the relative motion of the body with respect to the air. Even in "still air," without wind, as in a quiet room, there is some relative motion, the "natural convection," if there is a temperature difference or if there is a difference of vapor pressure between the skin surface and the general air. This natural convection sets a limit to the thickness of the film layer under windless or indoor conditions.

It is not accurate to think of the film layer as really still air: in fact, the rate of movement relative to the skin increases from its lowest value at the skin to the general average. The concept of "general average" air speed also requires reservations: The general environment is usually turbulent with gusts and eddies and changes of direction as well as velocity. However, it is useful to follow a concept introduced by Langmuir [271, 283] to think of a laminar air film, with velocity graded upward

Table 2-2. Insulation of Air Film and
Corresponding Wind Speeds, For All Temperatures[a]

Air insu-			Wind speed			
lation (Clo)	ft/min	cm/sec	(km/hr)	(mph)	knots	Beaufort scale[b]
0.1	4500	2280	83.1	51.0	46.9	9 Strong gale
0.15	2000	1015	37.0	22.7	20.8	5 Fresh breeze
0.2	1050	534	19.3	11.9	10.9	4 Moderate
0.3	425	216	7.8	4.85	4.48	2 Light breeze
0.4	210	107	4.0	2.39	2.19	1 Light air
0.5	120	61	2.2	1.37	1.26	1 Light air
0.6	75	38	1.4	0.85	0.78	0 Calm
0.7	50	25	0.91	0.57	0.52	0 Calm
0.8	35	18	0.65	0.40	0.37	0 Calm
0.85	30	15	0.55	0.34	0.31	0 Calm

[a]Reprinted from Ref. [83] by courtesy of Edward Arnold, Ltd.
[b]From Smithsonian Meteorological Tables, 5th ed., Washington (1939).

from zero at the skin to a steady flow equivalent in heat exchange capacity
to the disturbance level of the general environment, and to consider the
moving air with its velocity gradient as a film through which heat and water
vapor must diffuse. From the point of view of diffusion, such a laminar
layer is equivalent to still air. By this simplified view, the effect of air
itself as heat insulation or as resistance to evaporation can be measured.
Table 2-2 is Burton's table of standard values for insulation of moving air
with some additional air speed conversions. This table can be used at all
temperatures from -40 to $25°C$, since, as Burton has shown, the changes
in convective power of the air are very closely balanced by changes in the
radiation from the surface [83].

B. Air Layers between Fabric Layers

In the usual case, when clothes are worn, the same consideration applies
to air films outside the clothing. In addition, we have a new layer of air
in the inner side of each layer of fabric. The thickness of these internal
air layers depends on the pattern and fit of the clothing; for body-hugging
elastic knit wear, or for wet fabric adhering to the skin, this thickness may
be zero. But a requirement for fitting one garment over another, and for

motion within and between multiple layers, is progressive increase of circumference and of thickness along any radius from underwear to outer wear. This is illustrated by Table 2-3 which shows that nearly half the space within the clothing is air space between layers.

The insulative value of the air layers between fabrics, and of the fabrics themselves, can be approximated by a rule of thumb or tape measure, that each inch or 25 mm of clothing thickness equals 4 Clo of insulation (or 1 cm = 1.6 Clo), determining the clothing thickness from the radius difference, using a tape measure to get the circumference without clothing and as each layer is added. The increase per layer will be greater than the fabric thickness. Up to, but no more than, 5 mm (0.2 in.) of such air space may be counted as clothing thickness. In the first example in Table 2-3, 53.1 mm of internal air space exceeds this limit so that 22.5 mm of effective air, plus 27.5 mm of cloth, totaling 50.0 mm, would appear to correspond to 8 Clo at the chest level. The 4 Clo rating of the assembly as a whole comes from the lower effective insulation over other body areas where the air spaces are larger and the curvature greater.

The second example in Table 2-3 shows how, in a more recent version of arctic uniform, the girth and radius increase even more with each added layer. Corresponding fabric thicknesses are not available, but it is evident that the later model allows more air space, both for freedom of movement and for fitting a larger range of men with a limited number of sizes. In the greater air spaces, convection currents reduce the insulating effectiveness, so that there is not much insulation gain for further spacing. Indeed, by utilizing the chimney effect, one can get increased cooling with such air spaces, if the channel can be open all the way [156]. The larger spaces in heavy clothing can, however, be valuable in permitting more automatic decrease of insulation with increase of body motion.

The question of minimum air space between layers, or from another point of view, the difference between multiple layers and single layers, has been investigated by Morris [313]. She found that the thermal insulation of multiple layers was greater than the sum of the insulation for single layers, even though in each case the assembly or layer was measured at its thickness under a pressure of 0.02 psi (1.4 g/cm^2). The multiple layers averaged 1.53 Clo/cm; the single layers only 1.32 Clo/cm. This indicates either an effect of air layers trapped between the fiber surfaces, or an effect on heat conduction along the fibers, more of which continue a larger fraction of the distance from one surface to the other in a single thick layer than in two layers. Rees [341] also investigated the effect of multiple layers of a given fabric exposed to a wind; he found less

Table 2-3. Air Layers Between Fabric Layers

Arctic uniform, chest level[a]

Layer	Radius increase (mm)	Cumulative Air (mm)	Cumulative Fabric (mm)
Skin	0.0	0.0	0.0
Air	5.0	5.0	
Undershirt	2.0		2.0
Air	5.0	10.0	
Flannel Shirt	2.0		4.0
Air	8.1	18.1	
Jacket, field, pile	11.0		15.0
Air	5.0	23.1	
Parka, field, pile	11.2		26.2
Air	2.5	25.6	
Parka, field, cotton	1.3		27.5
Total	53.1	25.6	27.5
Total effective	50.0	22.5	27.5

Arctic uniform, chest girth for medium size[b]

Layer	Girth (in.)	Girth (cm)	Radius (in.)	Radius (cm)	Increase (mm)	Cumulative (mm)
Skin (35-39 in.) midrange	37	94.0	5.89	14.90	0.0	0.0
Undershirt, winter, M-50	40	101.6	6.37	16.18	12.8	12.8
Shirt, field, wool, O.G.-108	46	116.81	7.32	18.61	24.3	47.1
Liner, jacket, field, M-51	49 $\frac{5}{8}$	126.0	7.90	20.07	14.6	61.7
Jacket, shell, field, M-51	49 $\frac{1}{2}$	125.71	7.88	20.02	−0.5	61.2
Parka, liner, M-51	59	149.9	9.39	23.86	38.4	99.6
Parka, shell, M-51	59	149.9	9.39	23.86	0.0	99.6
Parka, field, over-white, M-50	66	167.61	10.51	26.69	28.3	127.9

[a]Data from Cochran, 1944 [104].
[b]Data from Winston and Kennedy, 1953 [460].

Table 2-4. Effect of Multiple Layers[a]

Fabric	No. of layers			
	1	2	3	4
	Relative insulation			
Wool	1.00	1.97	2.95	3.99
Cotton	1.00	1.89	2.77	
Viscose/cotton	1.00	1.75	2.55	
	Relative insulation per layer			
Wool	1.00	0.99	0.98	1.00
Cotton	1.00	0.95	0.92	
Viscose/cotton	1.00	0.88	0.85	

[a]Calculated from Rees [341].

insulation per layer for each additional layer, as shown in Table 2-4, for two of the three fabrics. It may be that this indicates differences in wind penetration, and an increasing effect with thicker layers of the more permeable fabrics. Further tests, with fabrics of known porosity and permeability, would be instructive.

C. Thermal Insulation in Relation to Thickness

Several studies of the variation of fabric insulation with thickness, collected in Table 2-5, indicate that the insulation gain is from 1 to 1.6 Clo/cm, with the 1.6 Clo/cm indicated by the tape measure rule at the high end of the range. Two chief reasons for this are: (1) thickness for fabrics is usually measured under a pressure which is large compared to the pressures while the fabric is being worn or tested for thermal insulation, and (2) in clothing, the air spaces between layers also contribute to thickness (up to 5 mm).

The results indicate that to a first approximation, the thermal insulation of clothing fabrics can be attributed to the air contained within them. This does not say that second order but worthwhile improvement cannot be obtained by careful selection of materials and structural forms for their thermal insulation per unit thickness relations. However, weight at given thickness, retention of thickness under pressure or tension, and recovery of thickness on release, durability, and flexibility and deformability in the ways needed for clothing, are often more important than the insulation/ thickness relations alone. Insulation per unit weight of fabric is probably the single most useful "figure of merit" where large insulations are required. Rees has proposed Thermally Effective Specific Volume (TESV) as a

Table 2-5. Variation of Insulation with Thickness[a]

Material	Method	Clo/cm	References
Blankets	To air in hood	1.35	[376]
Fabrics	To moving air	1.60	[330]
Fabrics	Between plates	0.94	[152]
Fibers	Between plates (density 0.5-0.3)	0.7-1.0	[397]
Fabrics	Between plates Single layer Multiple layers	1.32 1.53	[313]
Fabrics	Between plates	1.33	[307]
Foams	Between plates Highest	1.56 2.04	[307]
Fabrics	Between plates	1.18	[451]
Fabrics	To air	1.27	[451]

Comparison: Air

Air (practical maximum, in narrow horizontal spaces)		1.85	[84]
Air, spaces from 0.05 to 0.2 in.		1.07	[307]
Air, immobilized by diatomaceous earth, 5 lb/ft^3, 0.08 g/cm^3		1.87	[307]
Air (Rees)		2.56	[340]
Air 0°C (International Critical Table) 35°C 60°C		2.88 2.60 2.40	[315]

[a]Slope of regression lines, insulation/thickness. Most data fall within ±10 to ±20%.

measure, the ratio of equivalent air thickness to weight per unit area:

$$\text{TESV} \; = \; \frac{\text{cm air}}{\text{g/cm}^2} \; = \; \frac{\text{cm}^3}{\text{g}}$$

TESV avoids the problem of measuring fabric thickness, but adds that of the thermal resistance of air itself. If there were agreement on this, one could also use relative thermal resistance, the ratio of (fabric thickness): (equivalent still air thickness).

For the equivalent layer of air, Rees uses Kair = 0.0006 cal/cm² sec (°C cm⁻¹) or 2.56 Clo/cm. As shown in the figures for air collected in Table 2-5, this is much higher than the experiments on narrow horizontal air spaces. Burton has argued that the low thermal conductivity or high thermal insulation of air reported in International Critical Tables is an extrapolation to zero temperature gradient not applicable to problems involving substantial gradients, as in clothing [82].

D. Passage of Air through Fabrics

Not only does wind erode the external air film; it can come up our sleeves, down between the lapels of our coats, and indeed, apparently blow right through our clothing. Part of this "right through" feeling can be a feeling of cold rather than of wind itself, that is, can be the increased heat flow caused by erosion of the external film, and part can be caused by compression of the clothing fabrics themselves and the spaces between layers by the pressure of the wind. How much is direct penetration and flow through the clothing has not been determined on real clothing, although Fonseca et al. [140] have demonstrated the effects of within clothing flow in model systems, and Fonseca and Woodcock [142] have measured effects of loose or tight fit of head covers and face masks on models. Breckenridge and Woodcock have compared several arctic assemblies on heated manikins under severe outdoor conditions [68] and have measured the change of thermal insulation at various wind levels, but did not have the material to separate effects of fabric type from clothing design. Larose [273] has made a study of air permeability of outer shell, wind speed, and thermal insulation: Some of his results are shown in Fig. 2-1. These indicate that for single layer outer shells, low air permeabilities, below 40 ft/min, and better, below 15 ft/min, are desirable. Fonseca, Breckenridge, and Woodcock have indicated that two layers of material of higher air permeability can be as effective as one of low, and

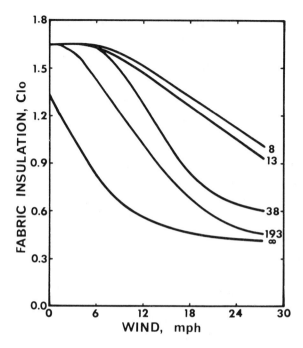

Fig. 2-1. Effect of wind on insulation of pile fabric and cover. Permeability of the cover in ft^3/ft^2 min at 0.5 in. water is given at ends of lines. From Larose [273].

that fuzzy, hairy fabric is better for reducing within clothing circulation than smooth fabric. Leach [274] has stated, without presenting data, that the actual air flow inside clothing is surprisingly small. The problem of defining thermal insulation of permeable systems with separate layers in relation to wind has not had as much study as it needs.

The actual effect of external wind in penetrating through fabrics may be smaller than is usually believed. The stagnation pressure of the wind, that is the pressure which prevents flow into a tube pointed directly into the wind (such as a Pitot tube), is proportional to the square of the wind velocity [328]. A wind of 32 mph (14 m/sec), however, is required to produce a pressure equal to a 0.5 in. water column (1.27 cm), the usual cross fabric pressure for measuring air permeability. Fig. 2-2 shows that at velocities corresponding to body movement, i.e., below 5 mph (8 km/hr) (220 cm/sec) the cross fabric pressures are quite low, although the erosion of the external air film is relatively large. This indicates why ordinary

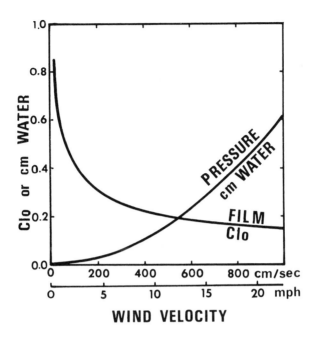

Fig. 2-2. Effect of wind on external air film, Clo, and the impact pressure of the wind, cm of water.

drafts and light breezes can have such a large cooling effect, by eroding the external layer, without real penetration. At higher speeds, penetration and compression are more important.

III. AUTOMATIC INTERACTIONS OF CLOTHING WITH THE BODY

At least five automatic interactions of clothing with the motion of the body can be listed. The first three, and usually the fourth, tend to increase cooling under the conditions of increased heat production which make more cooling desirable.

(1) Decrease of air film thickness outside the clothing.
(2) Increase of air flow inside or into clothing with body motion.
(3) Wetting out of clothing by sweat.

(4) Transient contact effects: warm or cool sensation.
(5) Inertia effects with respect to evaporation from the skin.

All of these automatic interactions can be augmented or reduced by choice of clothing materials or design.

A. Decrease of the External Air Film with Motion

Decrease of the external air film with motion is familiar to anyone who has been sweating while sitting still, but can feel a cooling breeze as he walks slowly. Whether this type of cooling by motion results in a net gain in heat removal is open to question, in view of the low mechanical efficiency of the body. A minimal motion, such as rocking in a rocking chair, or an amplified motion, as with a palm leaf fan may produce a real gain. Increased external wind does not prevent one from becoming warmer by running or by most work, but it helps. Table 2-6 illustrates estimates of the effect of walking at different levels of air movement, indicating that the effect is more noticeable in still indoor air than outdoors; or one reason why it is "cooler" outdoors than in the house.

Table 2-6. Effect of Activity on Insulation of
Ambient Air (in Clo Units)[a]

Air movement	Resting, sitting	Level walk		
		Slow	Normal	Fast
Normal indoors (20 ft/min)	0.78	0.37	0.33	0.29
Normal outdoors (5 mph)	0.30	0.24	0.22	0.20
Windy outdoors (20 mph)	0.19	0.18	0.17	0.16

[a] Reprinted from Ref. [166] by courtesy of the American Association for the Advancement of Science.

B. Increase of Air Flow inside or into the Clothing

Increase of air flow inside or into the clothing is also involved. Not only the effect of wind or motion upon the external air film but also the air currents generated by relative motion between the body and the clothing need to be considered. All who have gotten up on cold nights know that it makes a bathrobe much warmer to tie the belt snugly, even though not all the flapping is eliminated. However, very little is really known regarding the interactions of clothing design, body motion, and internal ventilation. Studies [310] have indicated disappointing or minor differences arising from insertion of vents in rain coats; the fault here probably is that the overall garment design is not sufficiently loose to permit air circulation within the clothing. Loose ponchos were less thermal burden than any raincoat. Use of smooth, nonhairy fabrics or thin fabrics which the wind can penetrate, or clothing design which will open with activity, such as a loose vest, open in front, or a loose cape, or application of the design principle of the grass skirt would enable more extensive use of this means of increasing cooling. The kilt is an example. At one time, slashed sleeves or ribbon sleeves were the height of fashion for men as well as women [447].

A study by Belding et al. is outstanding for presenting the possibilities of insulation variation by garment design [34]. In this, a 50% reduction in the insulation of an arctic uniform was obtained on marching men, in comparison with men standing still or sitting. This reduction in insulation with motion was obtained in a relatively loose fitting arctic uniform in which there was more opportunity for air movement than in close fitting clothing. The reduction in insulation was measured physiologically, and thus could be either a decrease in thermal insulation or an increase in evaporation from the skin. While there was evaporation, the main channel of heat loss was by the thermal gradient. The authors attempted to eliminate penetration by external air and escape of water vapor by control tests with an impermeable outer garment; this would not eliminate evaporation from the skin and condensation in the cold outer layers. The two-fold increase of heat flow was still observed with impermeable outer layers in tests on men, and also in tests with a mechanical model with no involvement of evaporation. This study by Belding and his associates is a pioneering one which suggests that heat transfer within clothing can be greatly modified by internal air flow which in turn can be facilitated or limited by clothing design. The study of the interaction of clothing with body motion is one which above all others requires tests on human subjects. The areas of military value are two: one for better dissipation of the heat of work in heavy arctic clothing; the other, for better cooling in hot environments while wearing protective clothing such as is required for fuel handling, and as protection against chemical, biological, or nuclear attack, or even against intense sun.

Yaglou and Rao [473] compared loose with close fitting clothing in warm environments with a high work load. The loose arrangement was cotton pajamas; the close fitting, a knit union suit. They also compared the Army poplin two-piece uniform, open at neck, sleeves, and trouser bottoms, or closed up and tucked into combat boots. Table 2-7 shows the sweat secreted and evaporated in two hours. Both indicators, and especially the sweat secreted, indicate increased burden with closer fit or less ventilation.

Table 2-7. Effect of Looseness or of Openings[a]

| Garment | Sweating in two hours | | | | |
	None	Loose	Close	Poplin, open	Poplin, closed
Weight, g	0	320	480	950	950
Sweat, g	521	610	694	756	984
Evaporation, g	518	546	548	584	610

[a]Reprinted from Ref. [473] by courtesy of Williams and Wilkins Co.

C. Wetting Out of Garments by Sweat

Wetting out of garments by sweat takes place with exercise or under hot conditions when further cooling is needed. This has a great advantage for increase of cooling: The evaporating surface is brought nearer to the clothing surface, so that there is less resistance to evaporation from films, interfabric air layers, or fabric layers [154, 358]. Tests with single-layer garments have shown that the evaporative cooling rate can be more than doubled by wetting the garment. Even if the fabric is water repellent, a film of water is rubbed onto the inner surface from the sweating skin, and thus the site of evaporation is brought closer to the external surface, removing the resistance of the space between skin and clothing. Of course, cooling by evaporation at a distance from the skin is not as effective for body cooling as would be evaporation on the skin itself. However, sufficient additional cooling can take place at the outer surface to overcome this inefficiency, while the evaporative cooling at the skin itself may be limited, if the clothing is dry and if there is a space, to levels which are insufficient [154]. Clothing wet with sweat has some disadvantages in clinging appearance and may have the more functional disadvantages of clinging to the skin and placing greater burden on motion. Use of knit fabric, or choice between different woven fabrics, to reduce clinging can reduce the drag effect. Most men working or exercising in the heat rightly welcome the greater cooling gained as the clothing is wet out.

D. Transient Contact Effects

Transient contact effects are familiar in the relatively cool feel of smooth, firm, solid fabrics, or the warm feel of hairy, less dense fabrics. There are two aspects of these contact sensations, the purely thermal and the combined effects of heat and moisture. The purely thermal effect arises from the greater thermal conductivity of fibers than of air, and the greater heat capacity and density.

There are not large differences of thermal conductivity for any of the fibers, which are rather similar organic compounds. We know from general experience that most fabrics feel "warmer" than oak (or other dense wood) and very definitely warmer than any of the metals. Besides the two intrinsic properties of the material, specific heat and thermal conductivity, a structural factor, specific contact area, is involved. When we touch smooth wood or metal surfaces, there is a maximum degree of contact between the skin and the heat absorbing surface. When we touch a fibrous surface, such as a fabric, only a fraction of the gross contact area is in contact with fibers; on a minute scale, much of the area of skin is still exposed to air. The wicker chair is a large scale version of the situation. This specific contact effect is one to which we are quite sensitive; a simple procedure such as singeing of the superficial fibers from a cotton fabric by passing it over a gas flame produces a surface which has a noticeably cooler feel. The cool feel of linen, or a filament rayon, in comparison with the warmer feel of cotton, or of spun rayon, is well known. Ironing a cotton fabric produces a definitely cooler feel by compacting the surface structure and by increasing contact between fibers in the fabric.

Another factor which can be involved in warm or cool feel is the hygroscopic one. If the fibers absorb moisture they will become warmer, releasing the sum of heat of condensation of the water and heat of chemisorption. In the usual conditions for observing warm or cool feel, with the fabric in a cool environment, the relative humidity of the air within the fabric if raised to skin temperature will be below that of the air layer close to the skin. Under such conditions, the fiber can adsorb moisture on contact by even "dry" skin, and will release corresponding heat. The release of moisture from "dry" skin can be noticed on handling gummed paper, such as postage stamps.

While hygroscopic effects are a possible component of the warm or cool feel, and a possible source of some of the difference between fibers, the structural factors of hairiness (specific contact) and density (extent of fiber contacts per unit volume) are probably more significant in most situations. An experimental test would be obtained by raising the fabrics to skin temperature, but at a lower relative humidity; any sensation of warmth on contact would then have to arise from adsorption. Such experiments could probably be carried out with "greater than" or "less than" reports of subjective warm or cool feel, or even scaled in intensity or matched to another kind of sensation range [408].

The hygroscopic problem is of considerable interest because of the traditional special warmth of wool, a fiber with unusually high adsorbed water content, especially in comparison with polyamide (nylon) or polyacrylic or polyester fibers which are quite low in adsorbed water content. However, the relative importance of hygroscopic effects and structure effects can be judged by recalling that Orlon (polyacrylic) sweaters are also warm to the touch, and have much of the bulky low contact character of wool, while rayon, which has high moisture adsorption comparable to that of wool, does not make bulky, low contact fabrics, and does not make "warm" sweaters by the usual processes. The question of methods of measurement of surface character of fabrics and the results obtained are discussed in Chapter 6. The warm or cool feel persists to some extent while the fabric is being worn as clothing, so that repeated intermittent contacts of the fabric with the skin have an effect on thermal sensation and on thermal flow, an effect which is automatic or intrinsic once the choice of fabric has been made.

IV. CONSCIOUS CONTROL OF INTERACTIONS OF CLOTHING WITH PHYSIOLOGICAL HEAT REGULATION

In contrast with the automatic interactions of a given set of clothing with the body, the large adjustments, of course, are consciously and purposefully made. We button up or open our jackets, choose light clothing for summer, or heavier for winter, put on sweaters or overcoats. Clothing for either civilian or soldier should be adjustable during the day, or during activity, so that one can take what he needs with him. The soldier in the field has more need to keep his whole clothing outfit with him, and has more dependence, therefore, on water-repellent and other protective finishes for multipurpose clothing. He also has more dependence on adjustment by closures or by means of carrying without wearing.

V. CONTROL OF CLOTHING USING AUXILIARY POWER

This discussion is restricted to clothing in the ordinary sense in which the thermal balance of the body is maintained by dissipating heat to the environment, or by evaporation. However, there are increasing numbers of industrial and military situations which use auxiliary power for either heating or cooling inside clothing. Aviation, space flight, and the Thermalibrium Suit [394-396] are examples. These developments must be considered outside the range of this discussion of comfort in clothing, which centers on heat and moisture passage through fabrics and the influence of fabric properties on perception of comfort or on conditions of utility.

VI. GENERAL FUNCTIONAL DESCRIPTION OF CLOTHING

The clothing provided as protection against the natural environment, and for that matter, clothing provided for protection against occupational or military hazards, has its structure and features specialized for the different areas of the body. Many different alternative designs and materials are available for each area and for most environments. It is no wonder that physiologists have preferred to study the heat regulation of the body without clothing. Indeed this is a necessary first step. However, for many environments clothing is a necessity, so that the physiology of the unclothed man is just a start on the problem. The fact, that a meaningful quantitative description of clothing from the point of view of heat regulation has been difficult, has retarded generalization in the biophysics or physiology of clothing. However, this has been the long term goal of physiologists and physicists concerned with the study of real clothing [75, 463]. This goal can be approximated if we substitute a functional description of clothing in terms of its resistance to flow of energy for the usual structural description of clothing in terms of garment items, design, and textile materials. The problem of describing clothing in terms of energy flow goes beyond mere passage of sensible heat along a temperature gradient, although this is the largest factor in cold environments. It is really a problem involving all the modes of energy exchange between the body and the environment, particularly those determined by vapor pressure gradients as well as those determined by temperature gradients. In special cases, the radiation exchange must also be considered. Several means of describing functions of clothing are taken up below.

A. Thermal Resistance: The Clo Unit

The expression of thermal resistance to heat flow along a temperature gradient has been put in readily recognizable "human scale" units by use of the Clo unit [166] which is roughly equivalent to the insulation given by a business suit (and associated shirt and underwear), or by an overcoat, that is, by a unit of clothing or a unit of increase of clothing. The minimum perceptible increase of clothing warmth or insulation is much smaller, on the order of 0.01 Clo or less [153]. The Clo has been discussed as a physical unit of thermal resistance in Chapter 1. Here we are concerned with its use in heat balance.

Along with defining the Clo, Gagge et al. proposed another practical unit, the Met, for metabolism, approximately the resting rate of energy production. Ideally, if there were only thermal loss, a simple Ohm's law relation would hold:

$$\text{Met} = \frac{K\Delta T}{\text{Clo}} \tag{2-1}$$

with a constant of proportionality K, dependent on the temperature scale, Centigrade or Fahrenheit. Here T is difference of temperature from environment. This is the basic form, but in actual use greater complexity is required, for this equation applies only to thermal exchange. Hence, the energy must be divided between thermal gradient loss and evaporation and, since the equation deals with the total thermal resistance, the insulation must be divided between that of clothing and inner air layers, and that of the external air layer. Because of the need to divide the energy flow, we will measure it not in Met units, but in smaller units, kg cal/m² hr. The heat flow equation then is

$$H_T = M - E = \frac{5.5\Delta T}{R_T} \tag{2-2}$$

where H_T is the thermal loss (kg cal/m² hr), M is the whole metabolism (kg cal/m² hr), E is the evaporative heat loss (kg cal/m² hr), ΔT is the temperature difference (°C), and R_T is the thermal resistance (Clo). In Eq. (2-2), radiation is not considered separately, and change of body temperature is ignored or considered to be zero, that is, the body is in a steady state of heat flow.

This equation, with extension for the case of gain or loss of heat storage in the body, and for energy exchange by other routes, provides the means for physiological measurement of clothing insulation. The experimental procedures are discussed in Chapter 5.

B. Resistance to Evaporation

The evaporation from the respiratory system, E_r, should be separated from the evaporation from the skin, E_s because only the latter is governed by a resistance which varies with the clothing and external air film. Since respiration increases with activity, the respiratory evaporation can be taken to a first approximation as a constant fraction (10%) of the total metabolism [199]. It could, of course, be directly measured, but the approximation is usually sufficient. In fact, few, if any, physiological tests have ever expressed the results on evaporation as resistance. The usual comparisons have been by rank order in terms of amount of sweat produced or evaporated.

However, resistance of clothing and of air layers can be measured by physical measurements (Chapter 6) and in principle, on sweating (moist surface) manikins or on men. Hence it is useful to develop the equations for evaporative energy loss in form similar to these for thermal heat loss.

The unit for physical measurement of evaporative resistance is the equivalent distance (cm) in still air. Hence, basically the evaporative loss through the clothing is

$$H_E = K_E \frac{\Delta P}{R_E} \qquad (2\text{-}3)$$

where H_E is the evaporative heat loss through the clothing (kg cal/m^2 hr), K_E is a constant of proportionality (dependent, however, to a small degree, on temperature), ΔP is vapor pressure difference between saturation at skin temperature and the general environment (Torr), and R_E is the evaporative resistance in centimeters of air. A more detailed form, taking account of respiratory evaporation, is

$$H_E = E - 0.1M = K_E \frac{\Delta P}{R_E} \qquad (2\text{-}4)$$

The value of K_E depends on the diffusion constant of water vapor in air, and on the total heat of evaporation and expansion, each of which is temperature dependent.

However, a considerable degree of approximation is appropriate here, in dealing with clothing problems, so we can follow Burton [79] in using a rounded value of 5 kg cal/m^2 hr per Torr. This is especially appropriate for cool environments, or for evaporation inside heavy winter clothing; in warm environments (above 25°C) and with light clothing, K_E = 5.3 would be a better approximation.

Hence, we can write, neglecting loss through the lungs and from the face

$$H = \frac{5.5\Delta T}{R_T} + \frac{5.0\Delta P}{R_E} \tag{2-5}$$

Woodcock [462] has suggested that the equation be written in the form

$$H = \frac{1}{R_T} \left(5.5\Delta T + \frac{R_T}{R_E} 5\Delta P \right) \tag{2-6}$$

On the basis that there is a nearly constant ratio between R_T and R_E for air, he assumes that there is also a nearly constant ratio for mixtures of air and fiber, although this ratio will be different from that for air. Thus, for air

$$\frac{R_{T\,(air)}}{R_{E\,(air)}} = S = 2°C/mm \text{ Hg of water vapor pressure} \tag{2-7}$$

where S is a constant whose numerical value depends upon the units. One may note that the thickness of the air layer has cancelled out. For air mixed with fiber, the ratio of the resistances will have different values, so that the ratio of ratios, i_m, can be defined:

$$\frac{R_{T\,(clothing)}/R_{E\,(clothing)}}{R_{T\,(air)}/R_{E\,(air)}} = i_m \tag{2-8}$$

This quantity, i_m, known as the permeability index, is a dimensionless number characteristic of any particular clothing system or system of air film layers. Woodcock assumed that this would be relatively constant for clothing during the period of a test, or during use, so that both the thermal and evaporative resistance of clothing could be encompassed in one equation:

$$H = \frac{1}{Clo} \; (5.5 \; \Delta T + i_m \; S \; \Delta P) \tag{2-9}$$

Equations (2-5) and (2-9) are theoretically identical; the differences, if any, lie in the means of determining R_E of (2-5) and i_m of (2-9). Experimental methods for determining R_E are presented in Chapter 6.

The factor i_m can be experimentally determined on a clothing assembly by exposing it over a saturated but nonwetting surface. Such a surface can be had by placing thin, plain transparent cellophane over a wet wick, with arrangements to keep the wick wet throughout the test. The wick should be well insulated on the side away from the clothing, so that all heat for evaporation of water from the saturated surface must come through the clothing. The saturated surface then acts as an imperfectly exposed wet bulb thermometer and falls in temperature as evaporation takes place, until the passage of vapor out through the clothing just balances the inward flow of heat through the clothing. Then,

$$i_m = \frac{\Delta T}{\Delta P \; S} \tag{2-10}$$

Since both the resistance to heat inflow and the resistance to vapor outflow involve the external air layers, there will be an i_m for layers of air alone. This will change with wind, as reported by Woodcock, because the transfer of heat by radiation is not affected by wind.

Table 2-8. Permeability Index of a Bare Cylinder[a]

Wind speed, ft/min	50	70	100
cm/sec	25	35	51
Permeability index, i_m	0.63	0.68	0.70

[a]Reprinted from Ref. [462] by courtesy of *Textile Res. J.*

The test system is essentially an imperfectly ventilated wet bulb thermometer, exposed to radiation, and the transfer of heat by radiation from the environment increases as the "wet bulb" falls to lower temperature. A ventilation above 300 cm/sec is required for good wet bulb measurements, with i_m approaching unity.

The great merit of Woodcock's development is that it supplies the previously "missing" parameter for describing the transfer of moisture and associated latent heat, and permits calculation of the effect of clothing on heat balance for hot or temperate conditions as well as cold. The i_m form has the advantage of being a dimensionless ratio, independent of the units of measurement or their system, and thus is a property of the clothing system itself, at ordinary atmospheric pressures and compositions.

VII. TIME COURSE OF VISIBLE WATER ACCUMULATION

In the hot environment, one of the automatic adjustment functions of clothing is progressive wetting out of the fabric as sweating goes on. The resistance to evaporation, R_E, decreases with time, and correspondingly i_m can be expected to change with time or with fractional area which is wet. After a certain period a steady state may be obtained, as we see from the definite wet shirt pattern on working men. There will also be changes in the dry thermal insulation, R_T, as water accumulates. To a first approximation, the same function can be used to modify both routes of energy loss. The fraction of the total area which is wet can be observed and represented by W. By plotting W against time, a rising curve, eventually leveling off, will be obtained. If the curve approximates a straight line, between the original dry and final steady wetted states, then a time, t_w, to reach maximum wetted area can be used to characterize combinations of clothing, environmental conditions, and work rate. If the approach to steady state is exponential, a "half time" may be more useful. This discussion applies only to visible wetting out of the clothing with liquid water from sweat. It is not likely that the same situation holds for the increase of adsorbed water. It is also unlikely that the same kind of time or wetness functions apply for heavy arctic clothing, and if this is indeed different, there must be transition situations for clothing of intermediate weight and thickness.

In heavy arctic assemblies, the total energy transfer through the clothing has one value for dry conditions, and a different, larger value for sweating conditions [157, 463]. This larger value continues unchanged for lengthy periods, while water is accumulating in the clothing. In such systems the time function may be relatively unimportant, and the whole story may be contained in i_m. It is not settled, though, whether or not R_T and i_m may each be changing constantly but in such a way as to permit a constant H during sweating and moisture accumulation.

VIII. EFFECT OF BODY MOTION

Another factor in the description of clothing in terms of heat balance is the effect of body movement on the movement of air within the clothing and the erosion of the air film layer outside the clothing. A proper expression for this factor requires further development. As a first approximation, it could be a function of metabolism, applying to both thermal and evaporative resistance. While metabolism can be increased without change of rate of motion, by change of posture as from lying down to sitting to standing, a rough equivalence of change of posture to motion may be found in the change with relation to the external air and to chimney effects. In the present state of knowledge, tests of the effect of body motion on clothing need to be made with human subjects: Mechanical models may illustrate the possibilities but our information is still too limited to permit specification of an adequate model. Modes of tests with human subjects can be specified at the present stage of development (Chapter 5).

Belding [34] has carried out experiments in the cold, in which apparent Clo values were determined at various rates of motion for arctic clothing. The plot of Clo against metabolism (Fig. 2-3) is probably not linear, but may be approximated by a linear portion between 2.8 Clo at 50 kg cal/m^2 hr and 1.3 Clo at 200 kg cal/m^2 hr. The corresponding plot against speed of progression (Fig. 5-1) is not linear. Each levels off at higher metabolism or speed. It may be possible to specify for clothing a range of decrease in resistance (here to 50%) and a range of metabolism or motion (here to 200 kg cal/m^2 hr or to 4 mph). Here the decrease rate is close to 0.5 Clo per 50 kg cal/m^2 hr (0.5 Clo per Met) but further tests with other materials are needed to relate such rates of change to design or such properties of the material as air permeability or density.

IX. EFFECT OF WIND

The effect of wind velocity can be considered as a coefficient K_V in an equation of the simplified form

$$H = H_B K_V \qquad (2\text{-}11)$$

where H_B is the heat transfer at very low wind.

A functional relation between wind velocity, fabric thickness, fabric

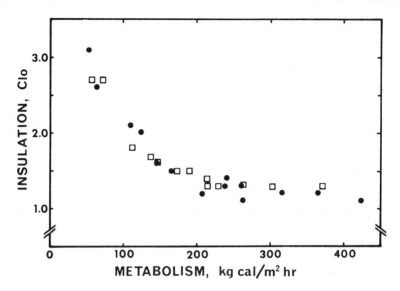

Fig. 2-3. Decrease of arctic clothing insulation with increased activity.
From Belding et al. [34].

compressibility under the influence of wind pressure, and fabric penetration
by wind, whether straight through or by ruffling pile or disturbing a ribbon
assembly or by coming up sleeves, is difficult to specify in general, but
could be established empirically for ranges of wind and types of clothing.
Chemical engineering studies on heat transfer from cylinders as a function
of stream velocity give a baseline, but do not cover the question of fabric
penetration and garment (e.g., up sleeves) penetration. This is an area for
further systematic experiments.

X. EFFECTS OF CONSCIOUS ADJUSTMENT

The range of conscious adjustment of a given outfit of clothing also requires measurement and quantitative expression. In any given test replicated
on several men, the clothing would have to be worn in the same way each
time. (For example, buttoned up or open front, collar open or closed,
sleeves down or rolled up, cuffs closed or open.) Nevertheless, an important
practical feature of clothing is the range of work and of environment in
which it can be used by conscious adjustment of its arrangement. This conscious adjustment range can be expressed as a set of terms Ka_1, Ka_2 . . . Ka_n,

one for each conscious change from the basic condition in which the combined energy flow is H_B, so that

$$Ka_1 = (Ha_1 - H_B)/H_B \qquad (2\text{-}12)$$

$$H \text{ combined} = H_B(1 + Ka_1 + Ka_2 + \ldots) \qquad (2\text{-}13)$$

XI. RADIATION RELATIONS

By becoming the surface exposed to the environment, instead of the skin, the clothing alters the radiation relations of the body. For cool environments, clothing acts to reduce the loss by radiation; for hot environments, to decrease the gain. It is important to keep in mind that radiation effects are all at exposed surfaces, where energy which within the surface was in the form of molecular motion is emitted at the surface as radiant energy, or where radiant energy from the environment is absorbed and becomes molecular motion.

In acting as a shield for radiation, the clothing has no specific interaction with the body; everything depends on the reflection and adsorption at the surface and the insulation between the surface and the skin. With regard to the emission of thermal radiation from the body, there is a small degree of interaction, for as skin temperature rises or as motion reduces the insulation of the clothing, the surface temperature of the clothing also rises, increasing heat loss at the surface by both convection and radiation.

This means to express the radiation effects of environments in terms of operative temperature and to calculate the radiation exchange of two surfaces are presented in Chapter 4, and in Chapter 6, Sect. IX.

The radiation characteristics of clothing are important in relation to sunlight, or to radiant heat as in fire fighting, or to the thermal pulses of nuclear weapons. All of the factors involved in the solar heat problem, including sun position, terrain, posture of the man, and amount of clothing have been analyzed and interrelated, with estimates of limits and typical values, by Roller and Goldman [363].

For the more intense radiant loads, the infrared and ultraviolet characteristics are also involved, but only tell part of the story because questions of flammability and decomposition under the heat load and of whether enough total protection is available are important.

XII. SUMMARY: FUNCTIONAL DESCRIPTION OF CLOTHING AND ITS ADJUSTMENTS

For simplicity, each of the variables of clothing has been discussed separately. The general description of clothing in terms of body heat regulation involves six sets of parameters:

For thermal insulation: R_T or Clo, units of thermal resistance.

For resistance to evaporation: R_E or i_m, evaporative resistance or permeability index.

For wetting out of light clothing: W, fractional wetted area, and the time required to reach the maximum or complete wetness at specified activity (other functions may be needed for heavy clothing).

For the effect of motion: the rate of decrease of insulation with increase of metabolism and the range of metabolism required to reach the maximum decrease.

For the effect of wind: K_V, coefficient of wind velocity effect.

For the effect of conscious change of arrangement: Ka_1 . . . Ka_n for each of the several possible arrangements, each being the ratio of change to base level.

For the effect of radiation barriers: The reflectivity (for intense heat or solar radiation) or the emissivity for body heat.

Most physiological studies of clothing have used some one or a few measurements, such as skin temperature (cooling) or sweat production or evaporation to compare clothing, rather than expressing the differences as numerical coefficients of properties of the clothing. It should be possible, however, to determine not only the thermal and evaporative resistance of clothing, but also several other functional characteristics by which the clothing can be described and the way shown to improve clothing design.

Chapter 3

CLOTHING CONSIDERED AS A
STRUCTURED ASSEMBLAGE OF MATERIALS

I. VARIED CLOTHING FOR DIFFERENT AREAS

What is really meant by clothing as a covering over the body needs to be considered. No clothing is usually worn on the face; rather different types of clothing items are worn on head, neck, hands, or feet than on the torso; clothing often is rather similar on torso, arms, and legs, but the dimensions of these "cylinders" are different. Development in clothing has tended to group one set of efforts on the torso, arms, and legs, and several special sets of effort on the head, the face, the hands, and the feet. Unless qualified with reference to one of the special areas, interest is centered on the torso, arms, and legs. This is about 80% of the body area [363]. Hall has defined the clothing for this area as "body clothing" in his measurements with a thermal manikin [192, 193].

II. COMPARATIVE CLOTHING–DESIGN POSSIBILITIES

Other peoples in other times have clothed the body differently than we do. An excellent discussion of native dress in stressful climates has been prepared by Wulsin [471], and studies of clothing styles through history and around the world are available [61, 114, 134, 194, 446]. The following outline intends only to indicate some of the major alternatives suggested by comparative study of costume.

The head is often protected against either cold or heat. This can be accomplished by a separate unit, a hat or cap or turban, or by a hood connected with the shoulder. A draped garment for head and torso can be suspended from the head in much the same way that a poncho or cape is suspended from the shoulders.

If the torso were protected by a draped cylinder or shell suspended from the head, and not in close contact with the neck, there would be wonderful opportunities for controllable ventilation by chimney effect, even without body motion, and for increase of ventilation within the clothing, when the body is in motion. Every point of close contact of clothing with the body, whether at the collar, on the shoulders, by belt at the waist, or by snug cuffs at elbows and ankles, reduces the possibility of convection or chimney flow, or of internal circulation of air by body motion, as well as reducing the inflow of external air. Thus, a beltless coverall permits more internal circulation than a garment belted at the waist and a skirt permits more air flow than trousers. Neck protection can come from a collar turned up from the shoulders (which if looser and larger would approach the idea of a hood) or by a separate tippet or muffler. The ears can be protected by flaps from the headgear or by special ear muffs. A muffler or scarf or shawl can also be used as a hood for the head and a cover for the face. A ruff around the opening of a hood can protect the face against cold wind and extreme cold, yet not cut off visibility. Masks can be used for the face, but the problems of fogging and condensation in the cold are severe. The idea of using a face mask containing a heat regenerator, to absorb heat from the outgoing breath, and warm the incoming, has been examined [399]; the available models did rewarm the breath, but a wool scarf over the lower face was even more effective. In aviation or space wear, complete pressurized head covers have been developed.

The arms can be protected by cylindrical extensions of the same type of material as covers the torso, the usual sleeves, or by a cape suspended from the shoulders or head. A poncho or cape needs to be open or openable in the front, for use of the arms and hands, or else should be short.

The legs can each be protected by a separate cylinder, the trouser pattern, or by a single cylinder, the skirt or robe pattern. The single cylinder pattern is often used in top coats, or overcoats, or raincoats over the double cylinders.

Avoidance of restriction to motion or of awkwardness in holding the arms is a requirement in clothing design. Too great a thickness cannot be used in the armpit, since the arm at rest is close to the body, and flexibility must be allowed at shoulder and elbow, hip joint and knee. Increase in number of trouser layers has its limits, for with the progressive lowering of the crotch the wearer will be hobbled. Fortunately, the armpits and the crotch are protected areas and do not need as much insulation as the truly external areas.

For the special protection of the hands, the basic variations are gloves with five fingers, mittens with only thumb separate, muffs, and the Chinese variation of the muff, inserting each hand in the opposite sleeve. The hands can also be warmed in pockets, if not needed outside; these pockets may be on the chest.

The clothing provided for the feet is more specialized because of the severe exposure to abrasive wear and to shock (stumbling or kicking) and the need for support and stiffening as well as protection. However, the general pattern of foot cover varies perhaps less than for other areas. The chief variations are in whether the ankle and lower leg are enclosed or not, or whether a sandal with largely open sides and only an underfoot element is worn instead of a shoe.

For the main body area (torso, arms, and legs), there can be underwear, a usual outer layer, and what might be called "overwear," added outer layers such as topcoat or overcoat. Other intermediate layers, such as vest or sweater may be added. The U.S. Army has carried the layer principle to four layers in arctic assemblies. On the hands, thin anticontact gloves can be worn for additional protection and some protection when thick mittens must be removed, and additional socks or overshoes are worn when needed on the feet. Thus, all over the body not only the thickness and weight of particular layers but also the number of layers can be varied, and the layers can have different functions. The outer layers are usually equipped with pockets, or with access means to the inner layers.

Although the variety of detailed clothing structure used on different body areas and the variety of choices of design are large, all clothing systems show successive stages of increased protection in which the cover over torso, arms, and legs is balanced by protection for head, hands, and feet. Siple [387] gives examples of balanced clothing capable of maintaining thermal balance for different climatic regions, from single layer with no cover on hands, face, or head to the four layer maximum clothing zone.

The "Clo unit" was deliberately chosen [166] to represent one stage of such a series, the usual protection, given by balanced clothing for a man in a conventional business suit. The defining example first calculates the thermal loss for the total resistance, external air film plus clothing; then subtracts the resistance of the external air films, averaged for the body as a whole.

It is not a great ambiguity, in a practical sense, to think of Clo values as determined for the main portion of the body, or for a local area, or by physical means, as between two plates. The variables of physiological condition, individual human variation, and above all, the variable of motivation make it difficult to make physiological estimates of Clo value. It is possible to be more precise about a physically determined value of thermal resistance of a fabric or a fabric and air space of a Clo determination on a thermal manikin but the variables of fit and air spacing from subject to subject rapidly erode this precision in terms of actual clothing on actual people. Thus, in speaking of the Clo value we may, according to context, be referring to the average, balanced value of a clothing assembly on an exercising man, or the local value of the insulation on his chest or on his foot, or the physical, thermal insulation of a fabric.

III. EFFECT OF CURVATURE

One important difference between Clo values determined on fabrics and those determined on clothing, in addition to the air spaces between layers, is the effect of curvature. For a physical determination on a guarded hot plate or between two surfaces, the warm and the cool surface each have the same area; however, in clothing the area increases as we go from the skin to clothing surface. The representative area for calculation for a cylindrical cover is the logarithmic mean area:

$$A_m \;=\; \frac{A_2 - A_1}{\ln(A_2/A_1)} \;=\; \frac{A_2 - A_1}{2.3 \log(A_2/A_1)} \tag{3-1}$$

where A_2 is the outer area and A_1 the inner area. The ratio of radii or diameters can also be used. The ratio changes more rapidly for small diameters, as on fingers or arms, than for large, as on the trunk, but does have the effect in all clothing of making the effective insulation as clothing less than that measured for flat surfaces.

IV. RELATION BETWEEN EXTREMITIES AND CORE

In severe cold, or with inadequate clothing, there is a general fall in skin temperature, which is greater for the feet and hands than for other areas. The question of how to combat this fall, to preserve mobility and manual dexterity, involves important connections between basic physiology and clothing choice and design. Belding [32] has summarized the practical solution, indicating that when electrical heat (or additional insulation) is available in limited amount, its application over the main body is more effective than only over the hands and feet. On the physiological side, these extremities obtain their heat mainly from the circulation, while on the physical side, the small diameter and large curvature effects limit the possible physical insulation, as has been shown by van Dilla et al. [428]. The whole problem of the hands has been considered in depth in the proceedings of a special conference [136].

The head also bears a special relation to the general heat balance of the body. Burton and associates [129, 164] measured the heat loss from the unprotected head, finding this to be very large: at 60°F (15°C), one-third of the heat production; at 5°F (–15°C), three-quarters. Even a modest protection for the scalp will conserve much of this heat. The sensations of chill or discomfort are a poor guide to the need for insulation, because the head is kept warm, rather than allowed to cool as do the arms and legs. The tip of the nose and chin, the forehead and tops of cheeks, and, of course, the ears are areas which do cool and require at least local protection from frost bite. Moreover, the head as a whole requires protection to balance the insulation of the rest of the body and to permit longer tolerance times in the cold. Conversely, exposure of the head can help dissipate excess energy production in hard work in the cold.

Chapter 4

HEAT AND MOISTURE
RELATIONS IN CLOTHING

I. APPROACHES FOR STUDYING HEAT AND
MOISTURE EXCHANGE IN CLOTHING SYSTEMS

A. Introduction

The concept that the body is in constant energy exchange with the environment and that clothing acts to moderate this exchange has been discussed fully in Chapter 1. Workers who have studied the role of clothing in moderating this exchange have generally agreed that heat transfer by conduction and radiation is almost always accompanied by one or more moisture transfer processes and that the total energy of exchange is made up of heat and moisture components operating simultaneously. Indeed if, following Winslow and Gagge [454], the body is treated as having a basic metabolism M, performing useful work W, under evaporative heat loss E, radiation loss R, and conductive heat losses S, the energy balance with the environment becomes

$$\text{Energy Balance} = M - W - E \pm R \pm S \qquad (4\text{-}1)$$

It is because the terms E, R, and S act through a common temperature gradient that heat and moisture losses are always coupled together. Three approaches have been used to study the role of clothing in this energy exchange.

B. Physical Sweating Models

A large number of attempts have been made to simulate the key aspects of body heat exchange functions and so make measurements on clothing fabrics under presumably realistic but well-controlled energy exchange conditions. The models have had a capacity for heat production and sweating and an early example of such a model is the Krieger Cylinder used by Rubner [366]. From studies on cotton, linen, wool, and silk clothing fabrics, he concluded that liquid water in the fabrics did increase the energy loss whereas the effects of change in relative humidity of the environment were much less important. Very sophisticated models simulating the torso and limbs of men have also been used. Day [115] describes one of these employed at the Climatic Research Laboratory, Lawrence, Massachusetts during World War II. In this case, the bellows action of clothing on a simulated arm was examined. Models have been useful in defining and measuring a variety of factors affecting combined heat and moisture transfer through clothing and these are discussed in Sect. III of this chapter.

C. Clothing Tests in Climatic Chambers

A very practical approach to understanding heat and moisture transfer processes has been to expose men to well-defined environmental stresses in climatic chambers and note the physiological, clothing parameter, and subjective changes brought about by these exposures. A good example of this approach is the work of Belding et al. [35] in the Harvard Fatigue Laboratory under contract to the U.S. Army Quartermaster Corps. The approach was straightforward. Soldiers in different arctic uniforms were exercised in the cold. Total sweat loss and water gain by the uniform were measured and this formed a practical basis for comparing the effectiveness of different uniforms. Controlled climatic chamber testing of clothing or subjects has no real substitute in assessing real clothing differences. Unfortunately, the energy transfer processes are sufficiently complicated in these realistic tests that no completely satisfactory overall view of heat and moisture has resulted. However, as discussed in Sect. IV, many insights into clothing function and design have resulted from real tests on men.

D. Physical Tests on Materials

A third approach used by many workers has been the measurement of energy loss through moist fabrics as a means of assessing the potential value of different clothing items. An excellent example of this approach is the careful work of Rees [341] using a hot plate thermal transmission apparatus (cf. Chapter 6). His work detected the "cool feel" of moist, smooth fabrics which later proved quite important in assessing the comfort of clothing fabrics in a heat and moisture transmission condition. However, as discussed more fully in Chapter 6, the fact that very precise physical differences in clothing fabrics can be measured does not insure that these, therefore, will be sensed by wearers in actual clothing use. Nevertheless, many physical measurements have been useful in defining clothing differences and this aspect of combined heat and moisture transfer is discussed more fully in Sect. V of this chapter.

II. HEAT AND MOISTURE FACTORS IN CLOTHING AS WORN

A. Ordinary Comfort

The concept that there exists a range of environmental conditions for which the clothed body is essentially in an equilibrium state is fairly well established in subjective comfort studies. Winslow et al. [457] provided a very useful parameter for estimating the net cooling effect of a given combination of air and wall temperatures. They called it the "operative temperature," T_O, defined as

$$T_O = \frac{K_r T_w + K_c T_a}{K_r + K_c} \qquad (4\text{-}2)$$

in which T_w and T_a are air and wall temperatures, respectively, and

$$K_r \text{ (radiation coefficient)} = A_r(4K_r T_s^3)$$

where A_r is the effective radiation surface of the body (m^2), K_r is the universal radiation constant, T_s is the mean body surface temperature (deg. Kelvin), and

$$K_c \text{ (convection coefficient)} = k_c V$$

with k_c the convection shape factor and V the velocity of air (ft/min).

These workers in studies on nude men found that at an operative temperature of $31°C$ and above, heat produced by metabolism was balanced by radiation, convection, and evaporative cooling, the last of these increasing as the temperature was raised. Below 31°C, evaporative cooling stayed at a minimum value and mean skin temperature fell as body storage of heat started to decrease. In a corresponding way, the effects of environment relative humidity were established [459] relating the wetted area in sweating to the relative humidity and dry bulb temperature. Indeed, the wetted area was identified with pleasant and unpleasant sensations. Thus, useful definitions arose for the zones of

(1) body heating
(2) evaporative regulation
(3) pleasantness
(4) indifference
(5) body cooling

Charts defining the comfort zones for clothed men were prepared and published by the American Society for Heating and Air Conditioning Engineers using these same principles and one of these is shown in Fig. 4-1 for air movement in the range 15-25 ft/min [286].

Winslow et al. [458] established a technique called "partitional calorimetry" measuring heat exchange between subject and environment in a climatic chamber using the energy equation

$$M + D = E + R + C \tag{4-3}$$

where M is rate of metabolism, D is rate of heat loss from storage or heat debt, E is rate of evaporative heat loss, R is rate of radiative heat loss, and C is rate of convective heat loss.

Using a limited number of measurements on men and the comfort chart concept (Fig. 4-1), they were able to predict subjective thermal response for other environments. A most successful application of this technique was made in 1948 using an electrically heated copper manikin and developing information for clothed men in submarines [212]. This particular study is a classic in presenting clearly the contributions to thermal comfort balance of radiation, conduction, and evaporation.

Within the pleasant or ordinary comfort zones, neither heat or moisture transfer through clothing are sufficiently great to pose a problem in terms of the clothing worn. There are, however, comfort sensations associated with the comfort zone encountered. Gagge et al. [168] have documented these for transient and long-termed thermal stress in terms of ambient temperature, skin temperature, and tympanic membrane temperature.

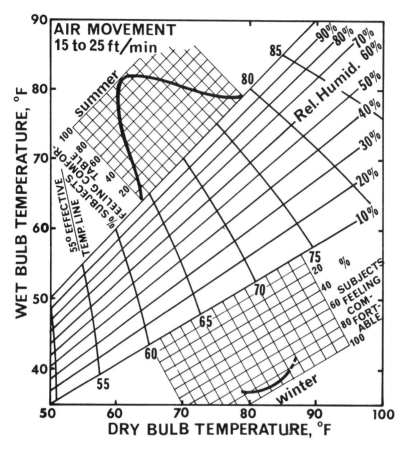

Fig. 4-1. ASHRAE comfort chart for the United States. Modified and used by permission from ASHRAE Handbook [286].

B. Cold Stress

A cold stress environment produces heat loss from the body which must be minimized by clothing in spite of a continuous, simultaneous loss of moisture. Thus, cold weather clothing in general must be thick, light, porous, and a poor collector of transmitted moisture. Belding [36], in a series of reports from the Harvard Fatigue Laboratory, was able to show the interaction of work load, clothing thickness, and sweat level in determining the effectiveness of cold weather combat uniforms. A list of these studies is given in Table 4-1. In all of these studies, the relation of cold stress to clothing worn was examined in terms of the factors in Table 4-2. From these tests on exercising men, the cold weather assemblies were found to be less insulating than anticipated from static measurements.

Table 4-1. Effect of Moisture on Clothing
Requirements in Cold Weather[a]

I	Methods: Ser. No. 141
II	Day to Day Variability and Differences between Individuals: Ser. No. 142
III	The Time Course of Sweating and Moisture Uptake of Clothing with and without a Pre-Cooling Period: Ser. No. 143
IV	Influence of Grade of Work: Ser. No. 144
V	Influence of Amount of Clothing Worn: Ser. No. 145
VI	Local Underdressing as a Means of Reducing Sweating: Ser. No. 146
VII	Partition of Sweating by Body Regions: Ser. No. 147
VIII	Effect of Impermeable Outer Garments: Ser. No. 148
IX	Cooling Efficiency of Sweat Secreted While Clothed: Ser. No. 149
X	Effect of Exercise in Reducing the Effective Insulation Provided by Clothing: Ser. No. 150
XI	Comparison of Post-Exercise in Relatively Dry and Wet Clothing: Ser. No. 151
XII	Relative Effectiveness of Several Methods of Drying Clothing in the Cold: Ser. No. 152
XIII	Theoretical Consideration of Insulation Requirements for Comfort during and after Work in the Cold: Ser. No. 153

[a]From Harvard Fatigue Laboratory Reports.

Table 4-2. Factors Assessing the Relation
of Cold Stress to Combat Clothing[a]

a.	Percent of sweat remaining in clothing
b.	Net efficiency of sweat for skin cooling (percent)
c.	Heat lost by evaporative cooling of the skin as a percentage of total heat loss (percent)
d.	Heat lost by radiation, convection, and conduction as a percentage of total heat lost
e.	Effective Clo value of the outfits (at 3.5 mph up a 6.5% incline)
f.	Grams of sweat remaining in undergarments and percentage of sweat remaining in undergarments

[a]From Harvard Fatigue Laboratory Reports.

There is a related cold stress condition worth mentioning in which the considerations for maximum insulation are much more critical. This involves the immersion of men in cold salt water. Turl [421] has reviewed this area and points out that the paramount need for protective clothing under these circumstances is that of waterproofness. A second desirable feature in the clothing is porosity to water vapor (from insensible sweat). In other regards, the requirements for cold dry stress apply.

C. Warm Stress

Woodcock [469] examined this problem for men starting with a wet bulb model and asking what cooling should be expected at different temperatures and humidities. This approach was then correlated with actual sweat rates observed on men and hence the water dissipation capacity desirable in warm weather clothing. Applied to actual clothing situations [468], the wet bulb theory was found to be only approximate in predicting heat stress imposed by different clothing in a variety of temperature, humidity, wind speed, and radiation environments. This was explained by the fact that real clothing on men can act in a variety of ways to evaporate moisture, e.g., from a variety of clothing surface layers. The wet bulb model does not simulate the different ways clothing can act in dissipating moisture under evaporative cooling conditions. Hence, climatic chamber studies provide the best guidance for the warm stress situation and these are successful in demonstrating heat and moisture relationships even with partially impermeable clothing systems [178].

D. Extreme Heat Stress

Although, in terms of heat and moisture relations in clothing, the comfort problems under heat stress are independent of the intensity, severe heat stress can be treated as a special case if the factors predominant for completely impermeable clothing are considered. Blockley and Taylor [50] documented the physiological effects from such stress and they evolved a new class of clothing to remove heat by forced circulation of cooling, drying air. Some of the principles of this approach and examples of its execution are covered in Sect. VII of this chapter.

III. MODEL SYSTEMS

A. Heat Balance and Physical Laws

The physical laws governing heat exchange of a sweating body with the environment have been treated thoroughly by Hardy [197], and reviewed more recently by Burton [76]. As most model systems are intended to simulate the body in these energy exchange functions, it is perhaps useful to at least restate the relationships which determine heat and moisture loss through a "clothed" model system.

For a single fabric layer the heat loss, H (kg cal/hr) is defined in terms of the surface area A (m^2), the model's surface temperature, T_s, and clothing surface temperature, T, by

$$H = \frac{A(T_s - T)}{I} \tag{4-4}$$

in which I is the clothing insulation.

For a completely wet simulated skin, the evaporative heat loss, E, is

$$E = \frac{A(P_s - P)}{R} \tag{4-5}$$

in which P_s and P are the vapor pressure of water at the skin surface and outside the clothing layer, and R is the vapor resistance of the fabric.

For additional clothing layers, the insulation and vapor resistance values are additive provided one takes into account the air layers at each fabric surface. Thus, the total heat loss through a multilayer fabric assembly can be stated as

$$H_t = A \left[\frac{(T_s - T_1)}{I_1} + \frac{(P_s - P_1)}{R_1} + \frac{(T_1 - T_2)}{I_2} \right.$$

$$+ \quad \frac{(P_1 - P_2)}{R_2} + \ldots \frac{(T_{n-1} - T_n)}{I_n}$$

$$\left. + \quad \frac{(P_{n-1} - P_n)}{R_n} + \frac{(T_n - T)}{I_a} + \frac{(P_n - P)}{R_a} \right] \quad (4\text{-}6)$$

in which I_a and R_a are the thermal and vapor resistance of the surface air layers and T and P are the temperature and vapor pressure of H_2O in the environment.

In some model systems, radiation heat losses, H_r, may also occur and are expressed in Stefans' law:

$$H_r = 1.37 \times 10^{-12 \, \epsilon_1} \, \epsilon (T_1^4 - T^4) \, A \quad (4\text{-}7)$$

in which ϵ_1 and ϵ are the emissivities of fabric and environment and T_1 and T are radiation temperatures of the fabric surface and environment, respectively.

Finally, there are also convective losses due to wind and these have been evaluated by the Pierce Laboratory [455] in terms of the change of the surface air layer by

$$I_a = \frac{1}{0.61 + 0.19V^{1/2}} \quad \text{Clo units} \quad (4\text{-}8)$$

with V the velocity (cm/sec).

Standard values of I_a at different wind velocities are given in Table 4-3.

Table 4-3. Air Insulation Values
at Different Wind Velocities[a]

Velocity of air movement			Insulation value
mph	ft/min	cm/sec	Clo
51.0	4500	2280	0.1
22.7	2000	1015	0.15
11.9	1050	534	0.20
4.85	425	216	0.30
2.39	210	107	0.40
1.37	120	61	0.50
0.85	75	38	0.60
0.57	50	25	0.70
0.40	35	18	0.80
0.34	30	15	0.85

[a]Reprinted from Ref. [83] by courtesy of Edward
Arnold, Ltd.

The work on models simulating human body heat and moisture losses has
been useful in delineating factors concerning heat and moisture transfer
through clothing. A specific result has been the characterization of construction and fiber factors important for comfort as well as the proper assembly on the body for greatest effectiveness. This work will be discussed
in terms of specific model type: flat plate, cylinder, and manikin.

B. Flat Plate Studies

Rees [341], using a guarded hot plate thermal transmission apparatus
with a water filled porous plate, studied the effects of water loss on the
thermal transfer process. He found, for example, in reference measurements on dry fabrics that the relative humidity of the air surrounding
the apparatus had very little effect on the heat loss. Using a very similar
apparatus in a small environmental chamber, Hardy et al. [196] interpreted the changes in thermal transmission in the presence of moisture
as variations in skin temperature and wetness as would be expected to
occur on a subject [459]. They made use of comfort prediction curves;
these are discussed further in Sect. V of Chapter 7. Similar equipment
was also used at the U.S. Army Natick Laboratories in examining the

relative merits of different clothing fabrics [65], and it was the use of this equipment on wicking clothing layers that led Woodcock to propose a permeability index to account for heat loss by evaporation [463] (cf. Sect. III, Chapter 6). Mecheels [298] has taken the same basic equipment and attempted to relate changes in thermal transmission of moist cotton fabrics to their water transfer properties. Cross-linking and water-repellent finishes on these fabrics were found to have only a modest effect on the thermal transmission properties even though the wetting properties of the fabrics were altered substantially.

C. Cylindrical Sweating Devices

Black and Matthews [46], in extensive work on the thermal transmission of clothing fabrics, tried comparisons on a "kata thermometer" or cooling bulb on which were wrapped dry and moist fabrics of different surface character. They were able to establish the effects of fabric surface responsible for the "cold feel" of clothing. These included weave, count, and finish of the fabrics, the smoother fabrics having the greatest effect on cooling. Air movement and moisture content of the fabrics were also studied. The importance of a surface air layer for added insulation and the loss of insulation due to moisture for single fabric layers were clearly noted.

Baxter [18], on the other hand, used a sweating cylinder hot plate device and measured thermal transmission values on fabrics of different thickness but made of cotton or wool. The diffusion rates of water through these structures calculated from the careful work of King [262] appeared to be consistent with the thermal transmission values obtained.

Hollies [218] used a constant temperature sweating hemicylinder to study the effectiveness of vapor impermeable layers on the insulation of cold-weather combat clothing. As shown in Table 4-4 describing the results from this work, partial coverage of an inner fabric layer with an impermeable film gave improved insulation in cold stress without undue hindrance of heat dissipation in a warm stress situation.

Fourt extended this work on a sweating hemicylinder to thick cold-weather ensembles of a variety of fiber and construction variations [145]. The change in thermal transmission with long-term sweating into these assemblies revealed a surprising fact that although energy loss increased at the onset of sweating, it remained at a new constant level independent of the amount of water collected in the clothing. At the same time this corresponded to a decrease in overall evaporation rate of water from the

Table 4-4. Heat Dissipating Capacity
and Insulation of Cold-Weather Assemblies[a]

Coverage with impermeable layer (%)	Relative heat dissipating capacity[b] (%)	Relative overall thermal resistance[c] (%)
73	95	143
87	90	155
93	84	170
100	76	190

[a]Tests were made on four-layer assemblies containing a water-vapor impermeable membrane of variable size next to the underwear layer, with wind velocity at 19 mph.

[b]At high metabolic conditions and relative to the value with no impermeable layer.

[c]Under low metabolic conditions and relative to the value with no impermeable layer.

body indicating that the evaporative mechanism of energy transfer was being retarded by water accumulation in thick clothing in a cold environment. Later Fourt [144] confirmed that although the total energy loss remained constant, the transfer of sensible heat increased, from the increased thermal conductivity of the moist clothing. Hence these results are compatible with those obtained by Hollies on thinner clothing assemblies [218]. Fourt [147] reviewed the possible interactions of heat and moisture transfer processes with clothing materials and body action. He pointed out that not only did the interaction change with level of metabolism but with body motion as well and suggested, following the approach used by Day [115], that this might be a fruitful area for further work in both understanding and constructing cold-weather clothing systems.

D. Heated Manikins

Heated manikins have had a very important part in comfort testing of clothing primarily because actual clothing items can be compared with their increasing complications due to fit and interaction with each other. Although many laboratories have used these devices, some have been more completely described than others and have served as a basis for new departures in assessing current problems connected with both heat and moisture transmission through the clothing.

Fitzgerald [138] provided a clear description of the copper man used so successfully at the Climatic Research Laboratory while Herrington [211] gave a detailed account of the human-body-model used at the John B. Pierce Foundation Laboratories. These devices have been particularly helpful in looking at heat exchange of the different body segments, but without a controlled sweating surface have had only limited application to heat and moisture problems in clothing.

The heated manikin has come into its own, however, in examining the effectiveness of ventilated clothing both in England [260] and in the United States [165]. But again it is not well suited to separate the interaction of heat and moisture transfer processes. Instead, studies on men have been much more effective, as discussed in the next section.

IV. CLOTHING TESTS ON SUBJECTS

A. Scope of Subjective Testing

Although it is easy to visualize how clothing comparisons on subjects may ease the problem of choosing optimum clothing systems, an understanding of what factors influence these choices becomes more difficult. This is a natural result of the fact that many physiological and psychological responses to clothing differences have no single physical cause in the clothing itself or the environment of exposure. At best, tests on men can help only to point out what clothing factors may be involved and thereby suggest other physical tests for direct comparison. This is true of heat and moisture transfer problems so far as they affect subjective preferences of one clothing system over another. The discussion of these problems is aided by considering the level of thermal stress placed on the subject, different stress levels invoking different mechanisms of heat and moisture loss.

B. Tests under Moderate Stress

Studies of the response of subjects to mild heating and cooling but with different clothing structures has received periodic attention, mainly in connection with civilian clothing. Andreen [10], for example, looked at coverall garments of nylon, cotton, and wool/acrylic blends in six different fabric types worn by men in environments of 60 to 100°F and

50 to 95% relative humidity. It was noted that body surface temperature, electrical conductivity of the skin, rate of sweating, and heart rate were useful for assessing the stress in a warm environment. However, subjective response of the subjects to the different clothing variations under mild heat stress was surprisingly similar. Differences between clothing were noted consistently in mild cold stress, the closely fitting smooth garments being least comfortable. In a sense, heat and moisture losses were both necessary to stimulate a subject response, but not much was learned about the mechanism causing it.

Behmann [24] had greater success in distinguishing between clothing fabrics using mild heat stress and a drying atmosphere. He proposed a "transition point curve" for each textile relating evaporation rate to moisture content as a useful practical index of comfort responses at different sweat secretion levels and suggested that subjective differences between a wool and polyamide fabric were due to different rates of water loss in the drying process.

In similar studies on women, Werden [441] followed the evaporative process closely to detect any possible relation to subjective comfort. In relatively still air (25 ft/min or less), the heavier assemblies apparently caused the most sweating and this was reflected in greater body weight losses. These, in turn, affected the objective skin temperature measurements and correlated well with the subject comfort votes. Galbraith and Werden [170] went further in trying to relate water loss properties to comfort. They chose suits of cotton, water-repellent treated cotton and of acrylic fiber in an environment of 94°F and 84% relative humidity. There were differences, especially when the subjects perspired freely, in the weight gain of the clothing. The subjects noted that the water-repellent fabrics did not remove as much moisture from the body as the cotton suit and they identified these cases as less comfortable but not hotter than the untreated cotton suit. Clearly, in this case, moisture removal from the skin was quite important.

Mehrtens [300] took the approach of asking subjects to rate clothing for sensations of clammy, clingy, damp, rough, scratchy, etc., under hot humid conditions (90°F, 80% relative humidity) and showed that clinginess and scratchiness sensations could be related to fabric properties in a qualitative way. Hollies [223] extended this approach to cold and warm stress studies on men and women and found that subjective sensations were intensified by the presence of water at the skin fabric interface. Hence, conditions of testing designed to produce sweating were most useful in making sensible comparisons between shirting fabrics. This work also revealed that skin fabric contact in the moist situation was translated into scratchy and clammy if the contact was high, but felt comfortable if the contact was minimized.

In recent work by Behmann [22], subjects under warm stress were able to distinguish between surface variations resulting from change in fabric density, yarn twist, and weave structure. The clearest results, however, were obtained where the subjects were asked to concentrate on comfort sensations [23].

C. Special Effects of Humidity Variation

Iampietro [246] exposed nude men to 50°F temperatures and humidity variations of 30 to 95% with wind variations of 1 to 10 mph. Chill by wind was noticed easily while relative humidity had little or no effect on any of the responses except heat production. The same subjects were tested with clothes [247] with much the same result; the relative humidity variations having no detectable effect on water or heat loss.

D. Extensive Heat Stress

Turrell and co-workers [424] in subjective work under warm stress conditions noted that the wetting properties of the fabrics were not closely related to response from men. Griffin [183], however, in tests on men wearing impermeable "exposure" suits noted a prolonged resistance to cold by the presence of a water impermeable layer. In addition, they noted that heat stress built up much more quickly in subjects wearing the impermeable layer.

Nelson [319] used partitional calorimetry to characterize the thermal exchanges and responses of three men while standing or walking in several hot environments. Although water transport was implied in the warm stress environment, no attempt was made to measure these changes in the clothing or the subject during the run. More useful information was obtained from men exposed for several days in Death Valley, California [275] using a wide variety of clothing items showing that impermeable layers preventing sweat loss resulted in enhanced heat stress. Veghte [433], in climatic chamber studies on high heat stress, showed that multilayer clothing substantially reduced sweating; indeed, provided much the same heat stress as impermeable clothing, and both should be avoided at temperatures of 90 to 160°F.

Impermeable protective clothing was also examined by the U.S. Navy [380], and this work was used to determine maximum physical activity tolerable with an impermeable suit. The immediate relief produced by a ventilating fan was also noted. Heat stress in CBR protective clothing [109] was also measured to determine the risk involved in donning this clothing and attempting to carry out hard work. The lesson from this heat stress work is that moisture loss is essential to achieving long tolerance times.

E. Extensive Cold Stress

The Harvard Fatigue Laboratory examined moisture distribution in arctic uniforms from the standpoint of sweat collection [37] with and without an outer impermeable layer. This work was extended to thermal responses and sweating efficiency of men exposed to temperatures of $-40°F$ to $+40°F$, and the distribution of sweat in the clothing layers obtained [38]. Good insulation was maintained over a wide range of sweating rates, while cooling from sweating was greatest under high sweating rates from exercise. This subjective study agrees quite closely with the findings of Fourt on model systems discussed in Sect. III. Belding and co-workers [34] assigned heat and moisture energy losses through the arctic uniform for a variety of activities and ambient temperatures. In addition, they could predict what insulation was required for each of these conditions as shown in Table 4-5.

Table 4-5. Predicted Requirements for Insulation from Clothing[a]

Activity	M	$+40°F$	$0°F$	$-40°F$	Actual Clo of arctic uniform
Sitting	50	(3.7)	7.0	10.3	2.9
Standing	60	(3.0)	5.8	8.5	2.7
Strolling, 2.25 mph	145	1.0	2.2	3.3	1.6
Level walking, 3.5 mph	200	0.6	(1.5)	2.3	1.4
Walking, 3.5 mph up 6.5% grade	300	0.4	(1.1)	(1.7)	1.3
Level walking, 4.5 mph	260	0.4	(1.0)	(1.7)	1.3

[a]The conditions were shade, a 2½ mph wind, and 3 ambient temperatures. Actual protection provided by the arctic uniform is given; where protection requirements are within 25% of actual protection provided by the arctic uniform, they appear in parenthesis. Reprinted from Ref. [34] by courtesy of *Am. J. Physiol.*

Another useful subjective study for heat and moisture dissipation in cold stress was carried out by Hall [189] for U.S. Air Force flying uniforms in a simulation of life raft exposure. Dry and wet clothing were compared and prediction curves for human tolerance prepared similar to Fig. 4-1. This illustrates again the great usefulness of chamber studies on men without necessarily understanding the complete heat and moisture loss picture.

F. Additions to Protective Clothing

The Harvard Fatigue Group was successful also in assessing the effectiveness of sleeping bags as an extension of the cold weather uniform using subjects in the climatic chamber [33]. Actually, insulation provided by sleeping bag materials with and without moisture from sweating is fairly well predicted from static studies as discussed in Chapter 6. Water-impermeable and water-repellent covers for these bags were quite adequately assessed in such subjective studies [102].

Renbourn [351] has reviewed how chamber studies can be used for a wide variety of military clothing items as carried out for the Royal Air Force for several types of climate. This is a very satisfactory approach for providing an acceptance level for new equipment. Equally useful are chamber studies for entirely new clothing concepts such as the water-cooled suit [439]. These well-established procedures should find wide applicability for full clothing studies of any type but should not necessarily be relied upon to answer questions on mechanism of heat and moisture transfer or new solutions for their control. Only specific physical tests can give these answers. A number are discussed in the next section.

V. HEAT AND MOISTURE TRANSMISSION PROPERTIES
OF CLOTHING MATERIALS

A. Concepts and Approaches

The foregoing discussion has served to show that there are several ways in which heat and moisture can pass through fabrics in a clothing environment. For example, sorption, diffusion, evaporation, condensation, and wicking of water through fiber assemblies all have their own associated heat transport mechanism. Each of these has been the subject of intensive study as governed by the specific fiber arrangements possible in clothing fabrics as well as in terms of the possible effects from individual fibers.

The approaches which have been used to study these energy transport processes in fiber assemblies have varied according to the skill of the worker and the need in terms of really understanding the problems of comfort. For example, Henry [205] took the classical diffusion approach to the uptake of water by cotton bales, showing that for a textile system there was an advantage in using individual diffusion coefficients for shape and heat factors in the numerical solution. Likewise, Cassie in his work on wool [95] set up the basic expressions for considering the simultaneous diffusion of heat and moisture. Later, Babbitt [15] rewrote diffusion expressions in terms of the Brunaur, Emmett, and Teller equations for sorption on a porous substance. For the student of sorption processes, it is convenient to couple these theories with actual sorption data on fiber materials. McLaren and Rowen [284] made such measurements on a wide variety of fiber substances over a reasonable temperature range.

The diffusion process has also been considered by Fourt [151] in the absence of a temperature gradient, but with and without water-adsorbing fibers. The Angstrom method for heat transmission has also been applied to water adsorbing porous substances [208], and this pulse technique with its associated wave equation appears suitable for application to the clothing fabric systems. A recent interpretation of the combined propagation of heat and moisture through fibers is that of McMahon and Downes [285]. They have suggested a number of practical means for establishing both the diffusion coefficients and boundary conditions for an actual coupled-diffusion process.

Heat and moisture transfer in clothing also occurs in the presence of actual water evaporation as well as diffusion. The heat of evaporation is large and this additional feature requires considerable modification in the transfer theory. Rust et al. [368] have proposed equations for these combined processes based on a somewhat simplified mathematical model of a real clothing system. Woodcock [462], however, took the somewhat simpler view that in the presence of water evaporation into and from the clothing, the total heat loss should be altered in proportion to the ease of water transfer. He proposed a permeability index [462] in the heat loss equation for fabrics (cf. Chapter 6) to take into account the extra heat loss caused by evaporating moisture.

Even in the absence of climatic chamber studies on men, or man simulants, there are far more physical factors to energy loss than just heat and moisture. Burton [85] reviews a number of these, including the interaction of wind on the transfer process. Fourt [147] has extended this thinking to many other aspects of comfort for combat clothing, including heat loss by radiation and the possible effects of body motion on the transfer processes. This appears to be an area open to considerable work to achieve full understanding of the most important factors for heat and moisture loss under actual wearing conditions. Mecheels [296] has considered properties of knit goods as related to their comfort.

B. Coupled Diffusion Studies

The very thorough work of Cassie and Baxter [96] on wool fiber systems showed that there were indeed two diffusion waves for heat and water vapor movement, respectively, through a hygroscopic fiber system. However, Hock et al. [214], on a very wide range of fabrics, established that moist fabrics in a thermal transmission apparatus gave a chilling effect at the hot plate surface in proportion to the degree of surface contact and the amount of moisture held. The work of Preston and Chen [333] on the drying of textiles is also related. The heating process gives rise to a constant rate drying period with a relatively low constant fabric surface temperature, and another higher but constant surface temperature when the fabrics are dry. These same changes must occur in the wearing of clothing starting at the very moist state.

Woodcock and Dee [466] also investigated heat loss in drying fabric assemblies and concluded that for thin fabric layers the amount of cooling at the evaporation surface depended very sharply on the ease of transport of water through the fabric layers. Evaporation from the outer fabric surface, for example, would be less cooling than evaporation on the skin, and, therefore, more comfortable in cold weather clothing.

The diffusion of water vapor, of course, even under essentially isothermal conditions, depends on fabric structure [445] and so has an effect on the total heat and moisture loss of any clothing item. The insulation of clothing to which water has been added falls in proportion to the amount of moisture. Hall and Polte [190] have shown clearly how the tolerance time of men partially immersed in cold water is shortened by having wet clothing. Hollies [230] has shown how to calculate this loss in insulation for a variety of clothing fabrics at moderate moisture contents.

C. Distillation Diffusion Studies

Energy losses through fabric assemblies are changed most radically by actual evaporation of moisture into the fabric from the skin and, if cool enough, recondensation, with ultimate reevaporation to the environment. Therefore, fabric measurements in this transfer mode can be useful for comparing the potential comfort advantage of several clothing fabric systems. Hardy and co-workers [196] took this approach in assessing the relative merits of several shirting fabrics. In this case, positioning of the shirting relative to the sweating skin was observed to make a considerable change in the total heat loss and its shifts with wind velocity.

Similar studies by Hollies [221] on a constant-temperature, sweating, heat transmission device showed substantial changes in energy loss with fabric surface, fabric thickness, and wind velocity, as shown in Table 4-6. The results with the wool serge at 4.7 mph indicate the existence of an effective barrier to the transport of water, probably a still air diffusion layer on the skin side of the fuzzy fabric surface. This is suggested by the lack of change in power and water losses upon napping as well as in experiments with a double layer of wool serge. If shearing were to decrease the thickness of the barrier which could be stabilized by the surface films, then penetration of wind on the exposed surface would be facilitated. This effect is seen in the small but significant increase in water loss and the corresponding increase in heat loss obtained by shearing the wool fabric. The single and double layers of wool serge exhibit appreciably higher moisture transfer in a wind stream of 15.2 mph than at 4.7 mph. The increase in heat losses is proportionally smaller because a greater fraction of the energy for evaporation is supplied by the windstream at the higher wind velocity.

Under similar conditions, the acrylic serge becomes wet and, after 2 hr, will have picked up 65% water. The water and heat losses are, therefore, large at both wind speeds. Napping is effective in interposing a barrier to the transfer of water as shown by decreased water losses for the napped acrylic fabric. A further decrease occurs with two layers of acrylic fabric because water transfer to the second layer is greatly limited. Thus heat and moisture losses through two layers of wettable fabric really resemble the losses through a corresponding thickness of nonwettable fabric.

The reverse effect is seen in thermal transmission measurements between two plates at 23 and $-10°C$ containing a moist underwear and dry serge layer. A sheared wool serge containing moisture has about the same thermal resistance as an acrylic serge of comparable thickness. These are both less insulating than the original wool. In a similar set of experiments, a wettable wool serge produced essentially the same thermal curve as its nonwettable counterpart, showing again that wetting and wicking were not very important in determining overall resistance of these two-layer assemblies.

Table 4-6. Heat and Moisture Loss Through Serge Fabrics as a Function of Thickness and Surface

Fabric	Condition	Thickness at 0.01 psi (mils)	Wind, 4.7 mph		Wind, 15.2 mph	
			Water loss[a] (g/cm hr)	Power loss[a] (W/cm)	Water loss[a] (g/cm hr)	Power loss[a] (W/cm)
17 (Wool)	Single layer	69	2.02	1.5	3.3	1.7
	Sheared	45	2.24	1.7	—	—
	Napped	106	1.93	1.6	—	—
	Double layer	118	2.03	1.6	3.5	1.8
20 (Orlon)	Single layer	35	3.50	2.0	4.4	3.0
	Napped	70	2.97	1.9	—	—
	Double layer	71	2.50	1.7	3.5	1.8

[a] Water and power losses are given per centimeter of mercury water-vapor pressure differential between skin and ambient air.

The water transfer diffusion equation (Chapter 6, Eq. (6-6)), and the
water content thermal conductivity equation (Chapter 6, Eq. (6-4)) were
applied to the data of Table 4-6. Agreement was poor, varying considerably
with the wettability of the fabrics used. Checks of the fabric surface
temperatures revealed that the site of water evaporation was different for
each fabric type and, therefore, the amount of cooling at the skin surface
depended on how closely evaporation was occurring. Hence, useful heat
and moisture transfer equations must take this into account.

Behmann studied the heat transmission properties of single fabric
layers of wool and polyamide on a sweating surface [21]. He confirmed
the importance of surface roughness of the fabrics in limiting the rate of
evaporation of water and this corresponded to higher skin temperature,
lower relative humidity at the skin surface, and lower total energy loss
for the wool fabric. Likewise, Woodcock's approach to heat and moisture
dissipation [461] was successful only for single fabric layers or in considering multiple layers as a whole, presumably due to the same problem of
moisture transfer between moist fabric layers. This approach was very
successful, however, in predicting which cold weather clothing ensembles
should feel warm or cool, depending on the ease of transmission of water
and its collection in specific fabric layers [464]. He showed also the strong
interaction between radiation from sunlight and moisture accumulation in
the clothing layers.

VI. HEAT AND MOISTURE TRANSMISSION
PROPERTIES OF AIR

A. Principles Affecting Clothing Insulation

In a study by Burton [73] to develop reflecting cloth for improved
insulation, the transfer of heat through air spaces was measured with and
without reflecting surfaces, and with and without a loose kapok filler.
The results of this work are summarized in Table 4-7. Not only did
energy transfer by radiation make a substantial contribution to insulation
loss, but convective transfer in the nonfilled space also contributed to this
loss. Burton [82] also reviewed the effects of wind and air pressure and
these are shown in Figs. 4-2 and 4-3. In both these cases, the loss in
insulation was associated with the stability of the still air layer at a fabric
surface. Fonseca and Hoge [141] looked at two other factors governing

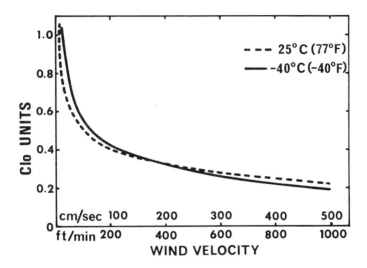

Fig. 4-2. Insulation of air around men. From Burton and Edholm [83].

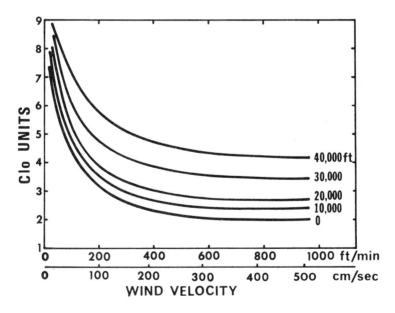

Fig. 4-3. Insulation of air on men at different altitudes. From Burton and and Edholm [84].

Table 4-7. Thermal Insulation of Air Spaces[a]

Thickness (in.)	Open space		Filled space	
	Black plates (Clo)	Reflecting plates (Clo)	Black plates (Clo)	Reflecting plates (Clo)
0.1	0.31	0.37	0.43	0.50
0.2	0.55	0.68	0.76	0.88
0.4	0.72	0.94	1.27	1.44
0.6	0.71	0.98	1.48	1.70
0.8	0.68	0.97	1.67	1.93
1.0	0.67	0.95	1.86	2.14

[a]Reprinted from Ref. [85] by courtesy of Edward Arnold, Ltd.

the effectiveness of air insulation in clothing systems. They showed roughly a twofold improvement in insulation in going from air at normal pressure and water contents to an evacuated space at 0.01 Torr. However, air of normal water content replaced by water vapor cut the insulation approximately in half. Part of this change was attributed to water sorbed by 50/50 wool/cotton underwear. These effects are shown in Figs. 4-4 and 4-5.

B. Design in the Use of Air Spaces

In relation to the insulation load produced by dead air on hot-weather clothing, Wing and Monego [452] studied the thermal resistance of a nylon oxford and mosquito netting in various configurations on the hot plate apparatus held in a vertical position to encourage convection. They concluded:

(1) For spacings less than 1½ in., the two fabric system exhibited considerably different thermal characteristics. For effective convective cooling, no special advantage was to be found in spacing low permeability fabrics from the body.

(2) The net fabric system, regardless of spacing, offered better cooling than the impermeable fabric. This effect was particularly noticeable for spacings less than 1½ in.

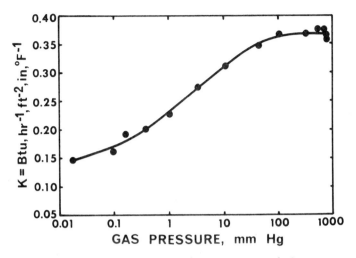

Fig. 4-4. Thermal conductivity, K, of underwear at several air pressures. From Fonseca and Hoge [141].

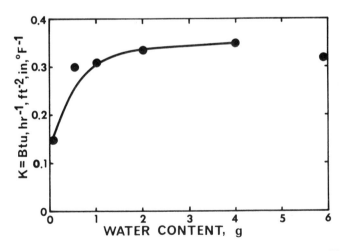

Fig. 4-5. Thermal conductivity, K, of underwear containing water. From Fonseca and Hoge [141].

(3) The net fabric system provided a peak cooling effect approaching that of nudity when the spacing was adjusted to about ¾ in.

(4) Neither system offered any marked advantage in cooling over the other when the spacing exceeded 1½ in.

Hollies [220] investigated forced and natural convection of air on a man-simulant surrounded by an impermeable clothing layer spaced at 3 in. and 1 in. from the sweating skin surface. He concluded that:

> The extent of cooling by moisture evaporation in spacer clothing depended on the interaction of the factors of spacer size, total air volume exchange in the spaces, and the actual direction of the air flow in relation to normal convection. With a moderate air flow of 7 ft^3/min through both three inch and one-inch spaces between the torso and outer shell, the coupling of natural and forced convection produced substantially greater heat transfer to the air, higher moisture loss, and lower skin surface temperature than if the air currents opposed one another. This increase corresponded to as high as 60 kg cal/m^2 hr in additional total cooling under conditions of restricted ventilation through the clothing and suggested that for large clothing spaces coupled natural and forced convection would be desirable for maximum cooling benefit. Although, in every instance, the higher the air flow volume up to 28 ft^3/min passing through the spacer clothing, the larger the cooling effect, the advantage of one-inch over three inch spaces in producing larger moisture loss, lower skin temperature, and hence greater total cooling was also clear from these studies.

Hollies [227] demonstrated that schlieren optics were well-suited to observation of the mixing of gases in clothing spaces and provided clear evidence that turbulence in convective cooling with moist air was the key to effective evaporative cooling. He showed further [228] that air and water vapor mixing could be observed directly by schlieren techniques. Fig. 4-6 shows such an optical system.

Carroll and Visser [89] also worked out a technique for detecting convective heat loss from men in subjective experiments. The method is based on the integration of heat in the wake behind the body by temperature integrating grids. All of these techniques for measuring air

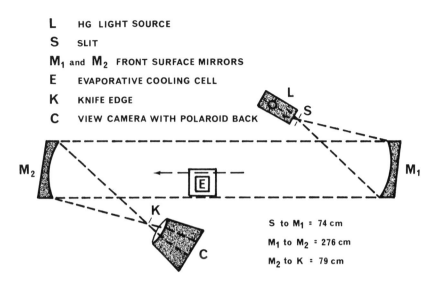

Fig. 4-6. Two-mirror schlieren system [228].

insulation work well in the presence of moisture and are potentially useful in a wide variety of heat and moisture transport studies concerned with body comfort.

VII. EXTENSIONS TO SPACE PROBLEMS

A. Fundamental Relations

The distinction between the cooling of a soldier dressed in an impermeable uniform under desert conditions and the cooling of an astronaut in a pressure suit held in a space cabin is really not very great. Efficient forced convective cooling is required for survival in both cases. Although a full coverage of space suit design is not anticipated in this monograph, certain points relative to the soldier are worth mentioning. Hanson and Dee [195] have outlined the extent of the thermal stress imposed by impermeable clothing on an active soldier in the desert, noting the critical dependence on evaporative cooling for survival. In addition, Colin and Houdas [106] have set forth the equations and the techniques for determining the convection with the human body.

B. Application of Heat and Moisture Techniques

The heated manikin [261] with modifications for a sweating function has been used in evaluating air ventilated suits. Full tests on men in a climatic chamber have also been carried out to determine the effectiveness of water cooling for impermeable protective clothing [176]. Sweating models have been equally effective in advancing understanding about forced convective and evaporative cooling in small clothing spaces [228].

Chapter 5

PHYSIOLOGICAL AND FIELD TESTING

OF CLOTHING BY WEARING IT

I. IMPORTANCE OF SUBJECTIVE AND HUMAN ELEMENTS

Field tests and physiological tests of clothing differ chiefly in terms of the degree of control over the activity and the environment, the thoroughness of measurement of the variables involved, and the degree of quantitative energy balance. Either form of testing should include the subjective response of the subjects wearing the clothing with regard to their own condition and any special reactions of the clothing on their bodies, and to the clothing itself and its fitness to the whole situation. In other words, the investigators and the subjects should take a "systems" or "operations research approach." It will often be a useful by-product, if someone in the test group asks "Does it have to be this way? What other way could we accomplish this?" It will help if the designers or planners serve as test subjects, or go into the field and use the clothing or equipment under field conditions. Siple writes feelingly [388] of arctic clothing. "Drop seats have been designed for underwear and outer garments, but in practice it has been difficult to reach fastenings behind due to the bulky clothing between the arms and body. Trousers have been designed which provide no opening facilities but require the whole trouser assembly to be lowered as a complete unit by unhooking from suspenders. Designers need field experience in these matters."

II. THE APPROACH OF USING SUBJECTS
FOR CLOTHING MEASUREMENTS

There are important features of clothing in use which can be observed and evaluated in no other way than by having live men wear the clothing. The environment can be controlled or natural, the activity of the men can be controlled or follow the variety imposed by environment, required duty, or personal choice. Whatever the degree of control or completeness of description of environment and activity, no mechanical or nonliving model has been devised to simulate the interactions between clothing and body. If we knew enough about a certain range of activity and condition, it is conceivable that limited models could be developed for testing specific interactions. On the whole, though, more needs to be learned before physical models can have much utility in testing the interactions of clothing with the body. While the purely thermal manikin is of value in testing the temperature gradient dependent effects of clothing and can be used in establishing i_m for clothing, if worn over a wet inner layer, tests involving moisture distribution through the clothing are suspect unless the moisture distribution has been established by evaporation from an inner layer, or unless the problem is one of saturation with water. Table 5-1 shows the types of measurement which require human subjects either for physiological or field tests of varying degrees between objective and subjective, extending to the purely "market research" type of preference acceptance or acceptability survey. The methods for each of these types of clothing measurements are discussed below.

The methods for quantitative physiological calorimetry have been well discussed by others [209] so that comments here on such methods will be directed to the conditions determining the choice between physiological or more physical methods or for personal reaction, general impression, subjective or market research type methods. The emphasis will be on the measurement of clothing characteristics in connection with physiological measurements and use tests. Clothing as distinct from its fabric components is the topic here; tests on fabrics are discussed in Chapter 6.

Table 5-1. Clothing Measurements Which Require Living Subjects

---

a. Water content; distribution over body areas and in clothing layers.

b. Relative humidity in each space, within each layer.

c. Temperature at each surface.

d. Onset of sweating; areas involved.

e. Overall and local rates of sweating.

f. Fraction of total sweat evaporated.

g. Efficiency of cooling by the sweat evaporated or in terms of total secreted.

h. Effect of movement in the clothing on insulation, evaporation, or combined energy loss.

i. Effect of wind, through physiological controls or end points; through evaporation from the natural distribution of water; in interaction with movement (purely thermal effects of wind can be determined from physical models).

j. Metabolic burden or cost of clothing; restrictions on motion. Includes effects of loads, load distribution, and load carrying equipment.

k. Cost of clothing or protective features in terms of performance; cost of too little or too much; alternatives to physical protection; cost-benefit analysis for field conditions, for base conditions, for voluntary choice civilian conditions.

l. Static electricity—ranges of environment and activity for its human significance: is static produced in clothing while naturally worn an explosion hazard, a noise source to electronic equipment, a discomfort factor (clinging, soiling, sensation on hairs and skin)?

m. Human significance of drag, cling, friction, against skin or between layers, for real movements in use and for real water contents and distributions. Effect of available choices in spinning, twist direction, weave, mechanical and chemical finishing, intermesh or relative direction of layers. How significant are physically recognizable differences for military or industrial effectiveness, or for customer satisfaction or advantage in competition in civilian areas?

n. Preference or acceptability.

III. CLOTHING MEASUREMENTS
WHICH REQUIRE LIVING SUBJECTS

A. Water Content in Clothing Layers

1. **Conditions of Observation.** An important related set of measurements which can be obtained in no other way than by wearing clothing, is the water content of the clothing, the distribution of water within the clothing, and the relative humidity and temperature, or the temperature and the vapor pressure, from point-to-point and layer-to-layer. Actual use is important because experiments based on wetting out clothing with arbitrary amounts of water can produce quite unrealistic conditions—except, perhaps, for the man who has just slipped while fording a stream, or has just climbed out of the sea onto a life raft, or reached the beach through the surf. Several types of observations which can be made, as the problem may require, are outlined. First, however, it should be recalled that all clothing fibers are hygroscopic to some degree; the water content increasing with increasing relative humidity of the air with which the fiber is in contact. Equilibrium between a single fiber and the surrounding air is obtained very quickly, within seconds, but in a larger mass of fibers, as in fabric or clothing, balance with respect to the general atmosphere requires care in exposing as much fabric surface as possible, opening up the garments, and allowing of several hours. The time scale for safety in reaching balance is not unlike that required for drying wet clothes on a line, although the time can be shortened if air can be blown over, or better, through the fabrics or garments. ASTM (Standard D1776) specifies a test for effective equilibrium in terms of change of weight no greater than 0.1% in a period of 2 hr. A room with controlled atmosphere and good circulation is valuable. The standard ASTM testing atmosphere, 21°C (70°F) and 65% R.H. (relative humidity) is convenient; this is a relatively high R.H. and will minimize the changes of clothing weight on being worn by subjects with only insensible perspiration, no frank sweating. However, any controlled atmosphere above 20% R.H. can be used—too low a R.H. is undesirable because it will produce unusually "dry" clothing with large changes in weight and large "heat of regain" or "heat of adsorption" effects. Whatever the working or "standard" condition of the controlled room atmosphere, or the day to day atmosphere of the laboratory outside the physiological test chamber, its actual R.H. and temperature during the experiments and conditioning periods should be measured. A recording thermometer and a recording hair hygrometer are useful;

faster responding instruments are not as appropriate as these time-averaging instruments, since the changes in textile masses as large as clothing items are slow.

2. Hygroscopic Relations of Textiles. The reason for standardizing the previous history of the specimens is that the more hygroscopic fibers may adsorb water up to nearly 40% of their dry weight, and that at intermediate levels of R.H. the water content in equilibrium with the particular R.H. will vary, depending upon whether the fibers are being dried (desorption) or are adsorbing water. Regain, based on dry weight, is used as the more convenient measure of the general concept of water content and has the advantage of a constant base, the dry weight, while water content has the constantly varying base of textile plus water. Speakman and Cooper [398] found that between 20% R.H. and 90% R.H. the desorption regain was from 1.2 to 1.4% higher than the adsorption (wool). For less hygroscopic fibers, the differences are smaller. For comparison, the water regain as percent of dry weight, is shown for several fibers in Table 5-2. The regain of textile, or polymeric, or porous materials in general, depends more on the R.H. than on the temperature. There is a small effect of temperature which is more noticeable in the more hygroscopic fibers: Data are shown in Table 5-3. The vapor pressure at 60% R.H. varies from 5.5 to 33.2 Torr, with only a small change of adsorption regain. Vapor pressure is not the direct determiner of regain; it requires to be related through relative humidity, i.e., fraction of saturation vapor pressure for water at that temperature.

3. Weighing to Determine Water Content of Clothing. After a period of use, the clothing can be weighed again, garment by garment. For experimental purposes, garments can be made quickly separable into local areas or parts, by basting parts together with pull threads (slick, strong, smooth threads such as nylon or polyester filament), or even by zippers (though these may be too stiff or bulky for this kind of test, interfering with normal relations). It is better to put the garments into tared tin cans or polyethylene bags, which can be quickly closed, as soon as they are removed. If cans are used, extra space should be minimal. The weighing can then be done later, although the effectiveness of the "weighing bottles" or sacks in preventing loss of weight should be checked for the time periods involved. Correction for air buoyancy is not required; other sources of error will be larger. The buoyance is about 1 mg per kg clothing per Torr barometric pressure difference.

Table 5-2. Commercial Moisture Regains[a]

Fiber	Regain, %
Glass, fluorocarbon, olefin, rubber	0.0
Polyester	0.4
Spandex	1.3
Acrylic	1.5
Acetate (triacetate)	3.5
Nylon	4.5
Acetate (secondary)	6.5
Cotton, dyed yarn	8.0
Cotton, mercerized yarn	8.5
Rayon	11.0
Wool	13.6

[a]Results are selected from ASTM standard
D 1909-68. These are not the equilibrium regains at
65% R.H., 70°F, but are in rough relation and indicate
comparative levels. Reprinted from Ref. [9] by courtesy of the American Society for Testing and Materials.

Table 5-3. Regain at Constant R.H., Effect of Temperatures

| Fiber | R.H. | Temperature °C | | |
		10°	25°	40°
Cotton[a]	20	3.2	2.8	2.5
	40	4.9	4.5	4.0
	60	6.8	6.3	5.8
Wool[b]	20		6.0	5.5
	40		9.65	8.8
	60		13.5	12.15

[a]Urquhart and Williams [425].
[b]Speakman and Cooper [398].

B. Determination of R.H. within Clothing

1. Use of Fabric Swatches. The facts regarding hygroscopic adsorption of water can be utilized to determine the R.H. at each surface of a fabric layer. If small, thin, porous swatches of a fabric made from a fiber of high water adsorption tendency, such as viscose rayon, are first raveled back from the edges, then hemmed so that they cannot lose threads by further raveling, and are basted to the surface of the regular fabrics by quick release pull threads, or attached by safety pins, the R.H. at that point can be determined by measuring the water content after exposure during a clothing test. Temperature measurement just under and just above the swatch is desirable, using the average for highest precision in R.H. estimation; at least one temperature measurement is necessary. For this work, the highest precision in weighing is desirable. The swatches should have been previously washed, with final rinse in distilled water; the yarns should be filament rayon, so that gathering of lint from other fabrics can be minimized; the fabric should be predried, then weighed dry (in a weighing bottle) prior to use. Immediately after removal from the clothing, the swatch should go into a tightly closed weighing bottle and be weighed promptly. It should then be dried again (105°C) and the final dry weight compared with the initial. Any large or systematic difference should be traced to its cause—such as adsorption of organic material or salt from sweat. If the gain in weight is due to solutes, another wash in distilled water should bring the dry weight back very close to the initial value. Such methods have been successfully used by Ogden and Rees [326] and by Turl [423]. Control regains at known R.H. (from salt solutions in equilibrium with air [442]) should be established for the fabric used.

2. Use of Humidity Sensors. There is a long and, on the whole, disappointing history of search for rapid, near instantaneous humidity sensors which can be used inside clothing without disturbing the relations which would prevail without the sensor. Any method which depends on creating air movement like dry bulb/wet bulb measurement, even with small thermistors to sense temperature, is suspect. Any humidity probe which requires a current of air across the sensitive surface or any which requires raising the temperature to balance the hygroscopic tendency is similarly suspect. Some workers [264] have sampled the air inside shoes using a syringe and flexible tube; this could be applied between clothing layers or could be applied to a fabric layer as a whole by drawing air through it. However, the accuracy possible with samples of convenient size which would not disturb prevailing conditions inside the clothing does not seem more than approximate, although the indications obtained might be informative and useful. Any continuous withdrawal method would be still more open to objections. The Dunmore type of sensor [367] can sense "in place" and is quite sensitive and rapid in response, but like the swatch method requires simultaneous temperature measurement. The lack of available appropriate thin shapes is the chief drawback. A second is the instability, especially if exposed to liquid water or high humidity. Conductivity type sensors have been used by Ogden and Rees [326] and Hollies has developed forms [331] which are directly metallized onto the cloth. However, these are somewhat difficult to prepare and of uncertain durability. Conceivably dielectric measurements depending on the water content and the type of fiber could be developed, similar to the means used for determining moisture content of fabric, or paper, wood, or bulk materials. No sensors robust enough for field or for severe exercise under laboratory conditions and high water contents have yet been developed, although the sensor methods are more satisfactory for milder conditions without frank sweating.

3. Results on Water Distribution and R.H. in Clothing. It can be clearly demonstrated by simple means, such as visual inspection, or by pressing filter paper or water sensitive indicator paper against each surface of a fabric [214], that the wetness of the two surfaces of the same fabric may vary. In general, the side closer to the source of moisture will be wetter. Hollies' conductivity gauge, metallized right onto each surface of the fabric [331] is especially useful in this field. As Hollies has shown in experiments with physical models [232], transfer of water from layer to layer, unless the fabrics are flooded with sweat, is more by distillation in the warmer regions near the skin and condensation in the cooler layers farther out than by direct wicking or blotting.

Ogden and Rees [326] found R.H. levels from 20 to 60% between the skin and clothing. Turl and Kennedy [423] found R.H. to rise above 80%, and finally, liquid water, after several hours use of most types of footwear. One of the most detailed studies of water relations in cold environment clothing, that of Folk et al. [139], found that after a bout of exercise, moisture was mainly held in the underwear layer; after longer wear at lower activity, it was found in the outer layers. The moisture content gain depended more upon the amount of sweating than on any other factor; this in turn depended on the rate of exercise, but at any rate of work and environmental temperature, the sweating could be reduced by under dressing, that is, wearing less clothing than would be suitable for rest or lighter activity. The accumulation in the cold outer layers is a result of low vapor pressure and low vapor pressure gradient to the environment.

C. Measurement of Temperature within Clothing

The first choice the experimenter must make is whether he is concerned with temperature at a number of individual points, which, if chosen in a representative way, can be averaged, or in a self-averaging report. For individual points, thermistors, thermocouples, or small resistance thermometer elements are usable. Radiation measurement is only suitable for external surfaces, unless a very small bolometer or detection device is developed, which does not change spatial or temperature relations. Means of using all these devices are well described by Hardy and Stoll [410]. If one wishes an automatically averaged temperature, one of the best means is a wire grid sewn to the fabric. Some wires can even be sewn in with a sewing machine, but a better procedure is to cross-stitch over the wire with low regain fine thread such as nylon or polyester. A metal of high thermal coefficient of resistance, such as high purity nickel, is convenient.

D. Indication of Onset of Sweating and the Area Involved

It may be of concern to know whether or not frank sweating has begun and over what areas. This can be valuable in assessing the influence of clothing on the borderline between vasomotor control without sweating and the beginning of increased evaporative cooling. This borderline may be taken as an objective definition of the high temperature side of "resting comfort" or "comfort" in the ordinary sense. Whether or not, and when, sweating has occurred can be observed by the method described by Kuno [267] which uses a dry powdering of starch over skin which has been painted with an iodine solution in alcohol or alcohol and oil and allowed to dry to a uniform light yellow color. Kuno used 15 g iodine, 100 ml castor oil, and 900 ml alcohol as his "paint." Variations on this method with particles of dye which spread and become visible when wet are possible. The subject must be cool and not sweating when the indicator is applied, and trials will be needed to judge when to remove clothing to inspect for the start of sweating, as well as to gauge individual and day-to-day variations.

E. Measurement of Rate of Sweating

1. Total Sweating Losses. The rate of sweating overall can be obtained by body weight measurement on a sufficiently sensitive balance. Platform scales weighing loads of 100 kg, enough for most body and clothing weights, accurate to 5 g are available. More sensitive and rapidly responsive devices can be developed with strain gauge load cells: Recent developments in bed weighing scales for hospitals, useful to detect imbalance in artificial kidney hemodialysis procedures, could be modified or adapted. The weight of the subject without clothing before the start of the test and his weight at the end are needed. A standardized method of wiping dry, and of weighing the towel, is required. This will give total sweat secretion, including that evaporated and that which runs off or is adsorbed in clothing or towel. Weighings of the clothing and the towel will establish the amounts secreted but not evaporated. Tared plastic sacks will be useful to minimize evaporation from the clothing. Accounts must be kept of any drinking of water or any voiding of urine. A baseline for insensible evaporation from lungs and nonsweating skin must be established though figures from the literature can be used. CO_2-O_2 differences can be subtracted.

2. Local Sweating Rate. Sweating over a small area on the order of 2 to 5 cm in diameter can be measured by small sweat collector boxes, containing a solid desiccant which is held 1 mm or so away from the skin, or by small chambers through which air is passed at known rate and total volume and is analyzed for water by R.H. measurement, or by adsorption or freezing out the water by a cold trap. With either system, error may be introduced by temperature changes: with the desiccant chamber, by rise of temperature of the desiccant; with the air flow, by introducing colder or warmer air, or by cooling the skin by too rapid evaporation. One can also err by incomplete evaporation; checks by visual inspection are needed, possibly aided by sweat indicators such as the iodine-starch system. Air can be prewarmed to skin temperature by initial adjustment or by passage through tubes or plenum chambers inside the clothing. Change of temperature of the desiccant cannot be completely eliminated, since each gram adsorbed gives off at a minimum the heat of condensation, 0.58 kg cal/g, but still higher heats of adsorption due to the heat of chemisorption, can be minimized by choice of desiccant and by deliberately avoiding extremely dry desiccants, because the heat of chemisorption is greatest in the dry end. At best, these measurements of rate of sweating are approximations and are more or less disturbing to the normal arrangement of clothing and its relation to the skin. For very heavy sweating, a blotting system, such as layers of filter paper in a small Petri dish, may be used. Petri dishes or similar small dishes with lids, e.g., flat metal pill boxes or ointment boxes, make reasonable equipment.

3. Sweat Collection. While total sweat secretion can be measured by weighing the subject, the amount evaporated is desired. If all excess sweat is absorbed in clothing or a towel there is no problem in making the measurements and finding the difference, but if light or little clothing is worn, and sweat drips off face, arms, or legs, or trunk as well, other means are needed. If the work is on a bicycle ergometer, or by stepping up a step, the working can be done over a pan containing a layer of nonvolatile oil lighter than water. The sweat will collect beneath the oil; once it reaches the oil, evaporation will be negligible. Evaporation from the step can be reduced by perforating it, or arranging it as a set of bars or a grill so sweat can run through.

F. Fraction of Total Sweat Evaporated

Knowing the total sweat secreted, from body weight change, and the total not evaporated, from the water gain of clothing or towel, or the collected drip, one can get a measure of the total evaporated by difference. Weight changes due to water taken in must be accounted for. The amount evaporated will almost always be overestimated since it will include any noncollected drip, and any evaporation from clothing or towel, but comparisons of similar overestimates with variation of environment, activity, or clothing are useful and informative.

G. Efficiency of Cooling by the Sweat Evaporated or in Terms of Total Secreted

The simple assumption that only water evaporated from the whole system, man plus clothing, is effective in cooling the man is not satisfactory. Belding and associates [38] in examining efficiency of sweating in heavy arctic clothing, considered that all the sweat condensed in the outer layers of the clothing must have evaporated at the skin or underwear layer. In condensing, the heat was returned, but its effect would be divided between body and environment in inverse proportion to the thermal insulation in each direction. On this basis, the water in each layer could be assigned a cooling efficiency, and an estimate of net effective sweating could be made. Burton [86] has suggested a similar system for estimating the efficiency of evaporative cooling.

H. Effect of Movement in the Clothing on Insulation, Evaporation, and Combined Energy Loss

Certain equations for expressing the effect of body motion or the effect of wind were indicated in the discussion of the functional description of clothing (Chapter 2). Another way of looking at the whole problem is to define a "Clothing Transfer Coefficient," C, for energy transfer by all routes, and "Environmental Stress Index," I_{ES}, for the potential (combined for both temperature and humidity relations) governing energy exchange, and a "Combined Resistance," R_C, of the clothing. The total energy transfer can then be obtained by physiological measurement of M, the metabolism, by O_2 consumption, and D, the heat debt as the body mass cools or (negative sign) its accumulation as the body warms, obtained by keeping track of regional surface temperatures and core temperatures as measured in the rectum. Then,

$$C \frac{I_{ES}}{R_C} = M \pm D = H \tag{5-1}$$

where H, as in Chapter 2, is the total heat (more generally, energy) loss from the body.

The advantage of this generalized equation is its usefulness in describing experiments in which the exact values of the environmental stress, represented by I_{ES}, are not known, although the environment can be described so that it can be recognized and reproduced another time. To do this, air temperature, air velocity, air relative humidity or vapor pressure, and radiation conditions (emissive or metallic walls), coefficients of emissivity for 10 to 100 micron infrared, presence and location or absence (or screening) of direct radiation sources will be sufficient. If cold conditions are chosen, the main environmental stress will be temperature, with the vapor pressure difference from average skin temperature to environmental vapor pressure a second factor. The actual environmental vapor pressure should be checked, since the coldest point in a circulating system will determine the vapor pressure in the absence of sources of evaporation such as the experimental subjects or frost. The presence of living subjects may raise the vapor pressure (and the temperature) in the general air of the chamber, depending upon the effectiveness of the cooling system.

The effect of motion in the clothing can be measured by keeping I_{ES} constant (or nearly so); motion will then change R_C, the combined resistance of the clothing, and C, the clothing transfer coefficient. The changes with motion are mainly in the air spaces between layers of clothing and in the external air film, since the fabric components or R_c are nearly constant. Belding et al., in a classic work [34], expressed all changes with motion as changes in R_c expressed as Clo units for purely temperature gradient dependent insulation, but the concept can be extended to include evaporative effects. Belding used controls with an impermeable outer layer and found that evaporation to the outside, as well as wind penetration, were not large factors. This does not rule out the possibility that motion may increase transfer within the clothing by evaporation at warmer, inner layers and condensation at cooler, outer layers.

The results of Belding et al. on the relation of effective clothing insulation to speed of level progression are shown in Fig. 5-1. The Clo value falls from 2.7 for standing to 1.3 at 3.5 to 6 mph marching, and C, the energy transfer, doubles. Although this curve resembles that for the effect of wind on the external air layer (Fig. 2-2) in being steep initially, the decrease of Clo with increase of rate goes farther, since the changes are in internal air layers as well as the external. Horvath [239] has examined the effects of closures, or of openings, on thermal balance for work in the cold. Some of these results, shown in Table 5-4, indicate that opening of the outermost wind-break layer had some effect, but that opening of the two outer layers had noticeably more effect.

I. Effect of Wind

The physical effect of wind can be more accurately measured on physical apparatus, but in clothing studies the use of living subjects to evaluate the effects of wind is desirable in some conditions. Examples are the effectiveness of arrangements for protecting the face, such as ruffs or face masks. Proposals for absorbing the heat (and moisture) of the expired air in regenerators which can warm the air breathed in have been tested in this way [399]. It was found that such systems could be used, but that the simpler expedient of breathing through a double layer of wool muffler was even more effective. Tests on living subjects are valuable to determine both effectiveness and practicality. In many cases the practical end point of a series of tests, or limit of effectiveness of a protective assembly will be set, not by general body cooling, but by critical cooling of some critical portion, such as hands, feet, or face.

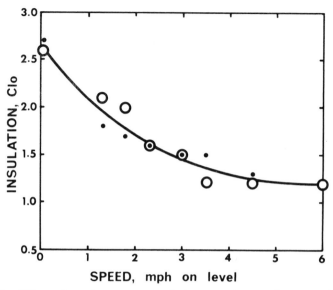

Fig. 5-1. Effect of motion on arctic clothing insulation. From Belding et al. [34].

Table 5-4. Effect of Ventilation by Opening Closures in Outer Layers of 4.5 to 5 Clo Arctic Clothing[a]

	No ventilation		Ventilation as permitted by garment	
Outer layer	Weight loss[b] (g)	Clothing gain (g)	Weight loss[b] (g)	Clothing gain (g)
Sateen	449	299	305	240
Sateen, zipper front	338	282	345	255
Sateen and pile, each with zipper	311	284	219	188

[a]Weight changes after 1 hr walk, 3.3 mph, 3% grade, –23°C. From Horvath et al. [239].

[b]Corrected for loss from lungs.

J. Metabolic Burden or Cost of Clothing—Restrictions on Motion

Several studies have shown that the cost of load bearing on the back, or in generally distributed weight as clothing, is the same as the cost of body weight [180]. The chief purpose of tests on living subjects should be to determine relative effectiveness of the man in the clothing and whether and how well he can carry out his tasks. Footwear is a special case, because the work of lifting the feet is different from the work of general body motion. The cost of added weight of footwear is four times greater than that of load on the back, according to Robinson [356]. More recent work with better statistical control indicates a ratio of 2.31 to 1, for load on the feet compared to load in a rucksack, with a standard deviation of 0.65 [125].

K. Cost in Terms of Performance

Beyond the measurable metabolic cost of clothing or equipment, there is another cost, in terms of performance. The cost in performance is much more difficult to really measure. The problem is related to that of measuring the effect of environmental stress on performance. The difficulty lies both in the measurement of performance and the many other elements— motivation, fatigue, stress—that enter into performance. Field, rather than laboratory, methods are required.

The best that can be done, probably, is to subjectively weigh the costs of protection against the cost of living without protection. The study of clothing armor, to reduce casualties from fragmentation weapons and low velocity missiles, illustrates the value of statistics on the relative frequency of wounds in different body areas [60]. For more conventional clothing features, a cost-benefit analysis is needed for military field conditions, for garrison conditions, or for voluntary choice civilian conditions.

L. Static Electricity

An example of a problem in which the use of living subjects is a valuable supplement to physical measurement is that of static electricity. As indicated in Chapter 6, measurement of surface conductivity permits classification with regard to static electrical effects. For any fiber or fabric, however, the conductivity is strongly dependent on the moisture content or on the relative humidity. Trials on live subjects in a variety of environments are needed to be sure what the R.H. and conductivity conditions will be in actual use. The difficulty may be personal; a matter of clinging to the body, or of sensations through effects on the hairs. It may be one of interference with electronic equipment. The conditions found with living subjects can also be used for tests (without the subjects!) of the explosion or ignition hazard.

M. Human Significance of Drag or Cling

The tendency of moist fabrics to cling to the skin or of one layer of fabric to drag on another can be measured physically, and altered by choice of yarn and fabric structure, but the real significance of such differences to the user can only be determined by the reports of people wearing the clothing. In evaluation, one must consider whether the reaction is one of noting a difference or represents a condition which would be really unsatisfactory in service. Two general rules regarding fabric surfaces are: (1) smooth fabrics make low friction linings, and (2) bulky, hairy fabrics are best for reducing internal air flow and filling spaces. Perhaps the best solution is to alternate smooth and hairy layers.

N. Preference or Acceptability

In the civilian, free choice market, the survival of a type of fabric or a design of clothing is governed by the cycles of style, and by factors of preference or acceptability, many of which, despite all efforts at physical measurement, remain imponderable. The test of acceptability or preference can also be useful in military trials of designs and types: Monego and Kennedy [308], after a series of wearing trials on a variety of summer uniforms, determined preference by allowing the subjects to retain one uniform. Questionnaire and interview methods are also used, as in civilian market surveys. These responses are more meaningful after actual use of the items than if based only on inspection and handling.

IV. COMPARISON OF PHYSIOLOGICAL AND PHYSICAL MEASUREMENTS OF CLOTHING INSULATION

One area in which a direct comparison of physical and physiological measurements can be made is in Clo value or thermal insulation. Belding [31] states that 91% of duplicate measurements on a given man, and 86% of measurements on different men, had a spread of less than 25%. The average percent differences between duplicates ranged from 9% to 17%, for arctic assemblies or sleeping bags. Hall and Polte [192, 193] have reported trials of a wide variety of U.S. Air Force equipment on heated manikins;

the range (as plus or minus) of percentage differences from the average for replicates on materials of the same kind as Belding's was from 0 to 7.6%, with a median at 2.1%. Hall found from direct comparisons of tests on men and tests on the thermal manikin that differences of 10 to 15% in Clo value could be demonstrated more clearly on the manikin [188]. The separate components of the manikin are particularly useful for measurements of the Clo value for headwear, handwear, and footwear. These values for small areas are difficult to determine by tests on men, where large variations in the individual area are only small factors in the heat loss of the whole man. Brown and Cotton, using a single trained subject and constant environmental conditions and daily schedule, were able to reduce the coefficient of variation for Clo determinations to 6%, but this leaves the manikin superior for purely thermal tests [70].

V. METHODS IN TESTS USING MEN

The full quantitative study of the thermal and evaporative features of clothing involves all the measurements necessary to evaluate the equation

$$M \pm D = H_T + H_E \qquad (5\text{-}2)$$

where M is the metabolism, D is the heat debt of the body (positive if the body is cooling; negative if it is warming), H_T is the temperature controlled loss, and H_E is the evaporative heat loss, all in kg cal/m^2 hr.

Methods for measuring the metabolism include direct calorimetry, partitional calorimetry, and indirect calorimetry through oxygen consumption. Direct calorimetry has been significantly improved in sensitivity and rapidity of response by the gradient calorimeter methods of Benzinger [42]. Partitional calorimetry is of special value if the radiation exchange with the environment is to be studied; it has been described by Winslow et al. [456]. The indirect methods through oxgyen consumption have been described by many authors; a recent reference to simplified and convenient methods is the paper of Liddell [279]. One of the best "how to" directions is that of Belding et al. [31].

The basic data require certain corrections before use in Eq. (5-2). Thus gas volumes as measured must be corrected to standard pressure and temperature, dry. The loss in weight because of the greater weight of CO_2 than O_2 can be calculated as 0.3 times weight of O_2. The heat lost in warming inspired air and the water loss in respiration can be calculated on the basis of saturation at 33°C. In cool conditions, without sweating, the insensible perspiration through the skin can be taken as 1.3 kg cal/m² hr [31].

The metabolism can often be specified from the grade of work. Wyndham [449] has used an economical method for assuring uniform work by different subjects. In this, each subject steps onto and back from a step, the height of which is adjusted so that the work in foot pounds will be the same for each. All the subjects in a given test series then step on and off of the adjusted steps in time to a metronome.

Where a comparison of the burden or metabolic cost of systems of clothing is required, without measurement of the heat relations, the minute volume of respiration can serve as a measure [125]. This method has been used to compare the cost of weight on the feet or on the back. It assumes that heat debt can be neglected or is the same for each condition tested.

The measurement of heat debt requires the measurement of body temperature, both core and surface. The core temperature is conveniently represented by rectal temperature; the surface temperature by the weighted average of a number of skin temperatures at points representative of principal body areas.

The number of points at which skin temperature is measured has varied for different investigators. Hardy and DuBois [200] used at least 20. Teichner [415] compared smaller numbers with the 10-point system regularly used at the U.S. Army Natick Laboratories, concluding that in many cases smaller numbers than 10 could be used. He found the medial (inner) thigh temperature to be the best single point representative of the average skin temperature. Ramanthan [337] confirmed the usefulness of the medial thigh measurement, but found an even closer correlation with the Hardy-DuBois measurement from 5 points (chest front and back plus three others). Points and weights for three systems are shown in Table 5-5. Burton [72] has brought out the point that the weighting should be in terms of body mass, when used for change of body temperature, and of body area when used for an average skin temperature. In fact, the differences on the whole are not large, compared with the other uncertainties, and most work is based on area.

Various investigators have used different mixing proportions for the relative weight of all the masses represented by skin temperature and core temperature. A division of one-third skin to two-thirds core is representative [72]. The value usually taken for the specific heat of the body is 0.83 [72, 80]. It is evident that there must be considerable uncertainty in measuring D, the body heat debt which results from body cooling.

Table 5-5. Locations and Weights for
Average Skin Temperature

Source location	Teichner [415] weight (%)	Burton [72] weight (%)	Ramanthan [337] weight (%)
Cheek	10		
Hand	6		
Upper arm	7		30
Lower arm	7	14	
Chest	12.5	50	30
Back	12.5		
Medial thigh	12.5		
Lateral thigh	12.5		20
Calf	15.0	36	20
Instep	5		

The body surface area is also required to reduce measurements on different subjects to a unit area basis. This can be obtained from tables [383], or by the DuBois height-weight formula (Eq. 5-3) [122].

$$A = Cw^{0.425} \, h^{0.725} \tag{5-3}$$

where A is the area (cm^2), C is a constant, 71.84, w is weight (kg), and h is height (cm).

A. Limits and Hazards

The normal ranges of variation, and the points at which the physiological variables indicate danger to the subject, should be considered so that the test can be halted and the subject may recover without lasting injury.

The hazards in the cold are frostbite or freezing. Watch should be kept of subjects faces; especially if there is high air movement: blanching or a white spot indicates the start of freezing and should stop the test. Temperature sensors on ear lobes, a finger tip, and a toe should be monitored for approach to $0°C$; the test should be stopped if the sensor reaches $5°C$. Subjects should be instructed to report if their cheeks, ears, fingers, or toes cease to hurt; this may indicate freezing and can be checked against the sensor in deciding whether to stop. Rectal temperature limits for survival have been discussed by physiologists concerned with survival from exposure or immersion in cold seas. However, for testing of clothing and sleeping gear, no great lowering of rectal temperature is required. A practical indication of tolerance limit is set by three signs: pain in the hands or feet or by severe shivering. Horvath and associates at Fort Knox [238] showed that there was a wide range of variability in resistance to cold. By observation on men sitting at $-27°C$ in arctic clothing, they classified the subjects as resistant, intermediate, or susceptible to cold. The susceptible group showed two of the signs within 2 hr, the resistant group did not show two of the signs within 3 hr, and the third not before 1.5 hr. Only the resistant group was consistent in repeated tests. These results indicate that in "tolerance time" tests, it is difficult to be very precise because of wide differences in subjects.

In field trials in the cold, it is desirable to have the men already trained in providing field shelter and to have reserve fuel available. Unexpectedly severe weather has been known to exceed the protective capacity of the equipment being tested (i.e., blow down tents).

Test programs which involve the prolonged exposure of the feet to the cold, but not freezing, conditions which lead to "trench foot" should be avoided unless it is the necessary control for the experiment.

The hazards of heat are fainting, heat exhaustion, and heat stroke. As with tests in the cold, field tests in the heat can present special hazards due to severe weather, such as sand storms, so that reserve water should be available. With healthy young subjects, the added load on the heart is not as dangerous as with older or less fit individuals, but most investigators regard a rise of pulse rate from the normal resting level near 80 per min to 160 or 180 per min [449] as a sign to stop. The rectal temperature of a man working in the heat will rise above "normal" $37°C$; it will arrive at a steady level which depends on the activity rather than the environment, until the environmental ability to accept energy (heat and moisture) is exceeded. Above this point, the rectal temperature will rise further with time of exposure and with increasing environmental stress; this process should be monitored, and the test stopped at $39.5°C$ [449] although tests to $40°C$ $(104°F)$ have been reported. Robinson has found that sweat secretion may stop after several hours at a high rate [357]; since body temperature will then rise rapidly, the test should be stopped. Lind, in discussing limits for exposure to heat [280], warns that the rectal temperature limit of $39.2°C$ $(102.5°F)$ is more applicable to conditions requiring an hour or more to reach this level; that in more severe conditions, the peripheral body temperature may rise so rapidly that rectal temperature can become a poor indicator of danger of thermoregulatory collapse.

Lind adds, "The judgment of the men exposed cannot be relied upon to prevent serious heat illness . . . the clinical judgment of experienced observers is the best method for assessing the limits of heat tolerance."

These limits, and the rate of approach to the limits, can be influenced by training, acclimatization, and motivation. Training and acclimatization are outside the scope of this discussion, except to note the need to assure adequate training and acclimatization and to arrange the order of tests to balance out residual changes. The extent of acclimatization combined with the differences between conservative, safe experiments versus motivated actual work under hazard are illustrated by a table presented by Lind [280] on mine rescue workers in England (cool) and heat acclimatized, trained men fighting a fire in a gold mine in India (Table 5-6).

New combinations of environmental conditions and activity should be undertaken with caution. Even an experienced group of investigators has been surprised at the high rate of heat transfer to the skin brought about by high humidity and high temperature combinations, above the saturation vapor pressure of skin. The skin and nasal passages acted as condenser surfaces, receiving the latent heat of the condensing vapor, an unexpectedly unpleasant and unendurable condition.

The general rule should be not to expose men to vapor pressures above that of saturation at 40°C (104°F), 55 Torr. The brief duration limit is set by the rate at which the blood can remove the heat of condensation from the skin, or by the thermal conductivity of tissue; the long-term limit, if the local heating can be endured, is set by the heat storage allowable, as reflected by the rectal temperature limit. Each could be calculated more closely, but here we are concerned with safety considerations and easily observed rules rather than precision experiments. An ideal rule might be for one of the principal investigators to be the first subject to be exposed to a new combination of conditions. Observance of this rule indeed prevented hazard to subjects in the high vapor pressure test.

B. Some Norms and Ranges

Every biological measurement shows a scatter about its mean; the scatter itself is a characteristic of the measurement. Some measurements which are frequently used are cited below, with ranges which approximately include 95% and exclude the two extreme 2.5% portions of the reported observations. Heart rates are given in Table 5-7.

Table 5-6. Comparison of Conservative Test Estimates
with Actual Performance by Heat Acclimatized Men[a]

Saturated environments		Tolerance time (min)	
		Unacclimatized (Britain)	Acclimatized (India)[b]
°F	°C	test estimates	actual fire-fighting
85	29.4	44	–
87.5	30.8	37	60
90	32.2	32	50
92.5	33.6	27	42
95	35.0	23	35
100	37.8	19	29
105	40.6	–	20

[a]Both groups fit and trained. Reprinted from [280] by
courtesy of Van Nostrand-Reinhold Co.
[b]W. B. Rountree, Trans. Inst. Mining Met., *60*, 513 (1950).

Normal temperature: Clinicians refer to measurement in the mouth,
under the tongue: 37.0°C (98.6°F), ranges 36.1-37.2°C, 97-99°F. Rectal
temperature averages higher; variation through the day is about 1°C (1.8°F)
with the minimum around 4 to 6 A.M., 36.3°C, the maximum in late
afternoon, 37.3°C [413].

C. Training and Experimental Design

Because of progressive changes in the subjects, especially if not already
acclimatized, attention must be given to experimental design. One should
not do all the tests on one kind of clothing first, then the tests for comparison of another kind; rather, the several kinds should be started together
and alternated between subjects, with a random sequence for each subject.
Use of acclimatized and trained subjects is desirable to minimize the rate
of change during a test; however, there is likely to be a degree of training
in putting on, working in, and removing a new kind of clothing.

Table 5-7. Normal Heart Rate[a]

Effect of age

Age	Beats/min	
(years)	Mean	(95% range)
15-19	79	52-112
20-24	74	41-100
25-30	72	52-102
35-40	72	52-100
45-50	72	49-100
55-60	75	48-108

Activity effects

College students	Mean	(95% range)
Basal	65	45-105
Recumbent	66	40-100
Sitting	73	48-105
Standing	82	54-104

28-year-old man		
Sleeping	59	53-67
Awake	78	61-112

[a]Reprinted from Ref. [251] by courtesy of Fed. Am. Soc. Experimental Biol.

D. Health Aspects of Tests of Clothing

There are two principal health aspects of clothing tests using human subjects: One concerns sanitation and personal hygiene; the other, the hazards of approaching physiological limits. The limit hazard will not be present in all, or even in many tests, but all test subjects should be medically screened for good general health or closely checked if the interaction with some medical problem is the point of study. To establish a LD_{50} of environmental factors in combination with clothing factors is not a proper objective for clothing tests although tolerance time determinations should bear a recognizable and probable relation to survival times.

The sanitation (general) and hygiene (personal) aspects of clothing tests require thought and supervision. Usual procedures for clothing care, by laundering or dry cleaning, should be used when different subjects must wear the same undergarment or other garment (such as a shirt) with extensive skin contact, in a series of tests. For socks, rinsing in a solution of a quaternary antiseptic after washing is desirable to avoid spread of athlete's foot. Outer garments with only limited skin contact may be more freely exchanged but the subjects should be medically screened for good general health, and medical observation should be maintained through the series. If infection (such as boils) or skin irritation should develop, the affected subjects should be eliminated from the test and the garments should be cleansed or sterilized. A balance is required, however, in choice of means of garment cleansing or sterilization and its frequency. Some procedures, such as washing fabrics or batts may cause excessive shrinkage, or compacting or migration of fibers, spoiling the insulative effectiveness and changing many characteristics. While the service life of a garment includes cleansing, items issued to one person will not be washed or cleaned after every use, so this high schedule of cleansing should not be used if it can be avoided.

Subjects should be no more likely to "catch colds" in the course of the tests than during other activities; however, some are likely to do so. While such subjects can usually carry out the tests, it would be better to exclude them, both to reduce exposure risk for the other subjects, and because temperature regulation is notoriously "odd" during the course of a cold. There is, of course, a very extensive clinical literature on body temperature, fever, and even differential temperatures between body areas. Local temperature differences have been suggested for indication of tumors or other pathology. The clinical area lies outside the present scope, but some of the methods discussed here may be useful there, and reciprocally. Local temperature differences revealed by infrared methods or by liquid crystal indicators are useful for showing the uniformity of insulation of clothing or the hot spots in an unbalanced assembly of clothing which does not properly adjust the insulation distribution to body surface temperature.

Chapter 6

PHYSICAL PROPERTIES OF CLOTHING AND CLOTHING MATERIALS IN RELATION TO COMFORT

I. INTRODUCTION

The concept that physical, optical, and even subjective differences in clothing materials are responsible for differences in comfort when worn as clothing is quite logical. Many test methods have been developed for assessing the physical properties of clothing fabrics and some of these can be measured with great precision. Unfortunately, these types of measurements, no matter how precise, cannot substitute for an actual measurement of comfort on people which takes into account the interaction of body physiology and its motion—and the motion of the clothing—as well as the microclimate of the exposure. However, there are physical techniques which can be very useful for screening potential clothing materials as to suitability for specific end uses and it is in this light that the different methods are discussed. In each case, an attempt is made to define the currently known relationships to real clothing comfort. The details of procedure are given in the references cited: We attempt here more a critique than a procedure manual, unless the method is not readily available.

The student of clothing needs a sense of *caveat emptor* even in using a test described by a standardizing body such as ASTM. Scopes are usually given and should be thought through carefully. Many tests used for purchase specifications are really only rather arbitrary comparisons, not measurements of basic physical quantities. One can often test applicability by such questions as "If this quantity (i.e., thermal resistance) should add up in series, do the measurements in fact add for multiple layers?" Frequently, arbitrary air or instrument conditions are included in measured values by "standard" tests. Intrinsic properties of the material or assembly are more likely to be of importance for thinking about various means of combining clothing elements. Again, in such combinations in actual clothing, the effect of intermediate and external air layers needs to be brought back into consideration.

As new relationships between clothing comfort and fabric properties become established, it is increasingly possible to draw on the wealth of test methods which have been established to make these assessments. The United States Government, the Canadian Government, the American Society for Testing Materials, the American Association of Textile Chemists and Colorists, and the British Standards Institute are the most widely recognized organizations which publish test methods in English. The U.S. Government publishes "Federal Specification Textile Test Methods," CCC-T-191b [97], ASTM Textile Committee D-13 publishes annually "ASTM Standards on Textile Materials" [9], the American Association of Textile Chemists and Colorists publishes an annual Technical Manual [1]. Wherever appropriate, these methods will be cited; new techniques will be described somewhat more fully.

II. THERMAL TRANSMISSION OR RESISTANCE

A. Methods for Clothing Materials

Because clothing is basically concerned with minimizing the thermal stresses, warm or cold, imposed on man by the environment, there is good reason to measure the thermal insulation of single layers of clothing materials, as well as multiple layers assembled more or less as in clothing during use.

Although there are many techniques for measuring thermal resistance of clothing, they fall essentially into three types as described by Morris [312].

(1) Constant Temperature Method. The fabric is placed on one side of an isothermal hot body insulated on all other sides, and the energy required to maintain the hot body at constant temperature is measured.

(2) Rate of Cooling or Warming Method. A hot body well-insulated on

all sides except where in contact with a fabric, or completely surrounded by the fabric, is allowed to cool freely, the rate of cooling determining the thermal transmission through the fabric.

(3) Disk or Heat Flow Meter Method. The fabric is held between a heat source and a heat sink (desirably of high heat conductivity and capacity materials) at different temperatures and the flow of heat is measured by a thin disk measuring device. Alternatively, or more basically, the disk can be placed in the thermal flow, and the gradient across the disk measured. From its known thermal resistance, the flow rate through all the layers in series is measured. If the temperature difference across any of the layers in the series is known, the thermal resistance of that layer can be calculated.

The guarded hot plate is the most common form of type 1 [100] in use today while the somewhat simpler rate of warming apparatus (type 2) by Cenco-Fitch [137] has had wide application to clothing items. Recent applications have also been made of the disk method (type 3) first introduced by Lees (1898) and described later by Baxter [19]. Benzinger [42] has made extensive use of this principle in his gradient calorimeters.

(4) Another method (not considered by Morris) is the measurement of propagation of thermal waves, a method originated by Angstrom [11] and more recently considered by several workers [126]. It is also related to single pulse measurements, which are of concern in connection with nuclear explosion heat pulses. As the technology of measurements has advanced, each of these techniques has been modified for application to specific textile clothing items and, therefore, is discussed separately.

1. Guarded Hot Plate Method. One of the earlier applications to textiles was by Schiefer [376], whose paper on blankets is a classic in the field. A fairly extensive body of work on the insulation value of clothing items was carried out by the Quartermaster Corps of the U.S. Army in the Climatic Research Laboratory at Lawrence, Massachusetts using guarded hot plate equipment [175, 314]. These techniques were later adopted as Standards and specified by ASTM Method D1518-64 [9]. The drawings and details of construction given there correspond to the equipment at the U.S. Army Natick Laboratories. A symposium comparing hot plate techniques was held in 1951 by ASTM and is available for study [355].

Modified hot plate devices shaped to human arm dimensions were also used [20] to simulate losses experienced by men in a moving air stream and wearing multiple clothing layers [155]. This approach was further extended both by the U.S. Air Force [187] and Army [138] to full clothing items on manikins using a combination of hot plate instrumentation and cooling technology to measure thermal insulation in Clo units. These same techniques have found extensive use in evaluating space clothing in a variety of environments. In most of these closely related approaches for measuring insulation of clothing items, the contribution of still air layers at a fabric surface and between layers has been included and in some cases discussed in terms of overall stability in a moving air stream [237]. Direct measurement with minimum air effect was carried out by Speakman and Chamberlain [397].

Various hemicylindrical or cylindrical test surfaces have been proposed, i.e., Freedman [162], Tallant and Worner [414], Hollies and Fourt [222], but are usually less satisfactory as physical measuring devices for the intrinsic thermal resistance. Insulation of bottom or ends, or provision of guard surfaces, has usually been inadequate, reducing the work to comparisons rather than absolute measurements. Heated man-shaped or hand-shaped models are, however, valuable for tests of clothing without the factor of body motion.

2. Rate of Cooling Method. An early modification of the Cenco-Fitch [137] device by Fourt and Fisk [150] permitted insulation to be measured under known applied pressures covering the range of 0.002 to 2.0 lbs/in^2 experienced in actual clothing use. In essence, the constant temperature heat source of the apparatus was mounted on a lathe milling attachment so it could be raised or lowered on the fabric sample supported by the temperature detector of the apparatus. Plate separation enclosing the fabric was measured with a thickness gauge and from thickness-pressure data could be interpreted in terms of applied pressure to the fabric. Wing and Monego [452] made a similar comparison of the definite thickness technique with the guarded hot plate in which there is no pressure on the fabric. These authors used three supports to separate the heat source and sink and control specimen thickness.

3. Disk Method. The modern terminology for disk devices designates them as heat flow transducers. These disks can be left in, because of their small size and ease of application to clothing items in situations and have found numerous applications to comfort problems. Woodcock and Goldman [467] applied them to specific body areas covered by clothing to assess local losses independent of the overall equilibration with the environment. On the other hand, Nelms [318] has applied these principles to measurements on fabric swatches, calling the new device a "Resmeter." Rees [103], in a most recent variation of this approach, has used temperature distribution between fabric samples and a standard insulating board placed in series in a constant temperature gradient as a fast and accurate technique for insulation measurement.

4. Heat Pulse Technique. An extension of the rate-of-cooling approach is that first reported by Angstrom [11] and applied recently to multicomponent structures containing air [208]. In this technique, multiple waves of temperature gradients are passed through the sample and the damping of the wave is used to calculate the heat flux through the sample. This technique along with several of the others is applicable to clothing materials containing moisture, discussed more fully in Sect. C.

B. Results on Dry Materials

Since the very careful study by Speakman and Chamberlain [397] on the relation of fiber type, fabric density, and fabric thickness to thermal insulation, not much has been added. Others [294] have used Speakman's and Chamberlain's data to bring out more explicitly the relation to density. Burton [84] cites wartime work on very low density in air spaces. Possible improvements result from the fact that new fibers do vary widely in their specific thermal conductivities and because of new techniques in making nonwoven structures. Very low density batts are possible. For systems made of one kind of fiber at similar density levels, thickness and thermal insulation are proportional over the whole range of available fabrics and several authors have written equations for converting thickness to thermal transmission. Examples of these are:

$$T = \frac{1}{3.0 \, t_{0.1} + 0.63} \; \text{Btu/}^\circ\text{F hr ft}^2 \qquad (6\text{-}1)$$

where T is thermal transmission and $t_{0.1}$ is thickness in inches at 0.10 psi, obtained by Schiefer and co-workers on a wide variety of blanket materials [376].

$$T = \frac{1}{1.38 \, t_0 + 0.252} \; \text{cal/}^\circ\text{C sec cm}^2 \qquad (6\text{-}2)$$

obtained by Rees on a variety of clothing fabrics [341].

The focus on clothing fabrics of new fibers has revealed that many new structures do not have a sufficiently random arrangement of the fibers to follow the early relationships between thermal resistance and thickness. Models assigning the contributions of fibers parallel and perpendicular to the fiber surface have thus been useful in interpreting thermal insulation figures [54].

The specific conductivity of a fiber-air assembly is given by

$$k = x(v_f k_f + v_a k_a) + y k_f k_a/(v_a k_f + v_f k_a) \qquad (6\text{-}3)$$

in which x and y are the effective fractions of fibers parallel and perpendicular to the direction of heat flow, respectively, and k_f and k_a are the specific thermal conductivities of fiber and air respectively while v_f and v_a are the corresponding volume fractions of each component.

A further variation in the use of materials for clothing purposes has been the use of foams and laminates to obtain a wider range of insulation for comparable weight than that achieved with conventional fabrics. Thermal insulation of these composites also follows a linear relationship with thickness, but of slightly different shape, as shown in Fig. 6-1.

C. Results on Moist Materials

A number of attempts have been made by various workers to assess the particular role of moisture in governing the insulation of clothing materials. These have covered rather wide ranges of moisture content consistent with the moisture actually retained by clothing in use on men (see Sect. V). Hock et al. [214] were one of the first to recognize that part of the effect of heat transmission in moist fabrics was sensed as coolness, particularly if the skin contact was extensive. Hall and Polte [191] examined the direct effects of sweat retention in clothing on thermal insulation and the changes brought about by compression over normal clothing pressure ranges. For example, Woodcock and Dee [466] studied wet clothing layers and concluded that the drying of fabric materials while conducting heat greatly lowered their insulating value, but that this occurred for shorter periods with bibulous fabrics than for nonbibulous types, such as cotton and wool underwear, respectively. They also noted that thermal losses were greater if the layer next to the heat source was wet rather than separated from it.

Later, Woodcock [464] determined the fluctuations in insulation of clothing on men under sweating conditions and found them to be much

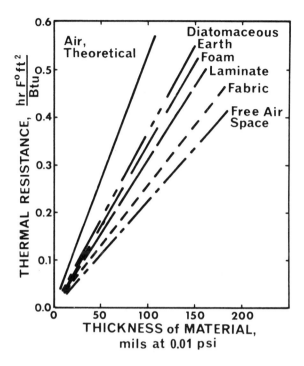

Fig. 6-1. Comparative thermal resistance of fabrics, foams, laminates, and air spaces. From Monego et al. [307].

smaller than predicted but attributed this to the low moisture levels achieved in these experiments. Hollies made actual thermal resistance measurements on clothing fabrics in this moisture content range and found that the loss in insulation was proportional to the moisture content, taking into account fiber arrangement as shown in Table 6-1 [230].

The specific conductivity data in Table 6-1 was calculated using the expression

$$k_3 = (1 - v_w)k + v_w k_w \qquad (6-4)$$

in which k_3 is the specific thermal conductivity of the fiber-air-water assembly, k is the overall conductivity of the air dry assembly (see Sect. VI), k_w is the effective specific conductivity of water in such an assembly, and v_w is the volume fraction of water ($v_w + v_f + v_a = 1$). The basic assumption used in deriving this equation is that water is held either

Table 6-1. Thermal Conductivity of Moist Fabrics

Fabric description	Fabric thickness[a] (mils)	Water content		Specific conductivity	
		Weight (%)	Volume fraction, v_w	Exp. k^b (cal in/m² sec °C)	Cal. k^c (cal in/m² sec °C)
Wool serge	73(0.01)	12	0.027	0.34	0.35
	75(0.01)	27	0.056	0.40	0.40
	79(0.01)	45	0.077	0.46	0.45
Orlon serge	42(0.01)	8	0.030	0.40	0.40
	42(0.01)	23	0.079	0.44	0.47
Cotton serge	47(0.01)	11	0.034	0.49	0.48
	46(0.01)	23	0.069	0.54	0.52
Nylon underwear	40(0.1)	15	0.041	0.47	0.47
Nylon underwear[d]	35(0.1)	16	0.048	0.47	0.47

Cotton underwear	32(0.1)	18	0.057	0.53	0.53
Wool underwear[e]	52(0.1)	17	0.028	0.37	0.38
Wool underwear	51(0.1)	15	0.031	0.37	0.38
70 wool-30 orlon serge	42(0.1)	13	0.061	0.46	0.47
	42(0.1)	30	0.120	0.54	0.57
	41(0.1)	15	0.089	0.54	0.54
	41(0.1)	31	0.142	0.63	0.63
Wool shirting	74(0.1)	15	0.035	0.37	0.36
70 wool-30 viscose shirt	67(1.0)	15	0.042	0.39	0.39

[a] Distance between plates of thermal apparatus. Numbers in parenthesis are estimates of pressure (lb/in^2) exerted on fabric.

[b] Measured directly on modified Cenco Fitch apparatus with cold source near 0°C.

[c] Calculated using Eq. (6-4).

[d] Water repellent.

[e] Shrink resistant.

within the fiber substance or on its surface and so contributes to the overall conductance as a group of conducting elements in parallel with the fibers already present. The equation appears to hold for applied pressures of 0.01 to 1.0 psi and for up to 15% water on serge, knit underwear, and shirting fabrics of cotton, nylon, acrylics, wool, and wool blends with these fibers. Further work at the U.S. Army Natick Laboratories [217] on underwear fabrics revealed that the replacement of air in fabric with water vapor substantially decreased the thermal insulation more than would be predicted from the specific thermal conductance of water vapor. They attributed this to the ease of accommodation of water on the fiber surfaces leading to a liquid film and agreed with the mechanism proposed by Hollies [230] for this effect.

III. WATER VAPOR DIFFUSION RESISTANCE

A. Introduction

Interest in the passage of water through clothing materials stems naturally from the fact the human body is continually losing water, mostly by evaporation and diffusion, and the loss of moisture through clothing is very important for heat balance and comfort. Even at low stress levels, the restriction of water passage by diffusion can be sensed subjectively.

The key factor for clothing materials involves sufficient openness such that the water vapor resistance of a fabric is not very different from that of an equivalent air layer. Indeed, for convenience the diffusion resistance is often expressed in terms of an equivalent thickness of air. As with thermal transmission, it is convenient to express the clothing impedance to water vapor in resistance units, permitting the summation of clothing layer components to achieve the total resistance of a clothing assembly. In terms of comfort, it is important to distinguish between the water vapor transmission properties and those of air permeability or the effects of wind on clothing effectiveness; the two are quite different.

B. Methods

Price [335] has reviewed the techniques which have been used for water vapor transmission methods. Fourt [151] described the two main methods which have been applied to fabrics. In the absorption method, an assembly of fabric and metal rings is sealed to small dishes containing a granular drying agent. The dishes are inverted and placed in a constant humidity atmosphere. The adsorption method is not well suited for high permeability materials, because the surface of the desiccant becomes moist, or for very low permeabilities, because the resistance of the material may be much higher when dry, or dry on one side.

It is important to distinguish between vapor permeability methods which are suitable for high resistance packaging materials, in which the resistance of air layers is only minor, and methods for high permeability materials, such as fabrics, where a major part of the resistance of the measuring system is in air layers. Because of this importance of air layers, an open dish is *not* a suitable control, a point which has been overlooked in some otherwise excellent work.

From Fick's diffusion law, the total resistance to water vapor transmission is

$$R = \Delta CAt/Q \qquad (6\text{-}5)$$

in which ΔC is water vapor conc. gradient (g/cm^3), A is area of transfer (cm^2), and Q is weight of water transferred in time t.

From several measurements of different numbers of fabric layers, the contribution per fabric layer can be determined.

The chief exponent of the evaporation method has been Goodings, who in a series of papers [444, 445] has shown how the technique can be applied to porous bodies in general and clothing fabrics in particular. In this technique, the fabric is sealed over the mouth of a small dish containing water, as shown in Fig. 6-2. The same equations applied, but in addition to variation in the number of fabric layers, the air space between water and fabrics must be varied to derive the contribution of a single fabric layer with or without its surface film of still air. Indeed, with these derived values of vapor diffusion resistance, it is possible to calculate the total resistance of a multicomponent system including a single air layer at the outer surface. Fourt and Goodings have shown that closely similar results are obtained using either one, two, or three layers, and constant air space [157], or one layer and a guard layer, with variable air space.

C. Results

Fourt [157] found that the resistance of a woven fabric depends on the thickness of the fabric and the tightness of the weave. Fabrics of cotton, viscose, rayon, and wool produced resistance two to eight times

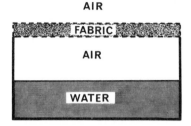

Fig. 6-2. Apparatus for measuring water vapor diffusion resistance of fabrics. From Whelan et al. [444].

that of air. Whelan et al. with Goodings went further in deriving an empirical formula expressing resistance in terms of thickness and fiber volume, excluding fabrics of very high and very low air permeability. These authors employed a "constriction resistance" for the blocking of streamline flow by the more solid parts of the fabric. Indeed, within the practical range of clothing fabrics there was no effect of air permeability on water vapor resistance. Furthermore, Whelan et al. (loc. cit.) showed that change in fabric vapor resistance with wind velocity was accounted for completely by the thickness of the still air at the fabric surface through which vapor must diffuse.

In terms of clothing uses, most fabrics restrict water loss by diffusion in proportion to their thickness and these characteristics of fabrics are easily assessed. For porous structures used in warm climates, the thinnest fabric seems advisable. For protection from rain, structures which breathe and are not completely impermeable are desired and the techniques for accomplishing this are discussed in Sect. IX.

Fourt et al. [149] have shown that the passage of water vapor through the fiber substance itself is very small compared with that through fabrics, that is, along fiber surfaces and especially through air spaces.

IV. WATER TRANSPORT IN CLOTHING MATERIALS

A. Transport by Wicking

Considerable attention has been paid to the ability of clothing structures to transport liquid water by capillary action. Although clothing fabrics in particular differ widely in their ability to act as wicks, not all these differences are translated into comfort differences. First of all, studies on men, particularly in the cold, have shown that water collection in clothing seldom reaches water content levels sufficient to induce wicking [224]. Water evaporating from the skin area may well condense in the cooler clothing layers but capillaries are not sufficiently water-filled, or continuous, to start the transport mechanism. In contrast, wicking may well be important in tropical clothing to promote quick-drying and cooling at higher water content levels [431]. A method of evaluating clothing in terms of wetted area was discussed in Chapter 2. In addition, capillary distribution in clothing materials is undoubtedly important in CBR protection of the soldier. (See Sect. VI.)

The classical work relating porous structure to capillary flow is that of Washburn [438]. On the basis of this wicking, tests have been devised for water absorption and capillary transport [232] to permit an easy interpretation of the results. For example, through the increase of wicking rate on horizontal samples, it is possible to assess differences in yarn evenness [233] and fabric structure [235].

Minor et al. [304] have studied transport of a wide variety of liquids in fiber assemblies and interpreted the penetration of fabrics by liquid drops [305] using single fiber and fiber-to-fiber wetting information. Schwartz [379] offered a thermodynamic explanation for this behavior and later applied it to two-component and two-phase liquid systems [336]. This information, although of key significance in CBR protection, has as yet had only limited use in normal sweat saturation of clothing or rain leakage.

The considerations of fiber parallelism and closeness which were studied in detail for CBR agent-simulants were also used as the basis of drop penetration rate tests and the degree of fiber randomness used by Bogaty [57] and Fourt [157]. These workers developed 100% wool-like characteristics in wool blends using fabrics of limited wool content, by applying drop penetration tests to assess the degree of randomness of the fibers used.

B. Water Transfer between Clothing Layers

The basic concept for achieving flexibility in clothing lies in the use of multiple layers, each designed for a specific function or to be added as needed to obtain more warmth. Moisture transfer in clothing fabrics, therefore, is very much concerned with the mechanisms operating between fabric layers. Several techniques have been developed to assess what actually happens at the moisture content levels of clothing in use [232].

Weight gain of a dry fabric in contact with a moist fabric and under load was used to assess the extent of blotting in casual contact of clothing layers. The corresponding transfer under a temperature gradient was measured between moist and dry fabrics placed in the modified Cenco-Fitch heat transmission apparatus [150] under a definite pressure. The temperatures of the fabric surfaces were measured with wire resistance grids.

This work revealed that with a wide variety of moist underwear-dry serge fabric combinations, all the water gained by the serge was through distillation from the underwear layer even at a pressure of 1.0 psi, generally in excess of the fabric loading by the body. Furthermore, it was clear that the surface hairiness of the component fabrics determined the distance over which distillation occurred. No underwear-serge combination, no matter how smooth, had so few surface fibers as to provide a continuous path for wicking.

An analysis of the temperature and water vapor pressure gradients across the fabrics showed further that both gradients were determined by the fabric thickness; fuzzy surfaced fabrics tended to produce a long distillation path and hence a slow accumulation of water. From this work, it was possible to derive an expression for moisture transfer.

$$m = \frac{\Delta CD}{l} \frac{(m_t - m)t}{m_t} \tag{6-6}$$

in which ΔC is the water concentration gradient, D is the diffusion constant of water in still air, l is the fabric separation distance, m_t is the maximum water holding capacity, and m is the amount of water transferred to dry fabric in time t.

C. Drying of Clothing Materials

There are some very practical aspects to the drying of clothing both as worn or in cleaning. At moderate water content levels, drying involves water transport within the fabric. Furthermore, the speed of loss of water from clothing can be very important to comfort under both cold and warm stress.

Generally, the moisture levels achieved in clothing fabrics under normal use are within the water content range through which there is a constant drying rate [158]. At this water content level, sufficient water is transferred to the fabric surface to keep it wet. The total drying time is chiefly determined by the total water content [404, 406]. The factors determining water holding capacity are discussed in Sect. V.

A new approach exists for achieving quick drying in cotton fabrics, at least, which may have an effect on subjective comfort [234]. It is possible to apply water repellent finishes to cotton in such a way as to lower the water holding capacity substantially without losing the ability to transmit water by capillary action to the fabric surface.

D. The Permeability Index

As developed in Chapter 2, the permeability index is a dimensionless expression relatable to vapor resistance and thermal resistance. However, it can also be measured directly.

Woodcock, in two classical papers [462, 463], handled the moisture transfer in clothing layers with a permeability index to account for the effective heat lost by moisture movement without specifying the specific contributions of condensation and evaporation of moisture. He postulated a coefficient describing the efficiency of fabrics or fabric systems in transferring moisture and the associated latent heat as an extension of the Clo system for describing dry clothing insulation. With his analysis, the total equation for heat loss becomes

$$H = \frac{5.5}{I} ((T_s - T_a) + i_m S(p_s - p_a)) \tag{6-7}$$

given in kg cal/m^2 hr in which I is dry insulation in Clo units, T_s, P_s are the temperature (°C) and vapor pressure at the wet skin surface, T_a, P_a are the temperature (°C) and vapor pressure at the ambient fabric surface, S is 2.0°C/Torr, a constant, from the slope in the psychometric charts, and i_m is the permeability index.

Values of i_m can be determined with fabrics wrapped on a wet cylinder in a controlled environment of temperature, moisture content, and air motion. The determination follows from measurement of the wet surface temperature, as an imperfectly exposed wet-bulb thermometer. In a modified hot plate type apparatus, heat loss can also be determined on fabrics collecting moisture and in the drying state. This type of measurement simulates two important phases of the use of clothing outside normal heat and moisture transmission and illustrates that clothing behavior does require more information than the static coefficients of I and i_m.

Goldman [179] has applied Woodcock's idea very successfully to the characterization of clothing systems and has been able to predict the tolerance limits for clothing under cold and warm stress using I and i_m for individual clothing components. Tables of insulation and permeability index values have been collected on combat uniform components, permitting such predictions without resort to subjective testing. The Woodcock approach is also described in Chapter 2.

V. WATER HOLDING PROPERTIES

A. Relation to Regain

Many textile fibers take up water internally due to their chemical structure, the so-called "regain" water. The way in which regain moisture relates to comfort is discussed in Chapters 2, 4, and 7. All textile structures, however, whether or not they absorb moisture, collect water on the fiber surface, or between fibers as capillary water, and this is called the water of "imbibition." Although water of imbibition and regain both contribute to the total water content, this section is concerned only with the imbibition component. As has been discussed in previous sections, the water content of clothing fabrics and motion of water in these fabrics both play an important role in determining comfort factors.

B. Methods of Measurement

The total water content of fabrics is easily determined electrically or by weighing while the water of imbibition can be determined by centrifuging the wet fabric [334, 429]. Although on a dynamic basis the amount of water held by clothing being worn is determined by the balance between collection in the distillation and evaporation processes (Sect. IV), it is the fabric structure which ultimately determines the peak moisture content to be expected. Generally, the fabrics of natural fibers with relatively random orientation of the fibers in the yarn hold the most moisture but there is no specific connection between these facts and their comfort. One possible connection, for thin filament yarn fabrics which feel wet at low moisture content, is the association, "It feels wet, therefore, I must be hotter and be sweating more." Liquid drops standing or trickling across the skin can be distinctly uncomfortable, as every public speaker knows, and damp fabric can also be uncomfortable.

C. Relation to Water Repellency

Although repellency will be discussed separately in Sect. IX, certain connections with the water content of clothing fabrics are worth pointing out at this stage. Variations such as yarn size, twist, and weave, and especially chemical finishes which lead to water repellency, also reduce the capacity. From extensive work on cotton fabrics [219], as illustrated in Table 6-2, Hollies and co-workers noted that the tightly woven twill, duck, and drapery fabrics of low specific volume were the most repellent of the group and also held relatively less water for their particular fabric weights. All of the structures given a water-repellent fluorocarbon finish became highly water repellent and as a result held one-half to one-third the amount of water, after spinning in a home washer, of their untreated counterparts.

D. Relation to Sweat Retention

The basic guides to the important practical ranges for water retention in clothing fabrics have come from actual measurements on men under stress. For example, Goddard [174] was able to give practical retentions for the various portions of arctic combat clothing and thereby determine the changes in overall insulation which might be expected. This work was extended later to other clothing items [133].

In a more recent study on men wearing cold weather combat clothing of different water permeability characteristics, and exercising in the cold, specific information was collected about the water content of underwear and outerwear layers in several experimental uniforms in a variety of environments [224]. This is summarized in Table 6-3.

Even in a warm environment, less than 10% water was added to the underwear layer unless the soldier wore an impermeable layer over the whole body. Without any impermeable layer, maximum water retained was only 2.2% for the first layer and 0.1% for the second layer. Thus, the ultimate water holding capacity of these uniform fabrics really did not play a role in determining the loss of comfort due to water penetration by sweating. Likewise, even when the impermeable fabric was applied to specific body areas and the underwear layer appeared wet, this wetness did not spread to other body areas and cause a loss in insulation. Thus, as discussed in Sect. IV, there was not enough water in any one layer to promote water transport along or between layers by capillary action. This is one of the main reasons that the first two combat clothing variations in Table 6-3 were so effective in these particular studies on men.

Table 6-2. Effect of Fabric Construction and Water Repellent Treatment on Water Retention

Fabric description	Print-cloth	Knit	Corduroy	Twill	Duck	Drapery	Terry towel	Upholstery
No.	1	12	10	3	4	5	11	8
Weight (oz/sq. yd)	3.25	5.00	6.25	6.50	7.75	9.00	9.00	10.25
Weave	Plain	Plain knit	Pinwale 16 ribs/in.	2/1	Plain double filled	Novelty	Warp pile	Plain
Spec. volume (cm^3/g at 0.1 psi)	2.1	5.7	4.1	1.9	2.1	2.1	10.0	3.2
Yarns/in. W	84	30d	96	112	94	84	52	25
F	76	24d	84	52	30	38	36	20

Yarn No. (tex)							
W	17	20/2	17	30	40	28	35	200/2e
F	14		25	33	35/2	70	60	200/2e
Twist[a] (tpi)							
W	22z	13s/20z	20z	14s	20z	16z	13z	9s/12z
F	22z	17z	17z	14z	18z/9s	9z	11z	7s/13z
Water content[b]							
Untreated, %	71	80	85	58	85	67	102	69
Treated,[c] %	36	28	31	24	27	27	40	30

[a]Ply twist/single twist.
[b]After spinning in a washing machine.
[c]Durable press and water repellent treated.
[d]Wales and courses.
[e]Novelty yarns; tex and t.p.i. are average values.

Table 6-3. Moisture Distribution in the First and Second Clothing Layers at the Completion of the Chilling Experiments[a]

Portion of underwear covered with a water vapor impermeable membrane		Weather[b] "cold"		Weather "moderate"		Weather "warm"	
		shirt (%)	pants (%)	shirt (%)	pants (%)	shirt (%)	pants (%)
Arms and legs	1st layer[c]	0.0	1.8	5.7	7.5	6.4	7.5
	2nd layer	0.0	-0.1	0.3	0.1	1.4	0.6
Torso (upper garment excluding arms)	1st layer	6.2	1.6	8.8	0.7	10.7	1.2
	2nd layer	0.1	0.5	0.1	0.5	0.3	0.5
Crotch and armpits	1st layer	0.0	0.7	0.9	1.3	1.3	2.4
	2nd layer	0.7	0.4	1.1	0.4	0.8	1.2

Complete (all sections)	1st layer	7.8	3.9	16.7	12.0	15.7	14.5
	2nd layer	-1.1	-0.8	-0.8	-0.6	-1.9	0.3
None (standard underwear)	1st layer	0.2	0.2	0.5	0.9	1.1	2.2
	2nd layer	0.7	0.4	0.7	0.5	0.7	1.0

[a] Average values for all men based on initial weights of individual clothing items.
[b] Definitions of weather conditions:

	Air temperature (°F)	Radiation temperature (°F)	Wind velocity (mph)
Average "cold" day	18.7	23.4	11.2
Average "moderate" day	25.2	38.5	7.1
Average "warm" day	37.3	43.3	4.2

[c] First layer: underwear; second layer: shirt and serge trousers.

VI. THICKNESS OF CLOTHING MATERIALS

A. Significance of Thickness

From the foregoing sections of this chapter, it is easy to recognize fabric thickness as a prime factor in determining the level of effectiveness for such comfort factors as insulation, water vapor transmission, and water holding capacity. This is true also in examining these properties as a function of clothing pressure and multiple layers.

B. Methods of Measurement

Fabric thickness can be determined with a number of different devices which all load the fabric to a specific pressure and determine plate separation with a gauge. The ASTM Method D1777-64 [9], and Federal Specification Method 5030 [97] use a dead weight loaded gauge, whereas the Schiefer Compressometer [372, 159] uses a spring-loaded presser foot, determining pressure from the compression of the spring. By loading to different pressures starting at low load, and then returning from a high load, compression and recovery thickness curves are obtained. Compression at very low loads can be achieved by loading with a microscope cover glass or a flat portion of paper, and observing the thickness change with a calibrated microscope. Likewise, the Instron or other recording force-displacement equipment can be used with a compression cell to obtain thickness pressure curves directly. Generally, a compression range covering that experienced in clothing is used [371]. For example, Bogaty et al. [58] characterized a series of blended wool fabrics for potential combat use at four pressures, 0.002, 0.01, 0.1, and 1.0 psi (metric, 0.14, 0.70, 7.0, 70 g/cm^2) to cover the range experienced in use. Loads comparable to another layer of fabric range from light (5 oz/yd^2) to heavy (20 oz/yd^2) and may be represented by 0.015 g/cm^2 to 0.07 g/cm^2. The pressures corresponding to fabric weights can be approximated by laying flat pieces of light paper on the fabric. This procedure can be used to measure a representative uncrushed thickness, by using a ruler, a cathetometer, or a microscope (40X objective) with a calibrated vertical scale to measure how far the tube must be focused upwards when the fabric is put under the paper. Thickness of clothing structures can be similarly measured, lying flat, but may or may not include the air spaces measured in the radial thickness as on a manikin or a living subject.

For ready conversion from pressure in lb/in^2 (psi) take 1 psi = 70 g/cm^2 (more exactly, 70.4). Usual pressure ranges in English units and close metric equivalents are shown in Table 6-4. In measuring fabric

Table 6-4. Conversion Table, Fabric Weight and Pressure

	psi	g/cm^2	g/m^2	oz/yd^2
	1	70	700,000	20,706
	0.1	7	70,000	2,071
	0.01	0.7	7,000	207
	0.001	0.07	700	20.7
Fabric wt.	20 oz/yd^2	0.07	700	(20.7)
	10 oz/yd^2	0.035	350	(10.3)
	1 oz/yd^2	0.0035	35	(1.03)

thickness, a pressure or condition of tension or both needs to be specified, except for firm fabrics which do not change much with pressure or tension.

C. Thickness Retention

From the measurements of thickness in compression and recovery, resilience and permanent set can be calculated. If the original fabric thickness was x, the compressed thickness was y, and the recovered thickness z,

$$\text{Resilience } (\%) = \frac{z - y}{x - y} \times 100$$

and   (6-8)

$$\text{Permanent set } (\%) = \frac{x - z}{x} \times 100$$

Bogaty et al. [58] used this approach to assess the relative suitability of blended serges for cold weather use.

D. Thickness and Pressure: An Equation of State for Clothing Materials

The concept of considering a fabric as a system invariant in two dimensions and compressible in the third dimension is not new. Several attempts have been made to treat compression and recovery data in more detail, particularly in reference to the easily recognized differences in behavior of lofty fabrics at low and high pressures. The approaches have generally been empirical, each worker expressing his thickness-pressure results in an equation having as few arbitrary parameters as possible. For example, Hoffman and Beste [216] used the expression

$$p = k(t_0 - t_p)\alpha \qquad (6-9)$$

in which k, t_0, and α were constants and t_p was the thickness at pressure p. With $\alpha = 5/4$, a fairly satisfactory fit to their data on clothing fabrics was achieved. A different equation was suggested by Van Wyk [430] for describing the compressibility of wool fibers in analogy to the compressibility of a gas. His expression was

$$p = \frac{KYm^3}{\rho_f} \left(\frac{1}{V^3} - \frac{1}{V_0^3} \right) \qquad (6-10)$$

in which m is the mass, ρ_f the density of the fiber, Y the Young's modulus of elasticity, K is a constant, V_0 is the volume at zero pressure, V is the volume at pressure p. Because of the way thickness is measured, i.e., the area parallel to the pressure foot remains constant, V in such equations can be replaced by t and in simplified form Van Wyk's equation becomes

$$p = \frac{C_1^\alpha}{t} + C_2 \qquad (6-11)$$

with C_1 and C_2 constants. In the work on wool, the best value for α was 3.

Schiefer [374] recognized the need for finding equations which would describe the thickness-pressure relationship quantitatively over a wide pressure range and proposed that the more extended equation

$$1/t = mp^{1/3} + 1/t_0 \qquad (6-12)$$

to account for the thickness t_0 at zero pressure, but still retaining a power function of 3.

In a similar approach but starting from the Van der Waals equation for gas compression, Bogaty and co-workers [56] examined the compressibility of a wide variety of blended wool fabrics using the expression

$$(p + c) (t - a) = b \qquad (6-13)$$

in which c is a constant and is analogous to the internal pressure at p = 0, a is a constant, the fabric thickness at a high pressure, and b is a constant related to the compressibility energy. In a survey of these approaches applied to measurements on pile fabrics, Larose [272] found the equation by Bogaty to be the most useful, the empirical parameter b reflecting very well the loftiness of these structures.

Hollies [225] later applied the Bogaty approach to a wider range of woven fabrics including smooth cotton structures and concluded that a single value of b would not be sufficient to characterize many of the fabrics. Indeed, the equation was not adequate over the whole pressure range for these fabrics. An attempt was made, therefore, to learn from the more general equations of state for gases whether a suitable form could be found for fiber systems in general. In the Beattie-Bridgeman equation [377], the interaction energy and real volume aspects are expressed as virial coefficients β, and γ, etc., in a series of equations of the form:

$$pv \ = \ RT \ [1 + (\beta/v) + (\gamma/v^2) + \cdots]$$

or $\hfill (6\text{-}14)$

$$(pv/RT) = f(v)$$

f(v) being a series equation in $1/v$. Using this concept and writing a similar equation for fabric compression, we have

$$pt = f(t) \qquad (6\text{-}15)$$

or correcting for the thickness a, at very high pressures and the fractional number of fibers in the area of compression (analogous to RT in the earlier equation)

$$\frac{p\,(t - a)}{1 - \bar{a}} \ = \ b_{\bar{a}} \qquad (6\text{-}16)$$

in which $\bar{a}$ is the fractional cross section of the fabric which is air and $b_{\bar{a}}$ is a compressibility energy function containing the virial coefficients of fiber-fiber interaction. For general use in which absolute values of the compression energy are not needed, the equation is

$$p(t - a) = b_0 \qquad (6\text{-}17)$$

It turns out that the real usefulness of $b_{\bar{a}}$ or b_0 comes from application of this equation to the surface properties of fabrics and this subject is discussed fully in the next section.

VII. SURFACE PROPERTIES OF FABRICS

A. Relation to Comfort Factors

As already noted in relation to thermal resistance and vapor diffusion resistance of fabrics [58], the surface hairiness of the yarns and fabrics themselves has a profound effect on the comfort factors of insulation and loss of body moisture. Because the surface fibers contribute substantially to fabric thickness at clothing pressures, changes in insulation and water transmission can be quite substantial. In addition, the type of surface contact of fabrics with the skin, especially when wet, may also affect the comfort level achieved by a clothing fabric system.

B. Surface Characterization by Thickness-Pressure Measurement

The use of thickness-pressure measurements for surface characterization of clothing fabrics has been discussed by Bogaty and co-workers [56] in relation to blended clothing fabrics. The equations of Bogaty were used to obtain a single compression energy value b and it was soon evident that the higher the value of b, the greater the hairiness. Table 6-5 gives data from this work relating subjective hairiness to b value, from which it can be seen that the two evaluations are positively correlated.

Using the compression energy b_0 as a parameter describing the change in surface contact with pressure (see Sect. VI), even smooth clothing fabrics can be described. If the surface changes with moisture content of the fabric, then the rate-of-cooling technique can also follow these changes as shown in Fig. 6-3 [223]. The peaks in these curves at high thickness are directly associated with the energy of compression and recovery of the surface fibers. As can be seen in this figure, the surface effects are largely removed by moisture.

C. Surface Characterization by Rate of Cooling

A heat transfer method was also developed for determining surface hairiness of fabrics [231]. The method measured the surface ratio n/l (number of surface fibers to their length), and was found to be applicable to wool, nylon, and rayon fabrics.

Table 6-5. Subjective Evaluation of Smoothness or Hairiness of Fabrics, Using Four Observers

Symbol	Fabric type	b value (lb/in)	
			Smooth
A	Viscose lining	0.17×10^3	AAAA
B	Tropical suiting	0.37	BCBB[a]
C	Tropical suiting	0.48	CBCC[a] CCCE
D	Tropical suiting	0.57	DDDC
E	Tropical suiting	0.73	EEED EEEE
F	Blended serge	1.32	FFFF
G	Cotton flannel	1.70	GGGG HGGG
H	Wool serge	1.94	GHHH HHIH
I	Wool serge	3.64	IIHI IIII
J	Blended covert	3.81	JJJJ
K	Wool blanket	12.5	KKKK Hairy

[a]These samples could not be differentiated by this observer. Samples were presented in groups of 3 or 4 as indicated in the table. Reprinted from Ref. [56] by courtesy of the *Textile Res. J.*

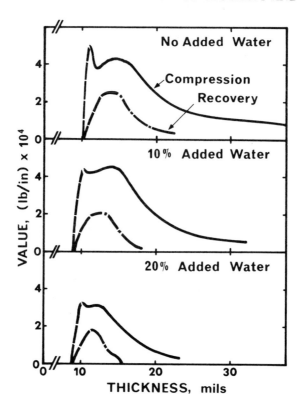

Fig. 6-3. Surface contact by compression measurements of untreated print cloth [223].

The technique defines that where a fabric surface has n fibers of length, l, and conductivity, k, per unit area

$$(nk/l) = C(m - m_0 - m_a)   \tag{6-18}$$

in which C is

apparatus constant = -2.303 Mc/A

M, c, and A are the mass, specific heat, and area of the heated metal disk contacting the fabric and m is the slope of the linear curve relating log fractional temperature drop of the metal disk with time, m_0 is the heat loss

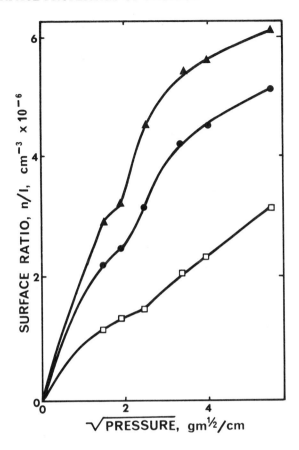

Fig. 6-4. Surface contact by rate-of-cooling measurements of untreated print cloth [223]. Amounts of added water: □, none; ●, 10%; ▲, 20%.

correction to the metal disk insulation, and m_a is the heat loss correction for air between the surface fibers.

A convenient parameter for relating rate-of-cooling data to surface hairiness is the time of cooling t½ (time taken for the heated disk to cool half way) [57]. As shown in Table 6-6, this is quite a sensitive measure of small differences in surface hairiness of blended fabrics.

Even in applications to very smooth cotton fabrics, substantial differences in surface ratio (n/l) occur. Results for a printcloth sample are given in Fig. 6-4 using for convenience (pressure)½ to condense the thickness range covered in this work [223]. Note that this technique distinguishes changes

Table 6-6. Surface Hairiness of Serges as
Estimated by a Rate of Cooling Method

Nominal fiber composition of fabrics		Time to cool 7.5°C ($t\frac{1}{2}$)	Specific conductance of the surface fibers[a] (nk/l)
Wool (%)	Other (%)	(sec)	(cal/°C cm² sec)
100	0	71	8.2×10^{-4}
85	15 Dynel	74	7.6
70	30 Dynel	76	7.2
50	50 Dynel	71	8.0
0	100 Dynel	53	13.2
100	0	68	8.9
85	15 Acrilan	71	8.0
70	30 Acrilan	65	9.3
50	50 Acrilan	58	10.9
0	100 Acrilan	49	14.4
100	0	73	7.7
85	15 Orlon	72	8.1
70	30 Orlon	70	8.4
50	50 Orlon	69	8.3
0	100 Orlon	49	14.2

[a]n is the number of surface fibers per unit area, k is the conductance of the fiber substance, and l is the mean length of the surface hairs. Reprinted from Ref. [57] by courtesy of the *Textile Res. J.*

in contact at low pressures due to surface fibers from fabric contact at high pressures and the changes of both of these with moisture in the fabric.

D. Surface Characterization from Photographs

Visual examination of a fabric surface has been found to be very useful in judging the relative hairiness of fabrics. The fabric to be examined is folded diagonally to the principal direction of the cloth and placed between two glass plates. The assembly is placed in a photographic enlarger and the image focused on a film to give a modest enlargement.

ALL WOOL SERGE (Sample WSC)

WOOL/NYLON BLENDED SERGE (Sample NSC)

Fig. 6-5. Photographs of fabric surfaces.

For quantitative work, a grid is photographed along with the fabric sample and the number of fibers at each grid level are determined by counting. A pair of these are shown in Fig. 6-5.

The number of fibers across the photographs at various heights above the bulk fabric were used to calculate the number of surface fibers, n, as a function of fabric thickness and with information from the compression measurements as a function of fabric pressure. Figure 6-6 shows surface ratio (n/l) values for the upper fabric in Fig. 6-5 obtained from rate of cooling, thickness-pressure, and photographic techniques.

E. Electrical Methods for Surface Contact

In connection with work for the U.S. Army Quartermaster Corps [52] on wool blends, it was possible to measure surface properties of fabrics using the electrical conductivity of the individual fibers as contact paths. Electrical conductivity between two metal plates of fixed area in contact with a fabric can be shown to relate to the surface ratio n/l using

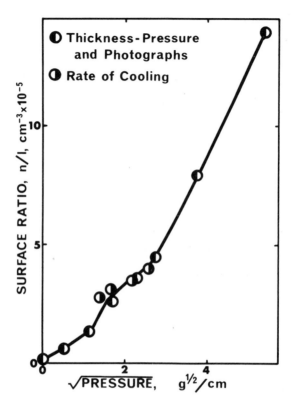

Fig. 6-6. Change of surface ratio, n/l, with pressure, wool serge WSC.

$$\frac{n}{l} = \frac{G_l}{G_h} \frac{4w_0}{\pi d^2 \rho_f s} \tag{6-19}$$

in which G_l is the conductivity at low pressure, G_h is the conductivity at high pressure, w_0 is the density of the base fabric. Fibers of diameter d have density ρ_f and s is the separation of the electrodes. Salt and moisture can be added to the fabric to make the electrical measurement easier.

Figure 6-7 shows how this method applied to a cotton serge fabric correlates with corresponding work using the rate-of-cooling method.

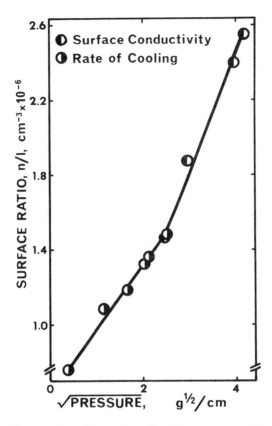

Fig. 6-7. Change of surface ratio, n/l, with pressure, cotton serge #28.

F. Significance of the Compressibility Energy Function in Terms of Fabric Surfaces

As discussed in the previous section on fabric thickness, the compression and recovery properties of clothing fabrics can be expressed in terms of an equation of state

$$\frac{p\,(t-a)}{1-\bar{a}} = b\bar{a} \qquad (6\text{-}16)$$

in which $b\bar{a}$ is an energy function containing the virial coefficients of fiber-fiber interaction. Such an equation becomes quite useful in application to

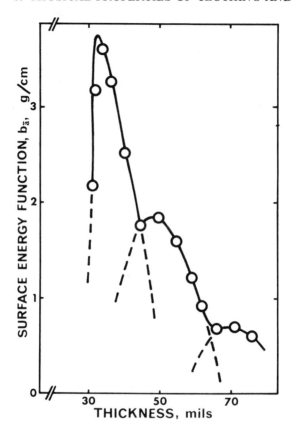

Fig. 6-8. Compressibility energy function, $b_{\bar{a}}$, as a function of fabric thickness, wool serge WSC.

the various methods for characterizing fabric surfaces since the biggest fluctuations in $b_{\bar{a}}$ occur at low pressures with corresponding large changes in fabric thickness.

The corresponding equation in terms of the number of surface fibers, n (per cm^2), the length, l (cm), and diameter, d (cm) is

$$\frac{4p}{\pi d^2} = \frac{n}{l} \, b_{\bar{a}} \qquad (6\text{-}20)$$

As we have seen, the fabric surface ratio may be evaluated from rate-of-cooling data or electrical conductivity data of the surface fibers while surface fibers can be counted directly using the photographic technique.

Values of the compressibility energy function, $b_{\bar{a}}$, were calculated from thickness-pressure, photographs, and rate-of-cooling data for the wool serge fabric shown in Fig. 6-5 and these are plotted against thickness in Fig. 6-8. For this fabric, in which n/l measurements were made down to 0.0005 psi using a special recording compressometer, three regions are noted in the $b_{\bar{a}}$ function.

At very high thicknesses at which only the long isolated surface fibers can be involved, there is a modest peak in $b_{\bar{a}}$ corresponding to their compression. At intermediate thicknesses, where only the scattered and slightly entangled surface fibers can be involved, there is a second peak in the function $b_{\bar{a}}$, while the final high peak must correspond to the compression of bulk fabric.

In terms of the model of a fabric surface used to develop the equation of state, $b_{\bar{a}}$ is a measure of the energy of compression per unit area of fabric independent of the number of surface fibers in that area. Accordingly, the value of this function should reflect any change in the mechanism of the compression process or change in structure of the assembly under compression. This approach to fabric surface characterization deserves further testing on a variety of clothing fabrics.

G. Fabric Surface and Subjective Comfort

One of the key reasons for placing so much emphasis on techniques for characterizing clothing fabric surfaces lies in the special role these parameters play in actual comfort situations. Aside from the cool feel produced by very smooth fabrics [214], other sensations are noted in connection with sweating and mild thermal stress.

In a recent study on the comfort of all-cotton men's shirts [223], the various shirt types were examined using the thickness-pressure approach to surface characterization. As shown in Fig. 6-9, there was a progressive loss in the energy function b_0 at large fabric thicknesses with an increase in water content of the shirting. This means that the oxford matted down at water contents seen in subjective experiments and the wearers noted this as an increase in the clammy, sticky feeling of the shirt.

The same oxford, however, napped and stabilized with a triazone treatment, was considered comfortable under most wearing conditions. Examination of the fabric with the rate-of-cooling technique (Fig. 6-10) showed that the napping had reduced the surface ratio, n/l, and hence contact with the skin even in the presence of moisture. Indeed, this effect was most pronounced in the low pressure range at which the surface fibers acted to maintain fabric separation.

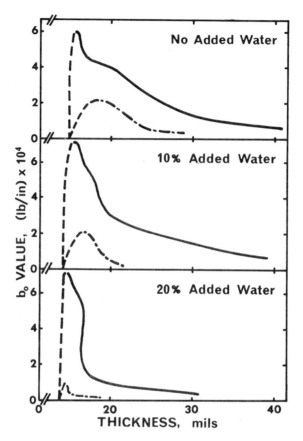

Fig. 6-9. Effect of water content on surface energy function, b_0, of oxford shirting [223].

VIII. POROSITY AND PERMEABILITY PROPERTIES

A. Porosity and Its Relationships

Whereas permeability refers to the accessibility of void space to the flow of gas or liquid, porosity is usually defined as the ratio of void space to the total volume encompassed by the boundaries of the material. The total porosity of a fabric can be visualized as having three components: (1) intra-fiber porosity—void space within the fiber walls; (2) interfiber porosity—void

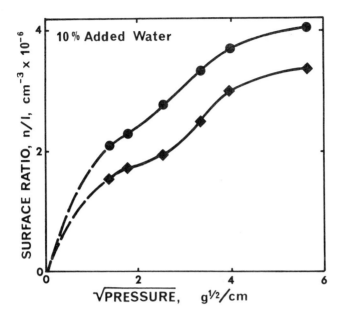

Fig. 6-10. Effectiveness of napping in stabilizing surface contact with resin [223]. Fabric types: ●, untreated, unnapped oxford; ◆, triazone-treated, very heavily napped oxford.

space between fibers in the yarns; and (3) interyarn porosity—void volume between yarns. Burleigh and co-workers [71] have reviewed the techniques for determining all types of porosity and most of these center on the penetration by weight of a liquid into the free space of the porous system. Because the porosity aspects most relevant to comfort are in the large size range (types 2 and 3), most of these techniques are satisfactory for studying differences in fabrics important to comfort.

It is possible, for example, to assess the distribution of pore sizes using mercury as the penetrant and observing the volume absorbed as a function of pressure. Studies on fabrics have shown that it is the interfiber and interyarn spaces which contribute the most to porosity and in turn are responsible for the main differences in air permeability.

Within the context of fabrics of similar structure, porosity is also a measure of water-holding capacity as mentioned in Sect. V, and so can influence substantially the drying rate [158]. Steel [405] was able to relate the distribution in capillary sizes of cotton printcloth, wool flannel, and nylon challis to their water holding capacity. More recently,

Coplan [107] has explored porous textile structures of high temperature fibers for reentry use in space in which the balance between air flow and temperature rise due to frictional effects is critical for determining which are useful structures.

B. The Measurement of Permeability

The Gurley permeometer [253] and Frazier air permeability [375] machines are used commonly for measuring air flow through fabrics. Other instruments have been described [97] but are less frequently employed. Although flow can be measured over a range of pressures, most textile permeabilities are quoted at 0.5 in. of water (ASTM D737-67). As discussed by Schiefer [375], the method of mounting the sample is important to avoid edge errors. From the practical standpoint, most fabrics exhibit air permeabilities in the range of 50 to 500 ft^3/min ft^2, well above the range corresponding to a partially impermeable film which would oppose water vapor transmission (cf. Sect. IV). This is the reason basically why air permeabilities of fabrics do not relate to the water aspects of comfort problems.

C. The Mechanism of Air Flow

Goodings [181] has studied the mechanism of air flow in clothing fabrics from the standpoint of a hydrodynamic flow and concluded that laminar and turbulent flow do occur. Much of the flow behavior is explained by the wide range of pore sizes involved. Also, flow through more than one layer is not merely an additive matter. The resistance to flow, however, becomes sufficiently high to make air penetration through multiple fabric layers quite unimportant over the air pressures met in clothing use. This work is interesting from another standpoint for clothing fabric considerations. Change of air flow through fairly permeable fabrics of the clothing range often follows an empirical logarithmic relation. This is consistent with the idea that internal resistance causing turbulent flow is due to the many abrupt changes in direction of air flow which occur in most fabrics. On the useful side, this relation makes it possible to calculate air flow through clothing under a variety of environmental conditions.

D. Air Flow over Fabric Layers — Wind

The air flow over a clothed man involves consideration of the effects due to air movement not normal to the fabric surface. The effect is partially that of permeability or penetration of the clothing but very largely that of air passage over the surface and a partial loss of insulation due to the still air trapped at the fabric surface. Day [117] made such studies on hot plate equipment and observed the very substantial contributions from windbreak layers as used in combat uniforms. Larose [273] extended this work to determine that windbreak layers need air permeabilities below 13 ft^3/ft^2 min, as measured at 0.5-in. water gauge, to give protection in winds (see Fig. 2-1). As the wind velocity is increased, a considerable portion of the insulation is lost due to removal of the outer still air layer. Above about 24 mph, no further loss occurs. In a two-layer system in which neither fabric is completely impermeable to wind, the effectiveness of the outer layer will depend very substantially on the nature of the second layer, open pile fabrics being less effective than low-density wool surface fabrics.

E. Fabric Systems for Wind Protection

Fonseca and co-workers [140] studied a wide variety of fabric layer combinations for combat soldier protection in the wind. This included the value of spaces between fabric layers, single and multiple windbreak layers with air permeabilities in the range of 5 to 720 ft^3/min ft^2.

In contrast to the findings by Breckenridge [68], Fonseca found no substantial advantage to spaces between layers in reducing wind chill. Both sets of work, however, showed that several combinations of windbreak and insulating layers can be effective and thereby modify the thermal losses predicted from wind chill tables of Siple [101]. In summary, the air permeability properties of clothing fabrics are mainly useful in cold environments and in the presence of wind.

In a practical study on civilian problems, Schiefer [371] did a very careful study on blankets and sheets in combination to determine which would be effective combinations. Sheets on either side of a blanket were found to maintain blanket insulation over a range of wind velocities. Likewise, Niven looked at a variety of overcoat [322] and laminated overcoat materials [323], noting how semipermeable layers in combination with low density insulators could be effective in winds to 17 mph.

F. Permeability to Water

Although clothing assemblies generally do not allow water to penetrate completely through, individual layers may be susceptible to penetration.

Fairly standard rain tests are available to assess this tendency, such as Federal Test Method 5-524 [97], ASTM Method D583-63 [9], or AATCC Method 35-1967 [1]. These all use a nozzle under pressure to achieve penetration. The tests are related directly to those for water repellency (Sect. IX).

G. Porosity Other than to Wind and Water

Although the relations to individual comfort factors are less well defined, the porosity of fabrics to other agents is also important. Protection from biting insects such as mosquitos involves consideration of low porosity outer layers of sufficient layer thickness to prevent penetration. Porosity is also involved in CBR protective clothing and this subject is mentioned in Sects. IV and X of this chapter.

IX. WATER AND OIL REPELLENCY

A. Introduction

Protection from rainfall is an essential requirement in a combat uniform, particularly for maintaining adequate insulation in the cold. As Weiner has pointed out [440], the use of a simple waterproof outerlayer is ineffective because moisture from sweating will collect in the clothing to as great an extent as if the outer layer had leaked. This results in not only a loss of insulation (Sect. II), but leads to excessive evaporation cooling (Sect. IV) when the waterproof layer is removed.

Protection from other liquid agents such as fuels and chemical warfare agents is also desirable. Again, the answer cannot be an impermeable protective layer which leads to sweating and loss of insulation. Rather, suitable clothing fabrics for any type of repellency must be able to breathe or maintain sufficient water vapor transmission to sustain the soldier close to physiological equilibrium with the environment.

B. Construction Approaches to Repellency

Construction factors promoting water repellency in wool fabrics were studied systematically by Sookne and coworkers [392]. Resistance to penetration increased very rapidly with increasing weight and thickness of the fabrics. Woven fabrics generally gave better resistance to penetration than corresponding knit structures. The generally good resistance of wool fabrics to water penetration was attributed to the difficulty of wetting out the wool yarns, and to shedding of water by the hairy surface. This was confirmed by Hollies [233] who showed that wool yarns had very high effective contact angles.

Segall [382] looked more closely at the effect of weave on water resistance showing that true water repellency was influenced by a combination of weave tightness and yarn porosity.

C. The Influence of Repellent Finishes

Chemical finishes, desirable and otherwise, were noted to contribute substantially to improved water resistance [382, 392] and especially when used with multiple fabric layers [140]. A wide range of material, including fatty long chain compounds, silicones, and fluorocarbons have all been shown to be effective. The mechanism of action is again an increase in effective contact angle with water for any structure so treated. Such finishes have no significant effect on water vapor permeability [151].

D. The Measurement of Water Resistance

A substantial number of tests have been developed for assessing the various aspects of water resistance. Related tests from the different standard groups are given in Table 6-7.

For screening purposes, the Spray Test has proved particularly useful for screening the relative resistance to external wetting of clothing fabrics. In addition, a modified permeability test was also devised for swelling-type fabrics [306]. Certain clothing items, however, really require testing in a rain room [440] to assess the contributions of openings and seams to overall water resistance.

E. Water Repellency of Seams

The U.S. Army Quartermaster Corps has also been active in determining how to sew water-resistant fabrics without losing their repellent features. As pointed out by Fredericks [160], this requires the production of a water-repellent sewing thread and controlled sewing practices. The treatment for water repellency can be evaluated by use of the Dynamic Absorption Test, #5500 (see Table 6-5).

Table 6-7. Water Resistance of Textile Fabrics

Description of test	ASTM Designation[a]	AATCC	Corresponding federal test[b]
Resistance to external wetting	Spray Test	22-1967	5526
Dynamic absorption	Tumble Jar	70B-1967	5500
Dynamic absorption	Launder-Ometer	70A-1964T	–
Static absorption	Immersion	21-1967	5502
Resistance to penetration	Simulated Rain	35-1967	5524
Resistance to penetration	Drop Method	–	5520
Resistance to penetration	Impact Test	42-1967	5522[c]
Water resistance, hydrostatic	Pressure Method	18-1967	5514[c]
Water resistance, hydrostatic	Permeability Method	–	5516[c]

[a]Under Test Group D583-63.
[b]Under Textile Test Methods CCC-T-19lb.
[c]This method differs in detail from the corresponding tests.

F. Water and Oil Resistance

Many commercial fluorocarbon-based, oil-repellent finishes are available today which also assure good water repellency in clothing fabrics. One of the first really durable treatments of this type came out of Quartermaster research in 1960 [119]. This involved a quarternary salt and a perfluoro compound, the treatment identified as Quarpel. A reliable screening test for the effectiveness of such treatments is found in AATCC Method 118-1966T [1]. The working mechanism in all of these treatments centers on coating the fiber surface with a very low energy film such as provided by close packed CF_3 groups. Zisman has described the preparation and operation of these films in some detail [476]. Such protective films are useful on protective clothing for handling fuels [393] and chemical warfare agents [257].

It is notable that silicone and fluorocarbon finishes for water and oil repellency have a large tendency to become soiled while immersed in water, as in laundering [43]. This is attributed to the low interfacial energy of these finishes in air and high interfacial energy in water [44]. If water and oil resistance of clothing is required, then there must be a balance in the fiber surface properties between those required for repellency and those required for soil release in water.

X. RADIATION EXCHANGE WITH CLOTHING MATERIALS

A. Radiation Heat Loads

Radiant energy exchange with the sun or with surroundings must be included in any assessment of thermal protection by clothing in cold or warm environments.

Wein's Displacement Law

$$\lambda_{max} = 0.3 \text{ cm deg} \tag{6-21}$$

states that as the temperature of a radiating object increases, the wavelength of maximum radiation is displaced towards shorter wavelengths. Thus, as shown in Fig. 6-11, for the sun's radiation (T = 6000°K), the maximum is about 0.5 μ, whereas a hot stove (T = 1000°K) has its maximum at about 3 μ. The human body on the other hand (T = 300°K) radiates maximally at 9.5 μ. Thus from Wein's Displacement Law and the spectral responses of the eye, it is clear why the sun appears white, a hot stove red, and the human skin gives no visible radiation.

Because of these different peaks and ranges of energy for different sources, and the different reflecting and absorbing powers of materials at different wavelengths, the radiation problems fall in distinct groups.

(1) High temperature sources—the sun, thermal pulses of nuclear weapons—peak in the visible or shorter wavelengths.

(2) Photographic infrared—the infrared region important for camouflage. Changes in reflectivity in this region will have some effect on adsorption of solar radiation but none on loss of body heat. Wavelengths extend to 1.2 μ.

(3) Low temperature sources—the human body, sun heated ground, interior walls. The energy from fires extends into this range. The absorption and emission of skin and textiles for this range is above 0.9, nearly unity; the reflectivity below 0.1. The only materials with low emissivity or high reflectivity for the low temperature infrared are the metals.

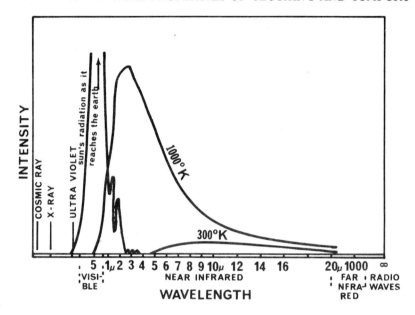

Fig. 6-11. Wavelength distribution of radiant energy sources. From Hardy, in *Physiology of Clothing*, L. H. Newburgh, ed. [197].

Rough measurement of low temperature infrared emissivity can be made with a radiometer and a thermostat with a painted metal wall. The thermostat can be operated at any convenient temperature above room temperature, such as 37 or 100°C. The radiometer, if calibrated for skin temperature, should be regarded as an empirical indicator in this application, with the reading from the warm painted metal surface taken as 100%. The reading when this surface is covered closely with thin, smooth aluminum foil should be about 10%. Fabrics of the same thickness, with and without metal, held against the painted metal surface, will each give lower readings than the metal surface, but an effective infrared barrier will be the lower of the two. The reading without metal, X_0, will be lower than the reading for bare painted metal because its surface temperature is lower; we may assume that its emissivity is 100%, so that the emissivity corresponding to the reading with metal, X_m, will be approximately

$$\epsilon = X_m/X_0 \tag{6-22}$$

The reflectivity, r, for long infrared is

$$r = 1 - \epsilon \tag{6-23}$$

The net transfer of radiation between a hot object (α) and its environment (β) thus becomes

$$H_r = S_b \epsilon_\alpha \epsilon_\beta (T_\alpha^4 - T_\beta^4) A_r \tag{6-24}$$

in which S_b is the Stefan-Boltzmann constant (1.37×10^{-11} kg cal m^2/hr), $\epsilon_\alpha \epsilon_\beta$ are emissivities, T_α, T_β are absolute temperatures, and A_r is effective radiating area.

For work in limited ranges of temperature, it is often sufficient to consider the radiation exchange as also proportional to the temperature difference and combine it with the convection exchange.

Herrington and Hardy [212] were able to make a careful assessment of the radiation exchange between the nude human body and the environment and relate this to contributions from other avenues of heat exchange. Part of the potential thermal stress arises because much of the body is exposed to direct sunlight and skin is a good absorber of energy over a wide spectral range [250, 203].

Woodcock and co-workers [465] were able to define the contributions of radiation to heat exchange of clothed men using these same relationships and this was confirmed in a similar analysis by Herrington [210]. Equation (6-25) was modified to include a weighting factor, f, equal to the ratio of the effective radiating surface to the DuBois surface area (f would equal 0.78 for an unclothed adult).

$$H_r = 4.9 \times 10^{-9} (T_\alpha^4 - T_\beta^4) \epsilon_\beta A f \quad \text{(kg cal/m}^2 \text{ hr)} \tag{6-25}$$

Recent studies of physiological stress due to radiant heat pulses simulating reentry of space vehicles [263] show that the effects of different clothing types is not predominant in determining the heat stress level. By taking into account the fact that the solar spectrum energy is concentrated below 2 μ while radiation from the body and clothing has its peak around 9 μ, it is possible to calculate the actual heat load using observed absorption and emittance efficiencies for the clothing fabrics [363].

Maximum calculated values of solar heat loads were shown to be 400 kg cal/hr for a nude Caucasian and 500 kg cal/hr for a nude Negro. These values fell to 200 kg cal/hr for either subject wearing a fatigue uniform and 125 kg cal/hr when wearing a multiple layer cold weather uniform. Radiant energy exchange with an atomic weapon involves many additional features and these are discussed later in a separate section.

B. Effect of Clothing Color on Radiation Exchange

In a classical investigation by Rees and Ogden [342], it was shown that for high-temperature radiation corresponding to that from the sun the absorption was dependent not only on the color of the fabric but on the type of dye used.

Dahlen [112], in his tour of Germany following World War II, noted dyestuff developments designed to make use of these facts for camouflage purposes and this approach was explored in an AATCC contest shortly afterwards [113].

Generally dyes giving minimum absorption in the near infrared were preferred. On the other hand, the absorption of medium temperature radiation such as that from the human body was independent of the color and the type of dye used. Thus, for this radiation range, a textile fabric approximates a "black body" emitting and absorbing energy to the maximum extent. This type of study was made on a group of combat fabrics using several spectrophotometers [118]. More recently, Rydzewska [369] has shown how visible and infrared reflection can be measured on fabrics and related to: (1) crystallite orientation in the fiber; (2) birefringence of fibers; (3) shape of fiber cross section; (4) fiber length; (5) yarn twist; (6) fabric structure; (7) type and concentration of dye; and (8) degree of delustering.

Indeed, the choice of colors for infrared reflection has been the subject of a recent work claiming effectiveness in protection from sunlight [120].

U.S. Army Quartermaster Corps work on these aspects of comfort was studied on men in the desert near Yuma, Arizona [67]. Black and white uniforms were compared during one summer, green and khaki during the next. The conclusions were derived from sweat evaporation data in the sun and shade, assuming that evaporative heat loss equaled total heat load.

The calculated solar heat loads were 145 kg cal/hr and 92 kg cal/hr for black and white uniforms, 113 kg cal/hr and 92 kg cal/hr for the green and khaki. In terms of the total heat load on the man, the differences with color represented increases of only 17% for black over white and 7% for green over khaki. The white uniforms had much less advantage than expected from reflectance measurements, possibly because multiple reflections in the vicinity of folds and creases increased the amount of radiation absorbed.

C. Problems of Conserving Body Heat by Prevention of Radiation

The fact that nude skin at comfort temperature will have a large fraction of its heat exchange by way of radiation has occasioned much investigation of the possibility of warmth without weight, by use of low-emission, high-reflection metallic surfaces. An earlier summary [152] shows that the difficulties in this approach make it relatively useless, unless:

(1) The metallic surface is exposed on the outside to the largest temperature differences.

(2) The metal is clean and bright. The adhesive used in popular commercial aluminized lining fabrics eliminates most of the low emission effect—what is left is further reduced by using the metallized cloth as a lining, in contact with other surfaces, so that hardly 5% of the theoretical gain is realized, in spite of the attractive, metallic appearance.

(3) The metal coating is durable to abrasion of wear and cleaning processes. Attempts to improve durability have hindered point 2 above.

(4) The system is not exposed to strong air movement: the non-emissive surface has a higher temperature than an ordinary surface which radiates more, and so is sensitive to heat loss by wind. One could almost say that a requirement for the insulation of clothing is that it reduce the surface temperature to within 10°C or 20°F of the environment.

(5) Finally, tests should either be by actual use in relatively critical conditions, or, if physical tests are used, the highest temperature involved should be body temperature, 37°, for test of protection against the cold. The use of high temperature sources has been misleading.

There have been several practical applications of these ideas. At an early stage, metal-coated fabrics were shown to be ineffective as thermal barriers while in contact with the next fabric layer [66]. Exposed reflecting metal coating system, however, were shown to be quite effective in the form of fire fighting suits [186]. Later work [185] revealed that aluminized asbestos-fiberglass gave the best balance of high reflectance and coating durability. Similar concepts of reflecting surfaces and layer separation were applied in designing an army helmet with good radiation protection [359].

D. Methods for Assessing Resistance of Clothing to High Temperature Radiation

McQuade and Kennedy [289] reviewed the techniques which were successful in screening fabrics as suitable barriers against nuclear blast. The prime methods involved exposure of fabric samples mounted on plywood panels at various distances from an atomic explosion, the peak temperature being measured with a suitable device. Some degree of correlation was achieved with results from exposure to a 24-in. carbon arc and corresponding peak temperatures. Related work was also carried out using animals for actual skin exposure.

The measurements of fabric effectiveness considered distribution of the energy in the exposure pulse in three sections: (1) energy reflected due to fabric color and surface; (2) energy transmitted through fabric to skin; (3) energy absorbed by the fabric.

Reflected energy was estimated by reflectance measurements prior to exposure. The remaining energy was assigned by carrying out multiple fabric layer exposures and noting how many were required to reduce transmission to the skin to zero. Zero effect was defined as no evidence of burn on the underlying skin. Practical tests revealed that non-fire-resistant treated fabrics tended to oxidize, then flame or glow after the initial heat pulse. Hence, the amount of glow in outer protective layers had to be considered in defining comparable tests.

In later work, Waldron [434] and the group at the U.S. Army Natick Laboratories were able to set up standard exposure tests using modified carbon arc and a solar furnace. In this way, the potential for heat blast protection was established on a wide variety of materials [435] including fabrics of graphite, quartz, fiber HT-1 (duPont) fiber 6 (Natick), and cotton/nylon blends.

E. Fabric Coatings and Assemblies for Protection from Intense Radiation

Early attempts to use fabric systems for radiation protection concentrated on spaced fabric layers and metallized reflector coatings or combinations of these [73]. Fabric layer separation was found to be effective, particularly if the surfaces facing each other were metal-coated to give high internal reflectance. Unfortunately, no durable reflecting finishes were found at that time. Nylon and cotton fabrics which have a favorable relation to the "burst into flame" problem were later combined with aluminum foil to give more effective radiation barrier systems [353]. Waldron [435], in a review of the other fabric parameters important to satisfactory radiation protection, has pointed out that weight (or thickness), choice of fiber, dyestuffs, and chemical finishes used all have an effect. Reflective sublayers add protection when used with a diathermous outer layer. As discussed in the next section, fiber properties are most important in resisting high intensity radiation.

Aluminum foil on fabric combinations were compared with: (1) aluminum deposit on fabric; (2) white organic coating on fabric; and (3) bleached white goods; in high intensity radiation exposure using a carbon arc [291]. All choices exhibited some radiation resistance provided they were separated from the backing in which pulse temperatures were measured. The bleached goods were least effective, the aluminum foil on fabric most effective, although the latter had very poor laundering durability.

McQuade [289] has surveyed all aspects of thermal protection from radiation afforded by clothing systems. In studies with a solar furnace, he noted that melamine formaldehyde finishes on cotton were able to increase energy absorbing power of the fabric. Man-made fibers were subject to melting and sticking to the second layer in two-layer clothing systems. Best protection again was achieved with the layers separated. He also suggested that shadowing of exposed body areas with clothing ought to be effective. The use of outer reflective layers obviously raised the threshold of energy required to cause serious damage. Flame-retardant materials in the outer layer were also found to be effective. Melt spun fibers, because of their low melting points, were best avoided. Shapiro has discussed clothing fabric effectiveness to reduce ionizing radiation hazards [384] with the general conclusion that only solid metal shields are appreciably effective. Seery [381] has summarized the many aspects to radiation protection, adding that further work on multiple reflecting layers and blended fabrics appears promising.

F. Colorant Systems for Radiation Protection

An extensive program has been carried out to examine the use of colorants for radiation protection from high-energy pulses [354]. This work showed that total absorption rather than selective absorption of specific wavelengths of energy caused damage to the outer fabric layer. Resin-bonded pigment systems appeared to offer enhanced protection from radiation.

Chromotropic colorants which change (darken) on exposure to radiation are now under serious consideration for camouflage purposes [105], and, in transparent layers, for protection of the face and eyes. It appears that their influence on radiation protection will not be substantially different from the contribution made by ordinary dyes.

XI. FLAMMABILITY OF CLOTHING MATERIALS

A. Introduction

There are two aspects of flammability which may affect the comfort of clothed men. Obviously, highly flammable clothing is inconsistent with pursuit of modern warfare, physical exposure of men to flammable materials being of such high incidence. The hazards of war, especially of the thermal pulse from nuclear weapons, or from napalm, are greater than ever, and seem likely to involve civilians also. Burning clothing can be quite lethal. On the other hand, very often flame-retardant clothing may be sufficiently loaded with retardant chemicals that the normal diffusion paths for water vapor from the body are blocked with serious consequences from overheating.

B. Methods of Evaluation

The relative flame resistance of fabrics can be established using the Flammability Tester with Federal Method 5908 [97], ASTM Method D1230-61 [9], or AATCC Method 33-1962 [1]. However, in terms of today's flame resistant goals, this is not a very severe test and the more stringent Vertical strip-Bunsen burner test 5902 [97], or AATCC 34-1966 [1], is recommended. Flammability is characterized by ignition time and char length of the specimen after the test. In a recent review, Richards [352] showed that flammability tendencies varied widely with the fabric used. He suggested other tests for assessing "flammability hazard" concentrating on ease-of-ignition and rate-of-burning factors.

C. Current Flame-Proofing Approaches

Structure choices and blending of fibers can reduce the flaming hazard, wool being particularly effective in this regard [58]. Chemical agents were tried at an early period on combat clothing [14]. Cotton structures are open to several approaches for flame proofing by chemical finishing [39, 302, 325, 416]. These chemical agents with high phosphorus content are also effective in other fibers providing they can be deposited internally. Flameproofing generally requires substantial quantities (10-20%) of these agents to be effective.

Waldron [436] has shown that for the military problems of protection against the nuclear explosion heat pulse, flame proofing is not enough, because it can lead to additional heat transfer to the skin by the decomposition products of the irradiated fabric. Clothing design to include internal spaces can help in this area.

Intensive work is current, with the aim of developing durable flame proofing for commercial civilian fabrics of cotton and other fibers. "Consumer protective" proposals have been heard which would outlaw most of the fibers now in use. There can be no denying that it is still necessary to teach fire safety as part of daily living, including textile use.

D. Relation to Work Load on Men

Thermal stress on men was studied wearing flameproofed and standard clothing in a hot environment simulating the interior of a tank [131, 132]. No additional heat load was imposed by the treated clothing containing a zinc oxide, aluminum stearate mixture. Antimony trioxide was also used in later work [130]. The amount of agent is probably more important than what agent, if nonirritating and not in quantities sufficient to seal the cloth.

XII. STIFFNESS AND BENDING PROPERTIES

A. Basic Relations to Harshness or Softness by Way of Fibers and Yarns

It is well known in the textile art, but not always appreciated by the users of textiles, that fiber fineness is the key property determining the fineness of the yarn which can be spun, and the softness or harshness of feel, and many of the features of drape or bending. This fact should be familiar to engineers, since it arises basically from the equation for the bending of a beam in which the deflection, D, produced by a load, m, at the end of a length of beam, l, from the rigid support is

$$D = \frac{gml^3}{4a^3 b \, Y} \tag{6-26}$$

where g is the acceleration of gravity, Y is Young's modulus, a is the dimension (of a rectangle) parallel to the direction of bending, and b is the dimension perpendicular to the direction of bending.

For a rod, substituting $12\pi^2 r^4$ for $4a^3 b$

$$D = \frac{gml^3}{12\pi^2 r^4 \ Y} \tag{6-27}$$

This equation shows that the amount of bending, D, is very strongly dependent on the fiber length, l (third power) and on the radius (fourth) power) or on the rectangular dimension being bent (third power). This is why fineness contributes so strongly to softness, and coarseness to harshness or scratchiness. In addition, the fiber length, l, from the support (or between supports: the equation has the same factors to the same powers) has a great influence, as shown by napping, which increases softness, or by fiber-cementing additive finishes or friction raising finishes, which shorten the fiber span. Increase of yarn twist also shortens the length within the yarn, and makes each yarn more nearly a monofilament of large radius than an assembly of parallel individual filaments of small radius. The hand and skin are very sensitive to these effects, which are basic to the skin contact aspects of comfort and to the ease of motion in the clothing.

One can see how the flattening of one dimension, as in cotton, increases the fiber flexibility, and how crimp in the individual fibers, as in wool or crimped man-made fibers, by increasing the fiber span, can contribute to yarn and fabric flexibility. The bulking of yarns of man-made fibers by the differential shrinkage process involves the tightening upon each other of the fibers which shrink, and the creation of loops or arches of the fibers which do not shrink, a mixed effect. Bulking is carried out with such a balance of fiber composition and shrinkage that the net effect is usually a gain in softness and fabric thickness, compared with the fabric prior to the differential shrinkage treatment.

B. Basic Relations to Hand of Fabrics

Peirce in an extensive monograph on fabric "handle" set down the basic equations for understanding the stiffness of a fabric [329]. The primary measurement is that of bending length, c, or the length of a strip of fabric which will bend to a certain angle under its own weight per unit area, w. He then defined stiffness in terms of the flexural rigidity, G.

$$G = c^3 w \tag{6-28}$$

To overcome the specific effect of fabric thickness, d, a further quantity, the bending modulus, q, was defined:

$$q = \frac{12G}{d^3} = \frac{12c^3 w}{d^3} \qquad (6\text{-}29)$$

Peirce identified flexural rigidity as the stiffness appreciated by the fingers whereas the bending modulus expressed the stiffness in dimensionless terms as an engineering material. He showed clearly that these functions of stiffness varied considerably with the water content of hygroscopic fibers and reflected the sensations noted in the hand of such fabrics.

C. Methods of Measurement

Abbott has reviewed some of the current methods being used for measuring fabric stiffness [2]. These included the Peirce Cantilever Test, Method 5202, CCC-T-191b in the Federal Specifications [97], the Heart Loop Test, also by Peirce [329], the Schiefer Flexometer [373], the Planoflex developed by Dreby [121] (which is really a measure of shear in the plane of the fabric, as will be discussed in Sect. D, not flexibility), and the M.I.T. Drapeometer [453]. He selected the Peirce Cantilever Test as being the most convenient to carry out in the laboratory and at the same time giving good correlation with subjective estimate.

Recently, Abbott and Grosberg have suggested a method for obtaining the elastic and nonelastic components in fabric bending [5] and have also examined the bending process in a cantilever test, pointing out the importance of interfiber friction in determining the recovery properties after bending [4]. Indeed, friction between fibers affects the free length of the fiber and through this the force to buckle or bend the fabric. Buckling and friction will be discussed in a separate section.

D. Relations to Comfort

Bogaty [53] made a study of subjective sensations in a variety of fabrics in the scale of soft to harsh, showing how accurate comparisons could be made using only small differences in the feel of fabrics. Noted also were substantial effects of fiber diameter and fiber length as discussed in Sect. A.

Mehrtens and McAlister [300], in a subjective study on knitted sport shirts, found that the greatest advantage in comfort was through lower scratchiness exhibited by fibers of lower bending or flexural rigidity and lower friction. The friction aspects will be covered in a later section.

Brand [62] also has attempted to establish a language of subjective comfort and hopefully relate this to objective fabric properties including resilience and shape. More recently, Hollies [223] has applied a combination of these techniques to subjective comfort tests on resin treated cotton shirts. Stiffness of shirting materials with and without moisture from sweating was found to be quite important in determining the comfort level.

XIII. CLOTHING FIT AND FABRIC SHEAR

A. Methods

The fit of clothing which determines contact with the skin depends not only on fabric stiffness but on ease of conformation in fabric length, width, and bias directions. Accordingly, tests have been developed for measuring fabric shearing and buckling. Dreby [121], for example, developed the Planoflex, a device designed for measuring fabric shear although it is sometimes classed with methods for measuring fabric stiffness (see Sect. XII). Later work at Fabric Research Laboratories [99] produced a practical approach to measure flexing and buckling together as they affect the drape of a fabric. Although this test was qualitatively useful, it was difficult to relate the appearance parameters to the fundamental structural stresses in the plane of the fabric or in terms of the buckling forces.

Behre [28], then Dahlberg [111], developed rather more sophisticated methods for measuring shearing and buckling of fabrics, respectively, making use in each case of the Instron tester for force and displacement measurements. Load-deformation curves were obtained characterizing the resistance of clothing fabrics to buckling and shearing.

B. Results on Clothing Fabrics

Lindberg, in cooperation with Behre and Dahlberg [282], made an exhaustive study of the shear and buckling parameters on 66 commercial fabrics of cotton, rayon, wool, nylon, silk, polyester, and saran. They concluded that to achieve a combination of high formability and low shell buckling load, the fabrics should have high thickness and low bending modulus. Wool-type fabrics do have this combination of properties and the meaning of this is discussed more fully in Chapter 7, dealing with specific fiber effects. Grosberg and Swani [184] have extended this work to a reasonable, satisfactory model for which a mechanical analysis is possible. This includes consideration of the bending resistance and initial frictional interaction in the fabric. The frictional aspects will be discussed separately.

XIV. FABRIC SLIDING PROPERTIES

A. Principles

The basic principles describing friction effects between solid materials have been examined thoroughly by Bowden and Tabor [59] and fiber-to-fiber friction is found to arise from surface roughness and welding of surface asperities as with other materials. As new fibers have come into use in clothing materials, the picture has not changed substantially. Meaningful friction coefficients have been measured on fibers, the frictional force being essentially independent of the area, showing Amonton's law to hold in most cases. DuBois [124] studied a number of these (Table 6-8) showing that the range in friction coefficients for fibers was not very large.

B. Specific Fiber Effects

Friction in wool fiber assemblies has received extensive attention, the difference in coefficient with or against the scales being cited as the main cause of fulling shrinkage or the main means of shrink proofing by fiber surface treatments. Essentially, treatments such as chlorination bring the lower directional friction coefficient up to match the higher one [163]. Lindberg has examined this problem in considerable detail in terms of wool tops with different surface properties [281].

In an interesting study on 12 different cottons in card sliver form, Mereness [301] showed clearly that the fiber-fiber friction values did not always determine the effect in sliver form. These workers describe several techniques for friction measurements evolving from incline plane and capstan techniques for static and dynamic friction, respectively. Much of the between fiber friction which holds staple yarns together arises from the twist, which, under tension presses fiber against fiber. Treatments which raise friction between fibers noticeably harshen the hand.

Table 6-8. Values of Friction Coefficient (μ)
of Different Fibers at Two Loads[a]

Sample	μ at 300 g load	μ at 600 g load
Untreated cotton	0.320	0.333
Decrystallized cotton	0.293	0.361
Acetate, dull 60 mm, 3 den.	0.476	0.432
Acetate, dull 40 mm, 3 den.	0.458	0.431
Cuprammonium rayon	0.278	0.258
Polyacrylo nitrile	0.325	0.310
Nymcrylon	0.327	0.311
Enkalon	0.384	0.357
Terlenka	0.349	0.323
Dynel	0.402	0.366
Merino, scoured	0.265	0.248
Crossbred	0.281	0.267
Teflon	0.273	0.239
Saran	0.322	0.272
Fibravyl	0.362	0.373
Nylon 66	0.459	0.436
Enkalon, high tenacity	0.425	0.398
Enkalon, low tenacity	0.419	0.371

[a]Reprinted from Ref. [124] by courtesy of the *Textile Res. J.*

C. Extension to Fabric Systems

The interrelation of fiber yarn and fabric has been reviewed most
thoroughly by Rubenstein [365]. Several workers found, for instance, that
fabric friction increased with moisture content of the air in equilibrium
with the fabrics, an important feature for clothing fabrics subjected to
wide fluctuations in moisture content.

When carefully cleaned yarns are in contact with smooth clean surfaces,
very high resistance to sliding can occur. The application of lubricants
reduces the coefficient of friction to 0.35 for a poor lubricant, or to 0.10
for a good lubricant. As recent studies on cotton fabrics have shown, this
has an important bearing on the softness of clothing fabrics. Harper
[47-49] recently has discussed permanent lubricants for textile systems.

Weaving choices have been used to produce fabrics of high friction character [236], and polytetrafluoroethylene coatings have been used to extend fabric friction into the very low ranges [339].

XV. STATIC ELECTRICITY

A. Background

Generation of electrical charge among high resistance materials is a fairly common phenomenon. As shown in Table 6-9, many fibers in extensive clothing use do have high electrical resistivities [252]. Materials can be arranged in a triboelectric series, indicating the sign of the charge produced by rubbing one on another, as shown in Table 6-10. Clothing worn in dry environments will exhibit this generation of electricity in sticking and riding up of clothing rather than assuming normal drape position. In houses heated in winter, static discharge from clothing may also be annoying in normal use.

B. Effects of Moisture

Hersh and Montgomery [213], in studies on a variety of yarns and fabrics from different fibers, showed that a decrease in resistivity with moisture content followed a log/log relationship (see also [202]). Moreover, the correlation between assemblies of different size was excellent. Ballou [17, 426] has discussed the clinging of fabrics to skin and how charge dissipation is related to fabric structure.

C. Methods of Measurement

Several commercial devices have been constructed for measuring surface and volume resistivity of fabrics as discussed by Kaswell [254]. These depend on measuring the discharge through a sensitive electrometer. Ballou [17] has suggested an alternate approach using a modulator for charging and discharging the fabric. There is an ASTM method, D257-66 [9], for surface resistivity of insulating materials which is readily applicable to fabrics and gives results which can be interpreted in terms of an analysis by Valko's Table 6-10 [426]. This approach and a more recent one by Henry [206] have advantages over other methods which are essentially comparative, without absolute quantities.

Table 6-9. Electrical Resistance of Textile Fibers[a]

Material	Resistance	Units	Test conditions
Cotton thread	0.132×10^5	MΩ/cm	70.8% R.H. 7.66% moisture regain. Applied voltage: 100
Silk yarn	1.79×10^5	MΩ/cm	70.8% R.H. 11.89% moisture regain
Wool yarn	17.0×10^5	MΩ/cm	70.8% R.H. 11.89% moisture regain
Viscose filament	8.1×10^5	MΩ/cm	75% R.H.
Nylon filament	14×10^7	MΩ/cm	75% R.H.
Creslan	4.5×10^5	MΩ/cm	50% R.H.

Nylon 66	1.21×10^9-9.80×10^{11}	Ω cm	64% **R.H.**, 20°C
Nylon 11	1.02×10^8-2.74×10^8	Ω cm	64% **R.H.**, 20°C
Cellulose acetate	2.69×10^{10}-4.36×10^{11}	Ω cm	64% **R.H.**, 20°C
Orlon	4.59×10^8-6.66×10^{13}	Ω cm	64% **R.H.**, 20°C
Acrilan	6.78×10^8-1.53×10^9	Ω cm	64% **R.H.**, 20°C
Dynel	2.79×10^7-2.17×10^{10}	Ω cm	64% **R.H.**, 20°C
Creslan	9.76×10^6	Ω cm	64% **R.H.**, 20°C
Terylene	7.79×10^7	Ω cm	64% **R.H.**, 20°C
Dacron	3.72×10^5-9.80×10^{13}	Ω cm	64% **R.H.**, 20°C
Vinyon	3.05×10^8-4.60×10^9	Ω cm	64% **R.H.**, 20°C
Saran	2.16×10^{10}	Ω cm	64% **R.H.**, 20°C
Thermovyl	2.31×10^7-2.97×10^9	Ω cm	64% **R.H.**, 20°C
Glass	2.79×10^8-4.22×10^8	Ω cm	64% **R.H.**, 20°C

aReprinted from **Ref.** [252] by courtesy of Wellington Sears Co.

Table 6-10. Triboelectric Series[a]
for Producing Electrostatic Charge[b]

Positive	wool
	nylon
	silk
	viscose
	cotton
	glass
	ramie
	acetate
	acrylic
	polyethylene
Negative	polyvinyl chloride

[a]Fibers above others in the series rubbed against the lower members, producing a positive charge on the upper member and a negative charge on the lower member.

[b]Reprinted from Ref. [426] by courtesy of Interscience Publishers.

Table 6-11. Relation of Surface Resistivity
of Fabrics to Susceptibility for
Electrostatic Charging[a]

Log R, Ω	Antistatic protection
13	none
12-13	poor
11-12	moderate
10-11	good
10	excellent

[a]Reprinted from Ref. [426] by courtesy of Interscience Publishers.

D. Elimination of Static

The most successful approaches to the present have been chemical and some of these have been discussed by Valko and co-workers [427]. The main approach has been to attach hygroscopic agents to the fiber surface which, by sorbing moisture, will have the same effect as raising the water content of the fabric. This approach has been applied successfully to polyester slips.

The approach by intimately blending fibers from opposite ends of the triboelectric series has not been widely used and may be basically unsatisfactory: More depends on dissipation of charge by conduction than upon avoiding or balancing production of charge. Blending with "conductive" fibers such as cotton or rayon will not be effective under dry conditions where the cellulose fibers themselves are high in resistance—in winter even a cotton T-shirt will crackle on being pulled off one's back.

XVI. CLOTHING WITH INTERNAL SPACES

A. Spacer Fabrics

The use of spaces between fabric layers to achieve protection from thermal blasts has already been discussed. The wearing of such clothing is satisfactory in cold weather but intolerable in warm weather. Brandt and Riddell [63] have discussed various means of supporting clothing layers from each other and still leaving room for convective cooling. Early studies on optimum cooling were made with hot plate thermal apparatus [309], and later a man simulant [148]. Chimney effects can be obtained, but hardly at spacings below 1 in. Optimum cooling by forced ventilation was shown by Hollies to depend on an interaction of space size and air flow [226]. For impermeable clothing, this cooling was not only necessary for comfort but essential for survival.

B. Water and Heat Detection by Schlieren Optics

Schrager and Monego [378] were among the first to use schlieren optics to study air layers over different fabric types and were able to illustrate visually the effects of surface hairiness in increasing thermal insulation. The schlieren approach is a very powerful tool because it reveals differences of refractive index arising from either temperature or moisture content and permits visualization of the convection currents in realistic models of the spaces within clothing. Later, Hollies [227] was able to apply the same equipment in the analysis of air mixing in the spaces of ventilated clothing. Improved cooling efficiency was achieved by observing which spacer designs improved the efficiency of mixing of warm, moist air from the sweating skin and the cooler, drier air of ventilation. Recently, Hollies has extended this approach to very small ventilation spaces of the type found in pressure suits [228]. As a result, evaporative cooling values of 375 kg cal/m^2 hr and total cooling values of 650 kg cal/m^2 hr have been achieved using 0.2-in. spaces and circulating air volumes of 10 ft^3/min at 85°F (based on the requirements for a man of 1.8 m^2 in area).

Chapter 7

DIFFERENCES BETWEEN FIBERS
WITH RESPECT TO COMFORT

I. TRADITIONAL AND COMMON VIEWS
OF FIBER DIFFERENCES

A. Natural Fibers and Environmental Stress

The history of clothing in tropical and subtropical civilizations records the use of flax and silk in fine weaves for lightweight comfortable clothing [345]. Cotton fibers were also used, presumably because they lent themselves to the production of thin comfortable clothing with sufficient cover to provide technical support to the modesty desired. In a similar way, wool and other keratin-based animal fibers have long been associated with protection in cold weather [349]. This natural association has grown up because wool yarns produce thick, lofty structures of high insulating value and fulled structures have excellent resistance to wind and mechanical impact. Indeed, the effectiveness of casein, silk, acetate, cotton, nylon, and orlon as fibers for cold weather clothing use has been weighed on the basis of their wool-like properties [332]. Systematic study of the performance of wool fabrics in military uses revealed other advantages also, for example, aesthetic appearance, ease of camouflage, and wear resistance [411].

B. Hygroscopic Effects with Natural Fibers

The natural fibers were also noted to sorb moisture in clothing use and laboratory work revealed this produced substantial heating of individual fibers [284], and presumably this was transferred to full clothing assemblies in normal use [361]. Rodwell et al. [362] in an up-to-date review of the contributions to comfort from heat of regain effects, have concluded: "Results, in brief, show no consistent statistically significant differences between wool and Terylene assemblies in exposure to damp-cold."

C. Acceptance of New Fiber Sensations

There is another aspect to comfort which predominates in the absence of thermal stress, warm or cold. This has to do with the feel of a fabric even in the dry state, i.e., "psychological factors" if you will, which can change as a result of training. Clothing made from filament yarns, for example, has been highly unacceptable to men [9], but not noticeably uncomfortable for women [341]. This presumably relates to the fact that most men are normally highly uncomfortable in filament underwear while women are quite accustomed to its definitely cool feel [341]. Knit structures do have an advantage in reducing contact with the skin [297], and, therefore, make filament yarns more acceptable. As a result, knit shirts of several filament fibers, for example, have become very common for everyday wear [204], illustrating that associations with a particular fiber do change along with technology and custom. The associated yarn changes due to texturizing which have made these structures truly acceptable have not come about easily; they will be discussed in a later section of this chapter.

II. ATTEMPTS TO MAKE SIMILAR FABRICS FROM DIFFERENT FIBERS

A. NRC Series

Kennedy [256], in a thorough review of the importance of the conservation of fibers for clothing items, reflected a clear trend on the part of the military to use available natural and man-made fibers to achieve high-performance, durable clothing. A specific assignment in this context was directed toward the conservation of wool. Stoll [412] has described how a cooperative effort with industry was established to produce serge, covert, shirting, and blanket fabrics of wool blended with nine different man-made fibers, the so-called NRC Series of fabrics. Physical property analysis of these fabrics [58] revealed that the blends tended to be lean and smooth, essentially non-wool-like, though they were produced on the same machinery as their all wool counterparts.

B. J.I. Series

A systematic study was made of the effect of the amount of man-made fiber in a wool blend, using the available acrylic fibers [57], and it was learned that it took very little synthetic fiber to produce thin, lean yarns in a wool shirting structure. The resulting shirts were more durable than their all wool counterparts but not nearly as warm. The effect was attributed very largely to the role of fiber randomness. Water transport properties of these yarns were able to give a quantitative description to the contribution made by noncrimped, short staple, man-made fibers [232].

C. Blends with a Wool Surface

A systematic program was undertaken for the U.S. Army Quartermaster Corps to produce truly wool-like fabrics from a variety of man-made components but using each step in manufacture to maximize randomness of the fiber orientation in the yarn and fabric [58]. As a result of this study, other fabric properties related to service use were in turn related to construction choices as summarized in Table 7-1. This work ultimately resulted in a patent [55] and a government specification for blended shirting fabrics [58]. Fourt [144] was able to show that high shrink fibers could also produce a more wool-like structure in blends with rayon and nylon. In addition, he was able to relate the resulting structure changes to the physiology of heat balance using model systems for assessing the heat and moisture transfer properties [157]. Again, changes in functional behavior of the blends in woolens and serges were attributed to shifts in fiber randomness. The techniques for assessing these changes have been described in Chapter 6, Sects. IV and VII.

The teachings from the Army programs on blends were applied to a series of serge fabrics for the Air Force with considerable success [450].

D. Blend Studies on Commercial Fabrics

The effects of various spinning techniques on blending were studied by Greenwood [182] using viscose rayon in several fabric constructions with wool. Likewise, Brown [69] examined the protein fibers from casein as blending components in yarns spun on woolen and cotton

Table 7-1. Fabric Characteristics Affected by Blending and
Construction Changes Related to Each

Fabric characteristics	Related construction features (fabric thickness affected by)
Thermal insulation	A. Yarn number
	B. Twist direction
	C. Fiber denier
	D. Fiber crimp
	E. Staple length
	F. Weave (effect on fulling)
	G. Texture (effect on fulling)
	H. Napping vs. shearing
Ease of wetting	A. Randomness of fiber arrangement in yarns and fabrics
	B. Water repellent finish
Flammability	A. Fiber type
	B. Fabric thickness
	C. Fabric weight
	D. Fabric cover
Tailoring behavior	A. Yarn balance
	B. Weave balance
	C. Other unknown factors

Muss resistance
   A. Fiber type
   B. Texture
   C. Weave

Pressing and drying behavior
   A. Fiber type
   B. Fabric weight

Sewing behavior
   A. Fiber type
   B. Sewing finish
   C. Fabric thickness

Handle properties
   A. Fiber type
   B. Fiber denier
   C. Fabric weave
   D. Fabric thickness

Durability
   A. Fiber type
   B. Fiber denier
   C. Fabric thickness
   D. Fabric weave

Dyeing
   A. Fiber type
   B. Dye selection
   C. Dyeing procedure

systems, showing that either is possible if care is taken to use similar denier fibers and good blending practices. More recently [269], structure factors in making cotton-like fabrics for durable press uses using substantial quantities of polyester have been studied.

III. PROPERTIES OTHER THAN THERMAL APPARENTLY RELATED TO FIBER TYPE

A. Contact with the Skin

The nature of the contact of a clothing fabric with the skin plays a very major role in determining subjective comfort in the range of acceptable thermal stresses. The special role that fiber fineness makes in determining the stiffness and bending properties of fabrics was discussed in Chapter 6. As stiffness is proportional to the fourth power of the radius, the fiber denier has a substantial influence on the type of contact. It is a natural result of the fineness of cotton and coarseness of wool used in clothing fabrics that gives them their soft and smooth vs. scratchy and prickly sensations on the skin. Bogaty [53] has documented this effect very clearly in a subjective study of the hand of blended fabrics of wool with viscose and nylon. Likewise, Mehrtens [300], in comfort tests under controlled environmental conditions, was able to assign scratchiness and stiffness sensations to individual fiber stiffness effects. The very fact that differences were due to fiber size rather than fiber type shows that contact variations to produce softness or harshness should be possible with any fiber providing the right denier range can be obtained.

A second area of contact has to do with coolness or warmness of the sensation. Rees [341] was one of the first to put these observations into quantitative form, identifying the cold feel with smooth fabrics of high surface contact. Hock et al. [214] extended this idea to clothing fabrics containing various amounts of moisture. They noted that the sensations were heightened with water present and attributed this effect to an actual lowering of the surface temperature of the fabric. These observations became the basis for a rate-of-cooling method [Chapter 6, Sec. VII] for measuring surface contact. Recent work on men's shirts [223] has shown that cold, clammy sensations do occur more with fabrics of high surface contact than with low contact. High contact, in turn, results from low crimp fibers in tight even spaced yarns, more characteristic of unaltered man-made fibers than natural fibers.

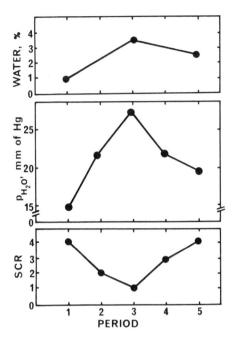

Fig. 7-1. Effect of water from sweating on subjective comfort rating (SCR), chamber at 95°F, and cycling relative humidity [223].

B. Water Distribution

Studies on clothing fabrics made from wool blends [232] have shown that extremes in wettability of fabrics can occur due to small changes in blend content. These are attributed very largely to the differences in the arrangement of the individual fibers forming parallel capillaries in a wetting system, or random orientation in a nonwetting system [233]. These extremes in surface wetness can be sensed subjectively and hold also for the removal of water from clothing fabrics [158]. Even differences in the passage of moisture vapor through clothing fabrics can be detected if the fibers are closely packed in the yarns and the yarns tightly woven [151].

A more recent assessment of the subjective aspects of this effect [223] has shown that moisture held at a clothing fabric surface, for example, next to the skin, enhances the sensation of discomfort if the fabric surface is potentially unacceptable for continuous wear. This effect is illustrated in Fig. 7-1 for a subject wearing a print cloth shirt at 95°F in an environment of fluctuating high relative humidity. The subjective comfort rating (SCR) is based on a summation of the factors of cold, clammy, clingy, rough, and scratchy, noted by the wearer.

C. Static Electricity

As discussed thoroughly in Chapter 6, the build-up of static electrical charges on clothing fabrics results from a combination of low electrical conductivity of the individual fibers and low moisture content of the environment (such as indoors in the winter in a temperate climate) [293].

In this case, the specific effect of static is very substantial and this has led manufacturers to produce new fibers with built-in hygroscopic groups to keep the fabrics from holding a static charge [474]. As pointed out by Valko [426], measurements of electrical conductivity can serve as a useful guide for determining the potential hazard from static electricity. The trend in industry is to solve this problem in fiber manufacture so this aspect of specific fiber effects may disappear as an important consideration in subjective comfort.

IV. CONCEPTS OF YARN AND FABRIC DESIGN FOR USING NEW FIBERS

A. Yarn Variations

A very substantial effort has gone into modifying filament yarns so they simulate, when woven, the bulkiness of staple yarns without losing their advantages in strength or ease of knitting or weaving. Four of the common bulking processes [171] show that several twisting and crimping techniques are available for introducing randomness into the yarns. In the use of staple yarns, the most effective randomizing effects can be achieved by twist variations [266], or by blending [146], and in the case of wool blends, by fulling after blending [232].

B. Fabric Variations

Knit structures have been found to make full use of bulked filament yarns for achieving clothing with a soft comfortable hand [51] and, where desirable, can be made into stretch fabrics with ease of body conformation [248]. Unfortunately, fabrics from highly bulked yarns tend to pill in use [321] and this has been the subject of a detailed analysis of the pilling mechanism [63] designed to circumvent its development.

In analogy with the fulling process for wool blends [232], surface softness and fabric loftiness in cottons can be achieved by napping, needling, tumbling, compacting, even ultrasonics [64]. König [265] has also demonstrated that foams, particularly in laminates, can produce clothing of·acceptable physiological effect on the wearer.

V. SUBJECTIVE STUDIES OF FIBER DIFFERENCES IN CLOTHING FABRICS

A. Hygroscopic Effects

Nelbach and Herrington, in climatic studies of heat loss from clothed subjects, noted transient heating effects not explained by the observed metabolic rates [316]. They attributed this effect to water sorbing or desorbing from the hygroscopic fibers used in their clothing tests. Wool, having a unique position in this regard [281], was examined closely by several workers in the Wool Industries Research Association. Cassie [92] summarized their findings, showing clearly that a heat pulse was definitely produced in taking wool samples from a dry to a moist atmosphere and he called this the "heat of regain" effect. He reasoned that this should be detected by wearers of wool clothing and temper their comfort during winter wear, as shown in Table 7-2. Hollies [218] evaluated this heating effect for a kilogram of each of four fibers used in combat clothing manufacture. The numbers revealed a potential heating effect comparable to that generated by a walking man. It was not known, however, how much of this heat would be felt by the wearer and how much lost to the environment.

Rodwell et al. [362] have reviewed recently the findings of various workers attempting to assess the "heat of regain" effect on the comfort of subjects wearing hygroscopic clothing. They carried out further subjective work on men using clothing with large differences in moisture regain characteristics and several realistic exercise/climatic variations.

(1) At rest under simulated damp-cold winter environment (indoors followed by outdoor exposure).

(2) At rest as in (1) in the presence of wind.

(3) Sweating from muscular work in a cool environment.

(4) Sweating slightly at rest in a hot, dry environment followed by exposure to damp-cold winter conditions outdoors.

Table 7-2. Water Sorbed and Total Heat Available
from Transfer of Fibers from Low to High Humidity[a]

	Viscose	Wool	Cotton	Nylon
Sorption regain (90% R.H., 15°C), g H_2O/kg fiber	275	237	130	69
Desorption regain (33.5% R.H., 30°C), g H_2O/kg fiber	98	105	69	20
Net water gain (33.5% R.H., 30°C to 90% R.H., 15°C), g H_2O/kg fiber	177	132	61	49
Heat of wetting, Q (33.5 to 90% R.H., 25°C), cal/g H_2O	8.0	7.2	3.5	1.8
Heat of condensation, L (22.5°C), cal/g H_2O	584	584	584	584
Unit heat of sorption, L and Q, cal/g H_2O	592	591	588	586
Total heat of sorption (33.5% R.H., 30°C to 90% R.H., 15°C), kcal/kg fiber	105	78	36	29

[a]Reprinted from Ref. [95] by courtesy of *Trans. Faraday Society*.

From this work they found no significant differences between wool and Terylene assemblies in exposure to damp-cold even though the clothing on hangers under warm conditions gave a "heat of regain" pulse.

B. Water Transport Effects

Hardy and co-workers [196] examined how the heat loss process from subjects might be modified by moisture transfer through clothing layers and set up comfort prediction curves from psychometric charts relating skin wetness to skin temperature as shown in Fig. 7-2. They reasoned that the subjects discomfort should be roughly proportional to the distance along the physiological curve from the comfort zone to the

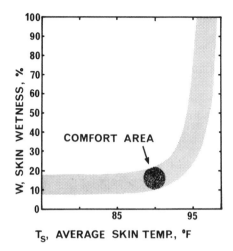

Fig. 7-2. Physiological comfort curve. From Hardy et al. [196].

equilibrium point for a particular clothing layer. In further subjective tests [10], the same group of workers showed that subjective response was not this clearcut, particularly in a warm, humid environment. In a cool environment, however, in the presence of moist fabrics, there was an apparent correlation of comfort with fiber type, but on closer examination the smoothness and wetness of the fabric on the skin produced the predominant effects. Spun nylon and other fabrics were consistently more comfortable than filament Dacron or nylon. Leach [274] reviewed all of these effects of the dissipation of perspiration on comfort sensations and concluded that for warm weather clothing, making clothing from filament structures had a potential advantage for ridding the body of perspiration. At the same time, he pointed out that the clothing was more comfortable if held away from the skin as achieved by spun yarn fabrics. Desirable also were porous structures to permit easy diffusion of water vapor through the clothing layer.

An interesting study was performed by Werden et al. [441] on women wearing summer clothing of cotton, nylon, acetate, and Arnel exposed to cool and warm heat stress. Physiological differences or those in comfort sensations were small, providing comparable relative humidities were used in the stress period. In general, the clothing gained weight from perspiration in proportion to the original fabric weight, but this effect was not noted by the wearers. Behmann carried out a similar study on men comparing wool and polyamid fibers in a tricot construction [26]. Actually, the wool fabric was thicker and heavier and had less air permeability so it felt warmer to the wearers. In addition, evaporation of moisture from men wearing the wool seemed to take place at the skin surface, while on polyamid clothing at the fabric surface. Again, this suggested a connection with fabric structure rather than fiber type.

In more recent work at the University of Illinois [170], women were subjected to warm, humid environment tests in which considerable effort was made to keep the clothing fabrics comparable in structure but different in wetting properties. Cotton, water-repellent cotton, and Orlon fabrics were used. In no instance did either the water-repellent treatment or fiber content have any effect on the physiological aspects of comfort. The water-repellent and Orlon suits, however, did not remove as much moisture from the body as the untreated cotton suit. The subjects classed the cotton suit as most comfortable although not necessarily cooler than the other suits. Recently, Mecheels [296] has examined moisture transfer and comfort of knit fabrics. He has pointed out the importance of fabric openness and ventilation in moisture transport independent of the fiber used. Hollies in a study on cotton shirts [223] has showed clearly that substantial differences in comfort are stimulated by moisture collection and high contact at the skin surface produced by unduly resin loaded fabrics. Likewise, he has shown that comfort can be maintained in cool and warm environments if the moist fabrics do not make high contact with the skin.

VI. DIFFERENCES IN FABRIC CHARACTERISTICS
OF DIFFERENT FIBERS

A. Structural Effects

As has been mentioned, there has been general agreement by different workers on the qualities of all-wool or all-cotton clothing fabrics in terms of high bulk and fuzzy surfaces for woolens and smooth, lean characteristics for cottons. The simulation of these structures with man-made structures with crimped, staple yarns on the one hand, and smooth filament yarns on the other, has been quite successful.

Information about what particular fiber differences give rise to yarn and fabric variations had come largely from the manufacture of blends designed to have specific end use properties. Various attempts to achieve these goals have already been discussed in Sect. II. Several others are worth noting.

Townend and Marsden-Smedley [420] made a clear study of the effect of nylon content on the strength properties of wool/nylon blends. They concluded that nylon content of the yarns far outweighed the influence of yarn twist in determining yarn strength properties and this effect was translated into improved abrasion resistance for the resulting fabrics. They showed also that it took very little nylon to make a substantial improvement in these strength properties.

Bogaty et al [57] went further in this regard by examining which associated fabric properties followed variations in blend composition. In a series of acrylic/wool blends, comfort-related properties of thickness, thermal resistance, surface hairiness, and wicking properties were all seen to follow blend composition. These are shown in Table 7-3. Generally, fabrics of high acrylic content were thinner, cooler, smoother, and more wettable than their higher wool content counterparts. Detailed thermal resistance measurements [54] on such blends revealed that fiber arrangement, rather than fiber type, could account for these differences and these effects were well-documented on a wide variety of blend fabrics in which construction factors were varied independent of fiber content [58].

B. Thermal Effects

One of the main features governing the introduction of man-made fibers into clothing items has resulted from the specific effects of thermal heating during or following manufacture. For example, Hynek [244] showed that acrylic fibers in wool blend fabrics were quite successful in protecting against strength loss due to heating to 450°F. He was able to separate the effectiveness of different acrylic fibers according to the softening point of the individual fibers. From the comfort standpoint, the preferred blends showed no stiffening in high-temperature exposure.

Sensitivity to local heating was also noted in the high-speed sewing of wool/nylon blend fabrics [161], resulting in seam puckering and poor fit of garments. These effects were largely overcome by suitable lubricants in sewing [475].

Many of the specific advantages of thermally resistant fibers have come into sharp focus because of specific needs for resistance to thermonuclear blast and the preparation of fire-resistant structures for space suits. These are discussed separately in the next section.

Table 7-3. Comfort-Related Properties of Wool/Acrylic Blend Fabrics

Nominal fiber content		Thickness at 0.002 psi (mils)	Thermal resistance at 0.002 lb/in^2 (°C sec m^2/cal)	Surface hairiness by cooling time (sec)	Wicking by drop absorption (min)
Wool (%)	Other (%)				
	Dynel				
100	0	97	0.198	71	>433
85	15	97	0.182	74	>433
70	30	99	0.185	76	>433
50	50	94	0.180	71	80
0	100	48	0.090	53	3
	Acrilan				
100	0	87	0.173	68	>433
85	15	93	0.200	71	>433
70	30	81	0.164	65	100
50	50	68	0.142	58	33
0	100	41	0.083	49	3
	Orlon				
100	0	103	0.198	73	>483
85	15	84	0.172	72	>483
70	30	86	0.172	70	166
50	50	74	0.148	69	25
0	100	38	0.076	49	16

VII. SPECIAL FIBERS FOR UNUSUAL STRESS ENVIRONMENTS

A. Thermal Blast Protection

Waldron [434] studied the ignition properties of wool/nylon fabrics used in combat clothing when exposed to intense thermal pulses of a carbon arc and a solar furnace. Resistance to ignition was found to improve substantially with increase in fabric weight and to some extent with nylon content of the blend. In a later review [435], he noted that although Fiber 6, a high temperature nylon was clearly advantageous for thermal protection, absorbency of dyestuffs on the fabrics and mechanical arrangement of the protective layers were equally important in determining overall effectiveness of the protection. A fire retardant finish on conventional cotton uniforms plus a suitable space between first and second layers was also found to be highly effective as a thermal barrier.

Ross [364] has reviewed the use of completely new fiber materials such as HT-1 (Nomex) and PBI (polybenzimidazole) (both polymers), Karma, Nichrome V, Chromel R (nickel chromium alloys), glasses, and refractories as potential materials for space clothing. These all have insensitivity to high temperatures and in some cases resistance to degradation in pure oxygen at high temperature. The mechanical factors which make them acceptable for clothing uses are not very different from those which are important in conventional fibers. Good strength and resilience in fine deniers are particularly important.

Coplan [108] in related work has examined fibers suitable for heat-protective shields and parachutes, wherein some of the same considerations are necessary as those for clothing items. There appears to be no practical limit for fiber composition use in clothing provided the mechanical properties of the fabric can be suitably controlled. Abstracts or preprints of 33 papers of a 1968 symposium on fibers of thermally resistant high polymers are available [7].

VIII. TRENDS IN FIBER USAGE

A. Consumption of Different Fibers

Mills [303] has reviewed recently the balance between cotton, wool, rayon, and man-made fiber consumption in the United States, a major portion of which goes to make clothing in a variety of forms. Clearly, man-made fibers have been used in increasing amounts over the last

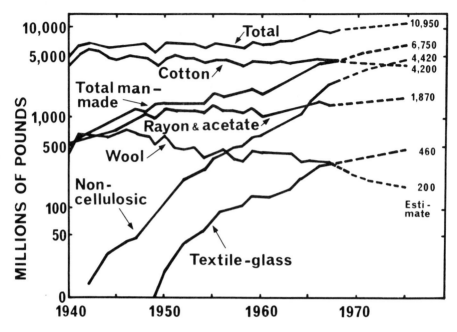

Fig. 7-3. United States mill consumption of fibers. From Mills [303].

30 years (as shown in Fig. 7-3), and Mills predicted they would surpass
cotton during 1967. As shown in Fig. 7-4 [241], this prediction came true
early in 1968. The large volume use of spun polyester blends with cotton
was mainly responsible for this trend. The use of wool for clothing on a
worldwide basis has continued to decline while rayon has maintained a
steady increase [242] due largely to the acceptance of high wet modulus
rayons for traditionally cotton containing clothing items [240]. The continued growth in use of man-made fibers worldwide for clothing was
reflected in the most recent International Man-Made Fibers Conference
[277]. Acrylics, for example, have shown substantial growth in Germany
and polyolefins in Switzerland. Presumably, this flexibility in the use of
different fibers for common clothing products is a real reflection of the
fact that mechanical similarity in structure and, hence, acceptability in
terms of comfort has been partially achieved.

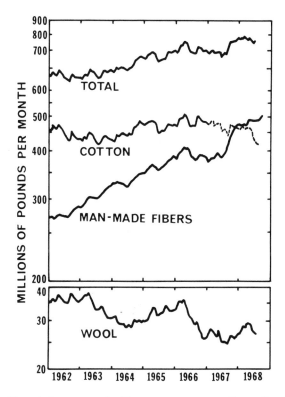

Fig. 7-4. United States textile fiber consumption. From Textile Organon [241].

B. Specific Fiber Uses

Data furnished to the U.S. Department of Agriculture by the Defense Supply Agency indicate that raw fiber content of 1967 deliveries of textile fabrics to the military amounted to 203,068,000 lb which was 46% larger than in 1966 [254]. Fabrics of 100% cotton continued to dominate military usage in 1967, accounting for 148,335,000 lb or 43% above 1966. Wool fabrics of 21,318,000 lb increased 39% and those of 100% man-made fibers increased 20% over 1966. However, blend fabrics of man-made fibers with cotton and wool were 86% higher in 1967 over 1966. This trend toward blends reflects quite dramatically the increased knowledge of how to make wool-like blends with substantial quantities of man-made fibers as discussed in Sect. II of this chapter. The special subjective qualities of silk have also been simulated directly [98] for use in the civilian market.

A recent survey of the use of different fibers in knit apparel [8] shows that not only a variety of fibers are now used successfully, but the combined use of wool and cotton accounted for only one-half the poundage used in 1967 for this particular clothing purpose. Again, the trend to use many different fibers in essentially satisfactory clothing uses is clearly indicated.

Chapter 8

CURRENT TRENDS AND NEW DEVELOPMENTS

IN THE STUDY OF CLOTHING

I. INTRODUCTION

The new trends in the study of clothing originate from three sources: (a) the continued development of new materials and finishes; (b) the availability of new methods of data gathering and handling, and the increased recognition of the utility of psychological scaling; and (c) new concepts of hazards requiring protection, new concepts of clothing design to utilize interaction between the body in motion and the clothing, and new concepts of the nature of comfort itself, with particular emphasis on contact between the fabric and the body. Each of these sources is considered in turn to suggest areas of work of both a fundamental and a practical nature worthy of further development.

II. NEW MATERIALS AND FINISHES

Not all the new materials developed for special mechanical properties, such as metallic filaments for high strength at high temperatures or graphite filaments for reinforcement of composite materials, can be expected to be utilized in clothing, because first of the expense and second of the lack of any advantage in the areas of ordinary clothing service. The requirements for fineness, for strength, and for recovery properties for textile fibers for clothing have been mapped out [45, 216].

As new polymers are introduced into the general textile market, it can be predicted that they will be tried in conventional structures for

195

clothing uses. Modification through fabric structure changes is a route to utilization of new fiber types in fabrics, on the one hand, and in non-wovens, on the other. The nonwovens offer a more uniform fabric density per unit area, but suffer the deficiency of lacking the lattice structure characteristic of fabrics made from yarns. This limits their acceptability in uses demanding easy deformation within the plane of the fabric. Modifications of nonwoven structures toward more lattice-like deformation and greater extent of deformation are possible, and uses will be developed in which this is less of a limiting factor.

The chemical finishing of clothing fabrics to obtain desirable end-use properties is not only extensive but in a constant state of flux due to new developments in this active field. Durable press [173], softeners [49], water and soil resistant materials [295c], and most recently, flame retardant chemicals [417], are used on the bulk of U.S. clothing fabrics with striking effects on the relative comfort of the finished goods. Finishes which act inside the fiber are least prone to affect the comfort properties [229]. Some attempts have been made to modify fiber substances to alter the comfort-related properties of man-made fibers for clothing uses [177]. Other finishes are applied essentially to the fiber surfaces for improved soil release or flame retardancy and there is general agreement that these surface coatings do affect water vapor permeability, hand, and other tactile properties related to clothing comfort. No systematic study has been made however of what levels of surface finishing are acceptable and this area awaits future workers in the comfort field.

III. NEW TECHNIQUES

Very practical types of clothing evaluation for space and deep sea programs have stimulated better techniques for the measuring of physiological temperatures and the handling of data collected on men under stress [292]. In addition, a whole new field of physiological monitoring has grown up for use in hospitals short of skilled nursing staff and for round the clock diagnostic attention to patients in intensive care. The temperature, heart, and breathing functions so monitored are well suited for comfort studies on new clothing [443]. A parallel, largely laboratory oriented development in time-shared computers makes it possible to record and analyze such data on a real-time basis [295b]. The combined potential of new monitoring techniques and of data handling has yet to be fully exploited in extending the basic understanding of comfort factors deserving attention in the design of new clothing of improved comfort acceptability.

Improved data collection and handling also will aid in climatological studies of clothing needs. The satellite data fills in the gaps between scattered observing stations, and new forms of data, never before available, such as infrared emission from the soil or from the clouds are now collected [290]. Improved records and improved statistical handling will permit better knowledge of the duration or frequency of given combinations of weather phenomena such as temperature and rainfall or temperature and vapor pressure. The frequency, duration, and direction of wind and its intensity, and the depth of snow in individual snowfalls can be better handled.

Appreciation of the utility of psychological scaling is certain to grow. Thurstone [419] showed that anything which the mind can recognize as greater or lesser can be scaled psychologically. Thus the several contact phenomena can be scaled and quantitatively expressed. Where psychological scaling can be combined with a set of material standards representing steps along the scale, even more convincing objective quantitation can be obtained.

A very closely related medical field is that dealing with the origin of skin sensations. The extremes in stimulus observable from direct contact with different clothing items of today [223] deserve analysis in terms of the electrical impulses in the nerves and their interpretation by the brain. Good ground work has been laid for such a study in work on patients [259] and the related challenge for clothing stimuli awaits the attention of a few courageous workers. This type of duality in the disciplines required for a skin surface study is fairly typical of that required for workers in the comfort of clothing field.

IV. NEW CONCEPTS

The third major source of new developments is from new concepts of hazards, of clothing design, and of comfort itself. Some of the new, workable uses of new materials have resulted from new clothing design concepts. An old concept applied to new resilient fiber materials is that of light weight batts and nonwovens for high thermal insulation. Aircraft survival kits have been made containing compressed blankets which can be back packed with a parachute and provide effective protection when opened. In the field of cryogenics, very highly effective insulating systems have been made using multilayer reflective coatings. This principle has been applied to radiation shields for aircraft and considered for extension to clothing items.

The increased emphasis on nonflammability in clothing for civilian use is an example of new concepts of hazard. The military problems of the resistance to ignition are more severe than the civilian ones, because it is not merely accidental contact with flame but the intense thermal pulse of nuclear weapons which must be avoided. Those who have seen the civil defense movies of the side of the wooden house bursting into flames can partially appreciate the problem. Another aspect of the military problem is the need for wearing a relatively heavy protective layer even in warm weather. This could be approached expensively by the encapsulated or fully air-conditioned clothing outfit. Work at the U.S. Army Natick Laboratories and on astronauts suits has shown that this is possible, but the expense is great and the problem of a power supply is very difficult.

More adaptable to large scale use would be a radical change in clothing design to permit internal ventilation by convection or chimney effect or by utilizing the interaction between the motion of the body and the clothing. The whole concept of clothing design can be refined both for warm climate clothing and for cold. If clothing is to be worn in warm climates with complete cover, internal ventilation is the only way to permit enough evaporation. The barrier to evaporation imposed by even the most permeable clothing is considerable. Channels at least an inch in clearance and completely unobstructed by any belts, flaps, or valves are required for natural ventilation. This has been discussed in Chapters 2 and 5.

The design of clothing for cold climates can be improved in two principal ways. One, as for warm climates, is by provision of better means for internal ventilation. These should, of course, be capable of being closed off when not required, but should be quite open to permit circulation when the body is in motion. Reports from Antarctic expeditions have stated that it is practically impossible with conventional cold climate clothing to avoid sweating during exercise [389]. The other line of improvement is by choice of fibers and fiber densities for the different layers. The layers nearest the skin, the warmest layers, can have a greater fiber density. If the exterior layers can have a low density, and be capable of having ice or frost brushed out of them, accumulation of water in the clothing can be reduced. The use of impermeable layers over portions of the body, especially for periods of low activity, has not been studied in sufficient detail. As with impermeable foot wear, which is now standard issue in the coldest regions, there is an obvious warm limit to the environment in which the impermeable clothing can be useful. This limit needs to be more carefully defined.

Other new concepts of comfort other than the purely thermal ones will have increasing importance for the ordinary concept of civilian comfort "at ease." Chapter 6 has outlined numerous methods of characterizing the surface of a fabric. These can be combined with psychological scaling procedures to identify the ranges for each fabric structure type which give optimum contact effects. The differences between fibers have been shown to lie very much in the area of effect of water content on the contact effects, as discussed in Chapter 6. The effect of clothing design, not only on ventilation, but also on mechanical impedence of the body in motion will also be worth a study and may indicate the desirability of rather radical changes in clothing design. The thing that is required is to study the system as a whole, the man in motion in his clothing in respect to the environment.

APPENDIX: CONVERSION TABLES

Tables for the insulation of external air layers at corresponding wind velocities in different velocity units are Table 2-2 and Table 4-3.

Table 6-4 converts pressure in lb/in^2 or oz/yd^2 into g/cm^2.

Table A-1 for velocity units, and Table A-2 for insulation, work, or energy, and metabolism follow.

Table A-1. Linear Velocity Conversion Table[a]

ft/min	cm/sec	km/hr	mph	knots
4 or 5 figure factors				
1	0.5080	0.01829	0.011364	0.009870
1. 9685	1	0.036[b]	0.02237	0.01943
54.68	27.78	1	0.6214	0.5396
88[b]	44.704	1.6093	1	0.8684
101.34	51.48	1.853	1.1516	1
1 or 2 figure factors for mental arithmetic				
1	0.50	0.018	0.011	0.01
2	1	0.036[b]	0.022	0.02
55	28	1	0.62	0.54
88[b]	45	1.6	1	0.9
100	50	1.8	1.1	1

[a]Read equivalents in horizontal rows.
[b]Exact.

Table A-2. Thermal Equivalents Insulation

---

1 Clo   = 0.18°C m² hr/kg cal

        = 0.155°C m² /W

        = 0.155 T-Ω

        = 1.55 Tog

        = 0.88°F ft² hr/Btu

        = about 0.62 cm or 0.25 in. of clothing

1 T-Ω = 10 Tog = 1°C m² /W

        = 6.45 Clo

        = 1.163°C m² hr/kg cal

        = 5.67°F ft² hr/Btu

Work or energy

1 kg cal = 1.163 W hr

        = 3.97 Btu

        = 3087 ft lb

        = 4.27 kg m

        = about 2.1 liters O_2 utilized

Metabolism/area to whole "Reference" man

1 Met = 50 kg cal/m² hr = about 100 W for "Reference" man with
        1.7 m² area

REFERENCES

[1] AATCC, *Technical Manual of the American Association of Textile Chemists and Colorists*, A.A.T.C.C., P.O. Box 12215, Research Triangle Park, North Carolina, 1968.

[2] Abbott, N. J., The Measurement of Stiffness in Textile Fabrics: Part I. A Comparison of Five Methods of Laboratory Evaluation; Part II. A Study of the Peirce Cantilever Test for Stiffness of Textile Fabrics, *Textile Res. J.*, **21**, 435-444 (1951).

[3] Abbott, N. J., and Goodings, A. C., Nylon Filaments: Moisture Absorption, Density and Swelling Properties, *J. Textile Inst.*, **40**, T232-T246 (1949).

[4] Abbott, G. M., and Grosberg, P., The Fabric Cantilever, *Textile Res. J.*, **36**, 930-932 (1966).

[5] Abbott, G. M., and Grosberg, P., Measurement of Fabric Stiffness and Hysteresis in Bending, *Textile Res. J.*, **36**, 928-930 (1966).

[6] Afaf, M., Determination of Thermal Insulation of Cold Weather Clothing and Equipment, Eighth Commonwealth Defense Conference on Clothing and General Stores, Australia, 1965.

[7] American Chemical Society, Polymer Division, Symp. Fibers of Thermally Resistant Organic Polymers, October, 1968. *ACS Polymer Preprints*, **9**, 1068-1464 (1968).

[8] American Fabrics, Fibers in the Knit Picture—1967, *Am. Fabrics*, **81**, 77 (1968).

[9] American Society for Testing Materials, Committee D-13, *ASTM St.*, **24**, **25** (1968).

[10] Andreen, J. H., Gibson, J. W., and Wetmore, O. C., Fabric Evaluations Based on Physiological Measurements of Comfort, *Textile Res. J.*, **23**, 11-22 (1953).

[11] Angstrom, A. J., Neue Methode, das Wärmeleitungsvermögen der Korper zu bestimmen, *Ann. Physik*, **190**, 513-530 (1861).

[12] Anon., Clothing Almanac No. 21, United States, Environ. Prot. Br., Quartermaster R. and D. Div., Natick, Massachusetts, Dec. 1951.

[13] Anstey, R. L., Clothing Almanac for Southeast Asia. Tech. Rept. 66-20 ES, Earth Sciences Division, U.S. Army Natick Laboratories, Natick, Massachusetts, Jan. 1966. AD 633 631.

[14] Ashe, W. F., and Bean, W. B., Fire Resisting Compounds for Clothing, Army Ground Forces Med. Res. Lab., Fort Knox, Kentucky, Mar. 1944. AD 657220.

[15] Babbitt, J. D., On the Diffusion of Adsorbed Gases through Solids, *Can. J. Phys.,* **29**, 437-446 (1951).

[16] Backer, S., Fisher, F. R., and Weiner, L. I., eds. Blend Fabrics and Their Impact on Military Textile Applications, Textile Ser. Rept. No. 119, Textile, Clothing and Footwear Div., Quartermaster R. and Eng. Center, Natick, Massachusetts, May 1960. PB 181360.

[17] Ballou, J. W., Static Electricity in Textiles, *Textile Res. J.,* **24**, 146-155 (1954).

[18] Baxter, S., Heat and Water Vapour Transfer through Fabrics, *J. Textile Inst.,* **37**, T39-T57 (1946).

[19] Baxter, S., Thermal Conductivity, *Proc. Phys. Soc.* (London), **58**, 105 (1946).

[20] Baxter, S., and Cassie, A. B. D., Thermal Insulating Properties of Clothing, *J. Textile Inst.,* **34**, T41-T54 (1943).

[21] Behmann, F. W., Differentiation in the Heat Transport Capacity of Textiles, *Melliand Textilber.,* **41**, 468-473 (1960).

[22] Behmann, F. W., Fibers and Fabric Structure as Factors in Clothing Physiology: Part 2. Experiments on the Thermophysiological Influence of Fabric Structure, *Melliand Textilber.,* **47**, 1193-1197 (1966).

[23] Behmann, F. W., Fibers and Fabric Structure as Factors in Clothing Physiology: Part 3. On the Subjective Perception of the Thermal Properties of Clothing under Controlled Experimental Conditions, *Melliand Textilber.,* **47**, 1315-1316 (1966).

[24] Behmann, F. W., The Influence of Climatic and Textile Factors on the Heat Loss in Drying of Moist Clothing, in *Biometerology,* Pergamon Press, New York, 1962, pp. 273-279.

[25] Behmann, F. W. (based on work by Behmann, rewritten by staff of *Wool Sci. Rev.*), The Physiological Properties of Wool Clothing: I. General Principles and Requirements, *Wool Sci. Rev.,* **21**, 40-50 (1962); II. Total Insulation of a Clothing Assembly, *ibid.,* **22**, 38-52 (1962); III. Wear Trials, *ibid.,* **23**, 1-12 (1962).

[26] Behmann, F. W., Heerd, E., and Heinrichs, H. J., Effect of Fibrous Material on the Effective Insulation Value of Clothing, *Melliand Textilber.*, **41**, 226-230 (1960).

[27] Behmann, F. W., and Meissner, H. D., Importance of the Physiological Behavior to Humidity of Textile Fibers in Garments, *Melliand Textilber.*, **40**, 1209-1214 (1959).

[28] Behre, B., Mechanical Properties of Textile Fabrics: Part I. Shearing, *Textile Res. J.*, **31**, 87-93 (1961).

[29] Behre, B., Mechanical Properties of Textile Fabrics: Part II. Buckling, *Textile Res. J.*, **31**, 94-99 (1961).

[30] Behre, B., Lindberg, J., and Dahlberg, B., Mechanical Properties of Textile Fabrics: Part III. Shearing and Buckling of Various Commercial Fabrics, *Textile Res. J.*, **31**, 99-122 (1961).

[31] Belding, H. S., Evaluation of Thermal Insulation Provided by Clothing, in *Clothing Test Methods* (Newburg, L. H., and Harris, M., eds.), CAM No. 390, Natl. Res. Council, Washington, D.C., 1945, pp. 9-21.

[32] Belding, H. S., Protection against Dry Cold, in *Physiology of Heat Regulation and the Science of Clothing* (Newburgh, L. H., ed.), Saunders, Philadelphia, 1949, p. 367.

[33] Belding, H. S., Darling, R. C., Turrell, E. S., and Robinson, S., An Evaluation of Sleeping Bags Designed for Use in Extreme Cold, Rept. No. 8, Harvard Fatigue Lab., Cambridge, Massachusetts, Nov. 1942.

[34] Belding, H. S., Russell, H. D., Darling, R. C., and Folk, G. E., Analysis of Factors Concerned in Maintaining Energy Balance for Dressed Men in Extreme Cold; Effects of Activity on the Protective Value and Comfort of an Arctic Uniform, *Am. J. Physiol.*, **149**, 223-239 (1947).

[35] Belding, H. S., Russell, H. D., Darling, R. C., and Folk, G. E., Effect of Moisture on Clothing Requirements in Cold Weather: I. Methods, OQMG Rept., No. 37, War Dept. Contr. No. 44-109-qm-445, Harvard Fatigue Lab., Cambridge, Massachusetts, July 1945.

[36] Belding, H. S., Russell, H. D., Darling, R. C., and Folk, G. E., Effect of Moisture on Clothing Requirements in Cold Weather: V. The Influence of Amount of Clothing Worn, OQMG Rept. No. 37, War Dept. Contr. No. 44-109-qm-445, Harvard Fatigue Lab., Cambridge, Massachusetts, Nov. 1945.

[37] Belding, H. S., Russell, H. D., Darling, R. C., and Folk, G. E., Effect of Moisture on Clothing Requirements in Cold Weather: VII. Partition of Sweating by Body Regions, OQMG Rept. No. 37,

War Dept. Contr. No. 44-109-qm-445, Harvard Fatigue Lab., Cambridge, Massachusetts, Dec. 1945.

[38] Belding, H. S., Russell, H. D., Darling, R. C., and Folk, G. E., Thermal Responses and Efficiency of Sweating When Men are Dressed in Arctic Clothing and Exposed to Extreme Cold, *Am. J. Physiol.,* **149**, 204-222 (1947).

[39] Beninate, J. V., Boylston, E. K., Drake, G. L., Jr., and Reeves, W. A., Conventional Pad-Dry-Cure Process for Durable-Flame and Wrinkle Resistance with Tetrakis, (Hydroxymethyl) Phosphonium Hydroxide (THPOH), *Textile Res. J.,* **38**, 267-272 (1968).

[40] Benzinger, T. H., On Physical Heat Regulation and the Sense of Temperature in Man, *Proc. Natl. Acad. Sci.,* **45**, 645-659 (1959).

[41] Benzinger, T. H., Peripheral Cold—and Central Warm—Receptors, Main Origins of Human Thermal Discomfort, *Proc. Natl. Acad. Sci.,* **49**, 832-839 (1963).

[42] Benzinger, T. H., and Kitzinger, C., Gradient Layer Calorimetry and Human Calorimetry, in *Temperature—Its Measurement and Control in Science and Industry,* Vol. 3, Reinhold, New York, 1963, pp. 87-109.

[43] Berch, J., Peper, H., and Drake, G. L., Jr., Wet Soiling of Cotton: Part II. Effect of Finishes on the Removal of Soil from Cotton Fabrics, *Textile Res. J.,* **34**, 29-34 (1964).

[44] Berch, J., Peper, H., and Drake, G. L., Jr., Wet Soiling of Cotton: Part IV. Surface Energies of Cotton Finishing Chemicals, *Textile Res. J.,* **35**, 252-260 (1965).

[45] Beste, L. F., and Hoffman, R. M., A Quantitative Study of Resilience, *Textile Res. J.,* **20**, 441-453 (1950).

[46] Black, C. P., and Matthew, J. A., The Physical Properties of Fabrics in Relation to Clothing: III. Heat Insulation by Fabrics Used as Body Clothing, *J. Textile Inst.,* **25**, T249-T276 (1934).

[47] Blanchard, E. J., Harper, R. J., Jr., Bruno, J. S., and Reid, J. D., Reactive Softeners Can Improve All-Cotton DP, *Textile Ind.,* 98, 100, 102, 104, 114, 116, 194 (October, 1967).

[48] Blanchard, E. J., Harper, R. J., Jr., Gautreaux, G. A., and Reid, J. D., Urethanes Improve All-Cotton DP, *Textile Ind.,* 115, 117, 118, 119, 122, 143 (January, 1967).

[49] Blanchard, E. J., Harper, R. J., Jr., Lofton, J. T., and Gautreaux, G. A., Stiffness, An Important Factor in the Abrasion Performance of Durable-Press Cottons, *Textile Res. J.,* **37**, 233-241 (1967).

[50] Blockley, W. V., and Taylor, C. L., Studies in Tolerance for Extreme

Heat, Second Summary Rept., AF Tech. Rept. No. 5831, USAF Air
Mat Command, Wright-Patterson AFB, Dayton, Ohio, Feb. 1950.
PB 110 069.

[51] Blore, J. H., Stretch and Bulk Yarns—What's Their Future? *Textile World*, **105**, 94-97 (1955).

[52] Bogaty, H., and Hollies, N. R. S., The Evaluation of Experimental Fabrics as Alternates for Standard Wool Fabrics, Repts. No. 2, 3, Contr. No. DA-44-109-qm-564, Textile, Clothing and Footwear Div., Quartermaster R. and D., Natick, Massachusetts, Dec. 1951. AD698445-6.

[53] Bogaty, H., Hollies, N. R. S., and Harris, M., The Judgment of Harshness of Fabrics, *Textile Res. J.*, **26**, 355-360 (1956).

[54] Bogaty, H., Hollies, N. R. S., and Harris, M., Some Thermal Properties of Fabrics: Part I. The Effect of Fiber Arrangement, *Textile Res. J.*, **27**, 445-449 (1957).

[55] Bogaty, H., Hollies, N. R. S., and Hintermaier, J. C., Mixed Fabric With Wool Surface, U.S. Patent 3,060,551 (Oct. 1962).

[56] Bogaty, H., Hollies, N. R. S., Hintermaier, J. C., and Harris, M., The Nature of a Fabric Surface: Thickness-Pressure Relationships, *Textile Res. J.*, **23**, 108-118 (1953).

[57] Bogaty, H., Hollies, N. R. S., Hintermaier, J. C., and Harris, M., Some Properties of Serges Made from Blends of Wool with Acrylic Type Synthetics, *Textile Res. J.*, **23**, 536-544 (1953).

[58] Bogaty, H., Monego, C. J., and Hollies, N. R. S., Blends of Wool-Type Fabrics, Textile Ser. Rept. No. 98, Textile, Clothing and Footwear Div., Quartermaster R. and Eng. Center, Natick, Massachusetts, Aug. 1958. PB136 730.

[59] Bowden, F. P., and Tabor, D., *The Friction and Lubrication of Solids*, 2nd ed., Oxford Univ. Press (Clarendon), London and New York, 1964.

[60] Boyer, J. C., ed., *Wound Ballistics*, Office of the Surgeon General, Dept. of the Army, Washington, D.C., 1962.

[61] Bradley, C. G., *Western World Costume, An Outline History*, Appleton, New York, 1954.

[62] Brand, R. H., Measurement of Fabric Aesthetics—Analysis of Aesthetic Components, *Textile Res. J.*, **34**, 791-804 (1964).

[63] Brand, R. H., and Bohmfalk, B. M., A Mathematical Model of Pilling Mechanisms, *Textile Res. J.*, **37**, 467-476 (1967).

[64] Brandt, H. H., and Riddell, A., Spacer Fabric Development, TELR No. 183, Textile, Clothing and Footwear Div., Quartermaster R. and D. Center, Natick, Massachusetts, Apr. 1957.

[65] Breckenridge. J. R., Closer Temperature Control Means Better Army Uniforms, *Instrumentation,* **11**, 21-24 (1958).

[66] Breckenridge, J. R., Evaluation of "Silver Slippers" Metal Coatings on Insulating Materials, Special Rept. No. 40, Environ. Prot. Sec., Quartermaster Clim. Res. Lab., R. and D. Br., Lawrence, Massachusetts, Aug. 1950.

[67] Breckenridge, J. R., and Pratt, R. L., Effect of Clothing Color on Solar Heat Load, Tech. Rept. EP-155, Environ. Prot. Res. Div., Quartermaster R. and Eng. Center, Natick, Massachusetts, June 1961. AD 263 355.

[68] Breckenridge, J. R., and Woodcock, A. H., Effects of Wind on Insulation of Arctic Clothing, Rept. No. 164, Environ. Prot. Sec., Quartermaster Clim. Res. Lab., Lawrence, Massachusetts, July 1950.

[69] Brown, H. F., An Introduction to the Preparation and Properties of Yarns Containing Ardil Protein Fiber, 37th Ann. Conf., Textile Inst., Edinburgh, June 1952, pp. 81-87; *J. Textile Inst.,* **43**, 584-592 (1952).

[70] Brown, J. R., and Cotton, L. M., An Experimental Method for the Determination of "Clo" Value of Clothing Assemblies, *J. Textile Inst.,* **48**, T379-T388 (1957).

[71] Burleigh, E. G., Jr., Wakeham, H., Honold, E., and Skau, E. L., Pore-Size Distribution in Textiles, *Textile Res. J.,* **19**, 547-555 (1949).

[72] Burton, A. C., Calculations of Heat Debt, in *Clothing Test Methods* (Newburgh, L. H., and Harris, M., eds.), CAM No. 390, Natl. Res. Council, Washington, D.C., 1945, pp. 5-7.

[73] Burton, A. C., Insulation by Reflection and the Development of a Reflecting Cloth, S.P.C. Rept. No. 116, Assoc. Comm. on Aviation Med. Res., Natl. Res. Council, Canada, Apr. 1943.

[74] Burton, A. C., The Range and Variability of the Blood Flow in the Human Fingers and the Vasomotor Control of Body Temperature, *Am. J. Physiol.,* **27**, 437-453 (1939).

[75] Burton, A. C., Symp. Physiologic Contributions to War Problems: Clothing and Heat Exchanges, *Federation Proc.,* **5**, 344-351 (1946).

[76] Burton, A. C., and Edholm, O. G., *Man in a Cold Environment,* Chap. 2, The Problem of the Homeotherm, the Heat-Balance and Physical Laws, E. Arnold, London; Williams and Wilkins, Baltimore, 1955, pp. 23-46.

[77] *Ibid.,* p. 35.

[78] *Ibid.,* p. 36.

[79] *Ibid.,* p. 37.

[80] *Ibid.*, p. 41.

[81] *Ibid.*, pp. 42-43.

[82] *Ibid.*, Chap. 3, The Thermal Insulation of the Air, pp. 47-57.

[83] *Ibid.*, p. 51.

[84] *Ibid.*, p. 54.

[85] *Ibid.*, Chap. 4, The Thermal Insulation of the Clothing or Fur, pp. 58-72.

[86] *Ibid.*, pp. 70-71.

[87] *Ibid.*, pp. 110-112.

[88] *Ibid.*, pp. 200-202.

[89] Carroll, D. P., and Visser, J., Direct Measurement of Convective Heat Loss from Human Subject, *Rev. Sci. Instr.*, **37**, 1174-1180 (1966).

[90] Cassie, A. B. D., Characteristics for Warmth in Underwear Fabrics, *J. Textile Inst.*, **40**, P444-P453 (1949).

[91] Cassie, A. B. D., Clothing: Warmth, *Textilwezen*, **4**, 45-48 (1948).

[92] Cassie, A. B. D., Moisture Relations and Clothing Comfort, presented to the British Assoc., Sept. 1952.

[93] Cassie, A. B. D., Physical Properties of Fibres and Textile Performance, *J. Textile Inst.*, **37**, P154-P167 (1946).

[94] Cassie, A. B. D., The Physics of Fibres with Special Reference to Wool, *Brit. J. Appl. Phys.*, **9**, 341-348 (1958).

[95] Cassie, A. B. D., Propagation of Temperature Changes through Textiles in Humid Atmospheres: Part 2. Theory of Propagation of Temperature Change, *Trans. Faraday Soc.*, **36**, 453-458 (1940).

[96] Cassie, A. B. D., and Baxter, S., Propagation of Temperature Changes through Textiles in Humid Atmospheres: Part 3. Experimental Verification of Theory, *Trans. Faraday Soc.*, **36**, 458-465 (1940).

[97] CCC-T-191b, Textile Test Methods, Federal Specification, GSA, Business Service Center, Washington, D.C., 1968.

[98] Chemical and Engineering News, Producers of Silk Substitutes Grapple for Fiber's Acceptance in Consumer Market, *Chem. Eng. News*, **46(46)**, 22-23 (1968).

[99] Chu, C. C., Cummings, C. L., and Teixeira, N. A., Mechanics of Elastic Performance of Textile Materials: Part V. A Study of the Factors Affecting the Drape of Fabrics—The Development of a Drape Meter, *Textile Res. J.*, **20**, 539-548 (1950).

[100] Cleveland, R. S., An Improved Apparatus for Measuring the Thermal Transmission of Textiles, *J. Res. Natl. Bur. Std.*, **19**, 675-684 (1937).

[101] Climatic Research Unit, Table of Wind Chill Values, Quartermaster, War Dept., Washington, D.C., Jan. 1943.

[102] Clinton, M., Jr., Galligan, A. M., and Morris, R. O., Methods of Reducing Evaporative Heat Loss from Soldiers Sleeping in Wet Clothing, Provisional Rept., Test No. 82, Quartermaster Clim. Res. Lab., Lawrence, Massachusetts, Mar. 1944.

[103] Clulow, F. E., and Rees, W. H., The Transmission of Heat through Textile Fabrics: Part III. A New Thermal Transmission Apparatus, *J. Textile Inst.,* **59**, 285-294 (1968).

[104] Cochran, M. I., Conductive Heat Transfer and Clo Values, in *Conference on Environmental Stress in Soldiers,* pp. 14-20, Climatol. and Environ. Prot. Sec., Quartermaster R. and D. Br., Natick, Massachusetts, Aug. 1944.

[105] Coleman, R. A., Foster, W. H., Jr., Kazan, J., and Mason, M., Synthesis of Chromotropic Colorants, U.S. Army Mat. Command, Natick Lab., Natick, Massachusetts, Feb. 1966. AD 630 908.

[106] Colin, J., and Houdas, Y., Experimental Determination of Coefficient of Heat Exchanges by Convection of Human Body, *J. Appl. Physiol.,* **22**, 31-38 (1967).

[107] Coplan, M. J., and Freeston, W. D., Jr., High Speed Flow and Aerodynamic Heating Behavior of Porous Fibrous Structures, WADD Tech. Note 61-58, Contr. No. AF 33 (616)-7222, Aeronautical Systems Div.; Wright-Patterson AFB, Dayton, Ohio, Oct. 1961. AD 271 960.

[108] Coplan, M. J., Freeston, W. D., Jr., and Powers, D. H., Thermodurable Textile Systems, *Textile Res. J.,* **32**, 777-783 (1962).

[109] Craig, F. N., Cummings, E. G., and Bales, P. D., Contribution of the E33 Hood to Heat Stress on Men Wearing CBR Protective Clothing, Tech. Rept. CRDLR3101, U.S. Army Chem. R. and D. Lab., Army Chem. Center, Maryland, Dec. 1961. AD 275 850.

[110] Cusick, G. E., The Dependence of Fabric Drape on Bending and Shear Stiffness, *J. Textile Inst.,* **56**, T596-T606 (1965).

[111] Dahlberg, B., Mechanical Properties of Textile Fabrics: Part II. Buckling, *Textile Res. J.,* **31**, 94-99 (1961).

[112] Dahlen, M. A., Dyestuff Developments in Germany during World War II, *Am. Dyestuff Reptr.,* **35**, 119-123 (1946).

[113] Dahlen, M. A., Chairman, The Effect of Dyestuffs on the Temperature Rise of Fabrics Exposed to Light, *Am. Dyestuff Reptr.,* **36**, 159-165 (1947).

[114] Davenport, M., *The Book of Costume,* Crown, New York, 1948.

[115] Day, R. L., Bellows Action of Fabrics on a Copper Cylinder, Rept. No. 50, Quartermaster Clim. Res. Lab., Lawrence, Massachusetts, Oct. 1943. PB 3410.

[116] Day, R. L., Regional Heat Loss, in *Physiology of Heat Regulation and the Science of Clothing* (Newburgh, L. H., ed.), Saunders, Philadelphia, 1949, pp. 243-244.

[117] Day, R. L., Relationship of Permeability of Windbreak and Nature of Underlying Fabric to Loss of Insulation Due to Wind, Rept. No. 43-A, Quartermaster Clim. Res. Lab., Lawrence, Massachusetts, Jan. 1944. PB 8249.

[118] deLhery, G. P., Derksen, W., and Monahan, T. I., Research Report on the Spectral Reflectance and Transmittance of Standard Fabrics for Thermal Radiation Effects Studies, Naval Mat. Lab., N.Y. Naval Shipyard, Brooklyn, New York, Aug. 1956. PB 171 838.

[119] DeMarco, C. G., Dias, G. M., and Smith, W. F., "Quarpel" Water- and Oil-Resistant Treatment for Textiles, Textile Ser. Rept. No. 111, Textile, Clothing and Footwear Div., Quartermaster R. and Eng. Center, Natick, Massachusetts, Apr. 1960.

[120] deThier, A. N., Infrared Reflecting Yarns and Fabrics, U.S. Patent 2,965,139 (Dec. 20, 1960).

[121] Dreby, E. C., Physical Methods for Evaluating the Hand of Fabrics and for Determining the Effects of Certain Textile Finishing Processes, *Am. Dyestuff Reptr.,* **31**, 497-504 (1942).

[122] DuBois, D., and DuBois, E. F., A Formula to Approximate Surface Area if Height and Weight be Known, *Arch. Internal Med.,* **17**, 863-871 (1916).

[123] DuBois, E. F., Heat Loss from the Human Body, *Bull. N.Y. Acad. Med.,* **15**, 143-173 (1939).

[124] DuBois, W. F., Frictional Measurements on Fibrous Materials, *Textile Res. J.,* **29**, 451-466 (1959).

[125] Duncan, J., Edwards, R. G., and Hardy, R. H., Method of Estimating the Respiratory Cost of a Task by Use of Minute-Volume Determinations, *J. Appl. Physiol.,* **6**, 287-303 (1954).

[126] Eckert, E. R. G., Hartnett, J. P., Irvine, T. F., Jr., and Sparrow, E. M., A Review of Heat Transfer Literature, 1959, *Mech. Eng.,* **82**, 47-61 (1960).

[127] Edholm, O. G., and Bacharach, A. L., eds., *Exploration Medicine,* Williams and Wilkins, Baltimore, 1965.

[128] Edholm, O. G., Fox, R. H., Adam, J. M., and Lewis, H. E., Exercise Bake: Acclimatization to Heat, Abstr., Proc. Intern. Union of Physiol. Sci., I, 24th Intern. Cong., Washington, D.C., 1968, p. 484.

[129] Edwards, M., and Burton, A. C., Temperature Distribution over the Human Head, Especially in the Cold, *J. Appl. Physiol.,* **15,** 209-211 (1960).

[130] Eichna, L. W., Horvath, S. M., and Shelley, W. B., Effects of Wearing Flameproofed Clothing in Hot Environments, Armored Med. Res. Lab., Fort Knox, Kentucky, July 1945. AD 657 222.

[131] Eichna, L. W., Horvath, S. M., and Shelley, W. B., Effects of Wearing Flameproofed Clothing in Hot Environments, Armored Med. Res. Lab., Fort Knox, Kentucky, July 1945. AD 657 225.

[132] Eichna, L. W., Horvath, S. M., and Shelley, W. B., Physiologic Effects of Wearing Flameproofed Clothing in Hot Environments, Armored Med. Res. Lab., Fort Knox, Kentucky, July 1945. AD 657 224.

[133] Eliot, J. W., and Winik, L. J., Moisture Absorption in Arctic Clothing, EPS Special Rept. No. 31, Quartermaster Clim. Res. Lab., Lawrence, Massachusetts, Feb. 1950.

[134] Evans, M., *Costume Throughout the Ages,* Lippincott, Philadelphia, 1950.

[135] Fisher, F. R., ed., *Man Living in the Arctic,* Quartermaster R. and Eng. Center, Natick, Massachusetts, 1961.

[136] Fisher, F. R., ed., *Protection and Functioning of the Hands in Cold Environments,* Washington, Natl. Acad. Sci.-Nat. Res. Council, 1957. AD 286 507.

[137] Fitch, A. L., A New Thermal Conductivity Apparatus, *Am. Phys. Teacher,* **3,** 135-136 (1935).

[138] Fitzgerald, J. E., A Study of the Copper Man: Phase I. Physical Characteristics; Thermometry; Air Clo Evaluations, Quartermaster Clim. Res. Lab., Lawrence, Massachusetts, Aug. 1946.

[139] Folk, G. E., Belding, H. S., and Darling, R. C., Rate of Sweating and Moisture Uptake of Combinations of the M-1943 Arctic Outfit as Functions of Grade of Work and Environmental Temperature, OQMG Rept. No. 36, Harvard Fatigue Lab., Cambridge, Massachusetts, Mar. 1945.

[140] Fonseca, G. F., Breckenridge, J. R., and Woodcock, A. H., Wind Penetration through Fabric Systems, Tech. Rept. EP-104, Environ. Prot. Res. Div., Quartermaster R. and Eng. Center, Natick, Massachusetts, Mar. 1959. PB 142 312.

[141] Fonseca, G. F., and Hoge, H. J., The Thermal Conductivity of a Multilayer Sample of Underwear Material under a Variety of Experimental Conditions, Tech. Rept. PR-8, Pioneering Res. Div.,

Quartermaster R. and Eng. Center, Natick, Massachusetts, Oct. 1962. AD 290 744.

[142] Fonseca, G. F., and Woodcock, A. H., Local Heat Transfer Co-efficients of Laboratory Facial Protective Systems in Wind, *Textile Res. J.,* **35**, 909-913 (1965).

[143] Forbes, W. H., Definitions, Miscellaneous Figures and Conversion Factors, in *Physiology of Heat Regulation and the Science of Clothing,* Appendix (Newburgh, L. H., ed.), Saunders, Philadelphia, 1949, pp. 445-450.

[144] Fourt, L., A. High-Shrink Fibers in Shirtings: Trials of Finishing. B. Effect of Moisture Content on Thick Clothing Assemblies, Rept. No. 27, Contr. No. DA-19-129-QM-1073, Textile, Clothing and Footwear Div., Quartermaster R. and D. Center, Natick, Massachusetts, April 1958.

[145] Fourt, L., Effects of Starting Sweating into Clothing with Constant Power Supply, Rept. No. 32, Contr. DA-18-128-QM-1336, Textile, Clothing and Footwear Div., Quartermaster R. and D. Center, Natick, Massachusetts, April 1960.

[146] Fourt, L., The Evaluation of Experimental Fabrics as Alternates to Standard Wool Fabrics: A. High-shrink Fibers in Wool-type 16-Ounce Shirting Fabrics: Plan of Trial to Evaluate the Resulting Fabric Structure, B. Cotton Battings, in Relation to Sweating and Cold, Rept. No. 24, Contr. No. DA-19-129-QM-331, Textile, Clothing and Footwear Div., Quartermaster R. and D. Center, Natick, Massachusetts, June 1957. AD 684 949.

[147] Fourt, L., Heat and Moisture Transfer through Fabrics: Biophysics of Clothing, TELR No. 256, Contr. No. DA-19-129-QM-331, Textile, Clothing and Footwear Div., Quartermaster R. and Eng. Center, Natick, Massachusetts, Nov. 1959.

[148] Fourt, L., Spacer Systems for Hot Weather Clothing, TELR No. 115, Textile, Clothing and Footwear Div., Quartermaster R. and D. Center, Natick, Massachusetts, Feb. 1958.

[149] Fourt, L., Craig, R. A., and Rutherford, M. B., Cotton Fibers as Means of Transmitting Water Vapor, *Textile Res. J.,* **27**, 362-368 (1957).

[150] Fourt, L., and Fisk, K., Thermal Insulation Measurements on Thin Fabrics, OSRD Contr. OEM cmr-506, Committee on Aviation Med., Washington, D. C., July 1945.

[151] Fourt, L., and Harris, M., Diffusion of Water Vapor through Textiles, *Textile Res. J.,* **17**, 256-263, 1947.

[152] Fourt, L., and Harris, M., Physical Properties of Clothing Fabrics, in *Physiology of Heat Regulation and the Science of Clothing* (Newburgh, L. H., ed.), Saunders, Philadelphia, 1949, p. 298.

[153] *Ibid.,* p. 299.

[154] *Ibid.,* p. 312.

[155] Fourt, L., Lyerly, G. A., Edwards, G. C., and Poland, E. W., Dry Thermal Insulation of Thick Clothing, TELR No. 263, Textile, Clothing and Footwear Div., Quartermaster R. and Eng. Center, Natick, Massachusetts, Mar. 1960.

[156] Fourt, L., Lyerly, G. A., and Poland, E. W., Net Direct Heat Loss in Spacer Systems with Simultaneous Evaporation, Quarterly Rept. No. 2, Contr. No. DA-19-129-QM-1328, Textile, Clothing and Footwear Div., Quartermaster R. and D. Center, Natick, Massachusetts, Dec. 1959.

[157] Fourt, L., and Monego, C. J., Influence of Blending on Properties of Wool-Type Fabrics, in *Conference on Military Applications of Blended Fabrics,* Textile Ser. Rept. No. 119, Textile, Clothing and Footwear Div., Quartermaster R. and Eng. Center, Natick, Massachusetts, May 1960. AD 260 575.

[158] Fourt, L., Sookne, A. M., Frishman, D., and Harris, M., The Rate of Drying of Fabrics, *Textile Res. J., 21,* 26-33 (1951).

[159] Frazier Precision Instrument Co., 210 Oakmont Avenue, Gaithersburg, Maryland.

[160] Frederick, E. B., and Zagieboylo, W., Water-Repellent Thread for Military Items, TMEL Rept. No. 128, Textile and Leather Div., Quartermaster R. and D. Lab., Natick, Massachusetts, Apr. 1954.

[161] Frederick, E. B., Zagieboylo, W., and Balas, F. F., Preliminary Investigation of Some Factors Governing Tailorability of Wool and Wool-Nylon Blended Fabric, TMEL Rept. No. 114, Textile and Leather Div., Quartermaster R. and D. Lab., Natick, Massachusetts, Dec. 1952. PB 121 114.

[162] Freedman, E., Thermal Transmission of Fabrics, *Proc. Am. Soc. Test. Mat., 30,* Part II (1930).

[163] Frishman, D., Smith, A. L., and Harris, M., Measurement of the Frictional Properties of Wool Fibers, *Textile Res. J., 18,* 475-480 (1948).

[164] Froese, G., and Burton, A. C., Heat Losses from the Human Head, *J. Appl. Physiol., 10,* 235-241 (1957).

[165] Gabron, F., and McCullough, J., Thermal Manikin, Contr. Rept. CR-644, Contr. No. NAS 9-3554, Manned Spacecraft Center, Natl. Aeronautics and Space Administration, Washington, D.C., Nov. 1966.

[166] Gagge, A. P., Burton, A. C., and Bazett, H. C., A Practical System of Units for the Description of the Heat Exchange of Man with his Environment, *Science,* **94**, 428-430 (1941).

[167] Gagge, A. P., Hardy, J. D., and Rapp, R. M., Proposed Standard Symbols for Thermal Physiology, *J. Appl. Physiol.,* **27**, 439-445 (1969).

[168] Gagge, A. P., Stolwijk, J. A. J., and Hardy, J. D., Comfort and Thermal Sensations and Associated Physiological Responses at Various Ambient Temperatures, *Environ. Res.,* **1**, 1-20 (1967).

[169] Gagge, A. P., Stolwijk, J. A. J., and Salting, B., Comfort and Thermal Sensation and Associated Physiological Responses during Exercise, *Environ. Res.,* **2**, 209-230 (1969).

[170] Galbraith, R. L., Werden, J. E., Fahnestock, M. K., and Price, B., Comfort of Subjects Clothed in Cotton, Water-Repellent Cotton, and Orlon Suits, *Textile Res. J.,* **32**, 236-242 (1962).

[171] Gastonia Combed Yarn Corp., Cotton Combing at Gastonia's Clara Plant, *Textile World,* **104**, 140-141 (1954).

[172] Geiger, R., *The Climate Near the Ground,* Harvard Univ. Press, Cambridge, Massachusetts, 1965.

[173] Getchell, N. F., Progress in All-Cotton Durable Press, *Textile Dyer and Printer,* **2**, 54-62 (1969).

[174] Goddard, W. L., Sweat Retention of Materials in Arctic Clothing, Rept. No. EP-153, Quartermaster R. and D. Br., Clim. Res. Lab., Natick, Massachusetts, July 1949.

[175] Goddard, W. L., and VanDilla, M., Physical Apparatus for the Measurement of Thermal Transmission, Rept. No. 85, Quartermaster Clim. Res. Lab., Lawrence, Massachusetts, Jan. 1946.

[176] Gold, A. J., and Zornitzer, A., Effect of Partial Body Cooling on Man Exercising in a Hot, Dry Environment, *Aerospace Med.,* **39**, 944-946 (1968).

[177] Goldberg, J. B., Textile Research Achievements in 1968, *Textile Ind.,* **133**, 59-74 (1968).

[178] Goldman, R. F., Preliminary Evaluation of the Work Limitations Imposed on Subjects Wearing Chemical Protective Clothing, Res. Study Rept. PHY-1, Environ. Prot. Res. Div., Quartermaster R. and Eng. Center, Natick, Massachusetts, Apr. 1961.

[179] Goldman, R. F., Systematic Evaluation of Thermal Aspects of Air Crew Protective Systems, N68-24878, Military Ergonomics Lab., U.S. Army Res. Inst. Environ. Med., Natick, Massachusetts, Aug. 1965.

[180] Goldman, R. F., and Iampietro, P. F., Energy Cost of Load Carriage, *J. Appl. Physiol.*, **17**, 675-676 (1962).

[181] Goodings, A. C., Air Flow through Textile Fabrics, *Textile Res. J.*, **34**, 713-724 (1964).

[182] Greenwood, R. S., Blends Incorporating Viscose Rayon Staple, 37th Ann. Conf., Text Inst., Edinburgh, June 1952, pp. 13-19; *J. Textile Inst.*, **43**, P511-P518 (1952).

[183] Griffin, D. R., Folk, G. E., and Belding, H. S., Physiological Studies of Exposure Suits in Hot and Cold Environments, Rept. No. 26, OSRD Contr. Nos., OEM cmr-54 and 328, Harvard Fatigue Lab., Comm. on Med. Res., Office of Sci. R. and D., Mar. 1944.

[184] Grosberg, P., and Swani, N. M., The Mechanical Properties of Woven Fabrics: Part III. The Buckling of Woven Fabrics, *Textile Res. J.*, **36**, 332-338 (1966).

[185] Hagan, E. T., Development of a Heat-Reflecting, Fire-Fighting Clothing Assembly, Tech. Mem. Rept. WCRD 52-110, Aero Med. Lab., Wright-Patterson AFB, Dayton, Ohio, Nov. 1952.

[186] Hagan, E. T., Suits—Protective, Fire Fighting, Mem. Rept. MCREXD-666-1L, Eng. Div., Aero Med. Lab., Wright-Patterson AFB, Dayton, Ohio, Dec. 1949. PB 100 200.

[187] Hall, J. F., Jr., Thermal Insulation of AAF Flying Clothing, TSEAA-696-105, Eng. Div., Army Air Forces, Air Mat. Command, Wright-Patterson AFB, Dayton, Ohio, Oct. 1946.

[188] Hall, J. F., Jr., and Hagan, G., Insulation Tests of Clothing Assemblies and Footgear, Mem. Rept. TSEAH-696-105D, Eng. Div., Aero Med. Lab., Air Mat. Command, Wright-Patterson AFB, Dayton, Ohio, Apr. 1947.

[189] Hall, J. F., Jr., Kearny, A. P., Polte, J. W., and Quillette, S., Effect of Dry and Wet Clothing on Body Cooling at Low Air Temperatures, WADC Rept. 57-769, Aero Med. Lab., USAF, Wright-Patterson AFB, Dayton, Ohio, May 1958. AD 155 639, PB 151 206.

[190] Hall, J. F., Jr., and Polte, J. W., Effect of Water Content and Compression on Clothing Insulation, *J. Appl. Physiol.*, **8**, 539-545 (1956).

[191] Hall, J. F., Jr., and Polte, J. W., Effect of Water Content and Compression on Thermal Insulation of Clothing, WADC Tech. Rept. 55-356, Aero Med. Lab., Wright Air Dev. Center, Wright-Patterson AFB, Dayton, Ohio, Oct. 1955. PB 130 359.

[192] Hall, J. F., Jr., and Polte, J. W., Thermal Insulation of Air Force Clothing: Part IV, WADC Tech. Rept. 56-482, Aero Med. Lab., Wright-Patterson AFB, Dayton, Ohio, Oct. 1956. AD 97296.

[193] Hall, J. F., Jr., and Polte, J. W., Thermal Insulation of Air Force Clothing: Part V, WADD Tech. Rept. 60-597, Aerospace Med. Div., Biomed. Lab., Wright-Patterson AFB, Dayton, Ohio, Sept. 1960. AD 256 875.

[194] Hansen, H. H., *Costumes and Styles,* Dutton, New York, 1956.

[195] Hanson, H. E., and Dee, T. E., Jr., The Influence of Thermal-Protective Ensembles on Physiological Stress in a Desert Environment, Tech. Rept. EP-146, Environ. Prot. Res. Div., Quartermaster R. and Eng. Center, Natick, Massachusetts, Feb. 1961. PB 154548.

[196] Hardy, H. B., Jr., Ballou, J. W., and Wetmore, O. C., The Prediction of Equilibrium Thermal Comfort from Physical Data on Fabrics, *Textile Res. J.,* **23,** 1-10 (1953).

[197] Hardy, J. D., Heat Transfer, in *Physiology of Heat Regulation and the Science of Clothing,* Chap. 3 (Newburgh, L. H., ed.), Saunders, Philadelphia, 1949, pp. 78-108.

[198] *Ibid.,* p. 85.

[199] *Ibid.,* p. 104.

[200] Hardy, J. D., and DuBois, E. F., Basal Metabolism, Radiation, Convection and Vaporization at Temperatures of 22° to 35°C, *J. Nutr.,* **15,** 477-497 (1938).

[201] Hastings, A. D., Jr., Climatic Analogs of Fort Greely, Alaska, and Fort Churchill, Canada, in North America, Tech. Rept. EP-108, Environ. Prot. Lab., Quartermaster R. and Eng. Center, Natick, Massachusetts, Apr. 1959. PB 143 230.

[202] Hearle, J. W. S., and Peters, R. H., *Moisture in Textiles,* Textile Book Pub., New York, 1960.

[203] Heer, R. R., Quantitative Studies on the Effects of Non-Ionizing Radiation on the Skin: Part II, Rept. No. 55, Project AMRL No. 6-64-12-08 (8), Army Med. Res. Lab., Fort Knox, Kentucky, May 1953.

[204] Heimbold, N. C., News About Fibers, Yarns and Fabrics, *Textile World,* **118,** 91-92 (1968).

[205] Henry, P. S. H., Diffusion in Absorbing Media, *Proc. Roy. Soc.* (London), **171A,** 215-241 (1939).

[206] Henry, P. S. H., Livesey, R. G., and Wood, A. M., A Test for Liability to Electrostatic Charging, *J. Textile Inst.,* **58,** 55-77 (1967).

[207] Henry, T. R., *The White Continent,* William Sloane Assoc., New York, 1950.

[208] Herminge, L., Heat Transfer in Porous Bodies at Various Temperatures and Moisture Contents, *Tappi,* **44,** 570-575 (1961).

[209] Herrington, L. P., Basic Procedures in the Calculation of the Heat Exchange of the Clothed Human Body, *Yale J. Biol. Med.,* **19,** 735-755 (1947).

[210] Herrington, L. P., The Body as a Heat Exchanger, *Mech. Eng.,* **79,** 1029-1031 (1957).

[211] Herrington, L. P., Full-Scale Human-Body-Model Thermal Exchange Compared with Equational Condensations of Human Calorimetric Data, *J. Heat Transfer,* **81,** 187-194 (1959).

[212] Herrington, L. P., Hardy, J. D., and DuBois, E. F., Temperature and Humidity in Relation to the Thermal Interchange between the Human Body and the Environment, in *Human Factors in Undersea Warfare,* Natl. Res. Council, Washington, D.C., 1949, pp. 269-309. PB 111 203.

[213] Hersh, S. P., and Montgomery, D. J., Electrical Resistance Measurements on Fibers and Fiber Assemblies, *Textile Res. J.,* **22,** 805-818 (1952).

[214] Hock, C. W., Sookne, A. M., and Harris, M., Thermal Properties of Moist Fabrics, *J. Res. Natl. Bur. Std.,* **32,** 229-252 (1944).

[215] Hoffman, R. M., Measuring the Aesthetic Appeal of Textiles, *Textile Res. J.,* **35,** 428-434 (1965).

[216] Hoffman, R. M., and Beste, L. F., Some Relations of Fiber Properties to Fabric Hand, *Textile Res. J.,* **21,** 66-77 (1951).

[217] Hoge, H. J., and Fonseca, G. F., The Thermal Conductivity of a Multilayer Sample of Underwear Material under a Variety of Experimental Conditions, *Textile Res. J.,* **34,** 401-410 (1964).

[218] Hollies, N. R. S., Comfort Properties in Cold Weather Clothing, Rept. No. 18, Contr. No. DA-19-129-qm-331, Quartermaster R. and D., Natick, Massachusetts, Dec. 1955 AD 698 441.

[219] Hollies, N. R. S., Development of Finishes for Cotton Fabrics to Render Them More Rapid-Drying, Rept. No. 4, Contr. No. 12-14-100-8158(72), Southern Utilization R. and D. Div., U.S. Dept. of Agriculture, New Orleans, Louisiana, May 1967.

[220] Hollies, N. R. S., Efficiency of Use of Air for Cooling in Spaces inside Clothing: III. The Combined Effects of Forced and Natural Convection at Different Air Flows in Three and One Inch Spaces, Quart. Rept. No. 1, Contr. DA-19-129-qm-1713, Textile, Clothing and Footwear Div., Quartermaster R. and D. Center, Natick, Massachusetts, Feb. 1961.

[221] Hollies, N. R. S., The Evaluation of Experimental Fabrics as Alternates for Standard Wool Fabrics, Rept. No. 10, Contr. No. DA-44-109-qm-564, Textile, Clothing and Footwear Div.,

Quartermaster R. and D. Center, Natick, Massachusetts, Dec. 1953. AD 698 447.

[222] Hollies, N. R. S., The Evaluation of Experimental Fabrics as Alternates for Standard Wool Fabrics, Rept. No. 13, Contr. No. DA-44-109-qm-564, Textile, Clothing and Footwear Div., Quartermaster R. and D. Center, Natick, Massachusetts, Sept. 1954. AD 698 448.

[223] Hollies, N. R. S., Investigation of the Factors Influencing Comfort in Cotton Shirts, Final Rept., Contr. No. 12-14-100-7183(72), Southern Utilization R. and D. Div., U.S. Dept. of Agriculture, New Orleans, Louisiana, May 1965.

[224] Hollies, N. R. S., Mt. Washington Feasibility Test, Rept. No. 20, Contr. No. DA-19-129-qm-331, Textile, Clothing and Footwear Div., Quartermaster R. and D. Center, Natick, Massachusetts, June 1956. AD 698 450.

[225] Hollies, N. R. S., The Nature of a Fabric Surface: Interaction of the Surface Fibers, presented to the Fiber Society, Montreal, Canada, Oct. 22, 1964.

[226] Hollies, N. R. S., A New Approach to Optimum Cooling in Ventilated Impermeable Clothing, Abstr. of paper presented at the 38th Ann. Meeting, Aerospace Med. Assoc., Washington, D.C., Apr. 11, 1967.

[227] Hollies, N. R. S., The Schlieren Method Applied to Air Mixing and Boundary Layers in Model Clothing Spacer Systems, Clothing Branch Rept. No. 23, Textile, Clothing and Footwear Div., Quartermaster R. and D. Center, Natick, Massachusetts, June 1961.

[228] Hollies, N. R. S., A Study of Effective Means of Body-Temperature Control Using Ventilated Clothing, Rept. No. NADC-AC-6813, Aerospace Crew Equip. Dept., Naval Air Dev. Center, Johnsville, Warminster, Pennsylvania, July 1968. AD840 081.

[229] Hollies, N. R. S., Wet Fixation Durable-Press Process: Polymer Deposition, *Textile Res. J.*, *37*, 277-288 (1967).

[230] Hollies, N. R. S., and Bogaty, H., Some Thermal Properties of Fabrics: Part II. The Influence of Water Content, *Textile Res. J.*, *35*, 187-190 (1965).

[231] Hollies, N. R. S., Bogaty, H., Hintermaier, J., and Harris, M., The Nature of a Fabric Surface: Evaluation by a Rate-of-Cooling Method, *Textile Res. J.*, *23*, 763-769 (1953).

[232] Hollies, N. R. S., Bogaty, H., Monego, C. J., and Donegan, J. H., Jr., The Movement of Water through Apparel Textile Systems, Textile Series Rept. No. 96, Textile, Clothing and Footwear Div.,

Quartermaster R. and D. Center, Natick, Massachusetts, May 1957. PB 132 922.

[233] Hollies, N. R. S., Kaessinger, M. M., and Bogaty, H., Water Transport Mechanisms in Textile Materials: Part I. The Role of Yarn Roughness in Capillary-Type Penetration, *Textile Res. J.*, 26, 829-835 (1956).

[234] Hollies, N. R. S., and Krasny, J. F., The Development of Quick-Drying, Easy Care Cotton Fabrics, *Am. Dyestuff Reptr.*, 55, 17-19 (1966).

[235] Hollies, N. R. S., and Watson, B., Water Transport Mechanisms in Textile Materials: Part II. Capillary Type Penetration in Yarns and Fibers, *Textile Res. J.*, 27, 8-13 (1957).

[236] Horowitz, H., Woven Friction Fabrics, U.S. Patent 2,835,279 (May 20, 1958).

[237] Horvath, S. M., Studies of Cold Weather Clothing, Project No. 20-4, Immobilized Air (OQMG Test No. 57-IV), Armored Med. Res. Lab., Fort Knox, Kentucky, May 1944.

[238] Horvath, S. M., Golden, H., and Wagar, J. E., Some Observations on Men Sitting Quietly in Extreme Cold, *J. Clin. Invest.*, 25, 709-716 (1946).

[239] Horvath, S. M., Wagar, J. E., and Golden, H., The Effect of Leakage from Closures upon Thermal Protection, Report on Sub-Project 20-1, Armored Med. Res. Lab., Fort Knox, Kentucky, June 1944.

[240] Hunt, S. B., ed., *Textile Organon*, 39, 57-72 (1968).

[241] Hunt, S. B., ed., *Textile Organon*, 39, 185-200 (1968).

[242] Hunt, S. B., ed., *Textile Organon*, 39, 201-216 (1968).

[243] Huntington, E., *Civilization and Climate*, Yale Univ. Press, New Haven, 1915.

[244] Hynek, W., Effect of Temperature on Acrilan and Dynel Blended Wool Serges, TMEL Rept. No. 97, Textile and Leather Div., Quartermaster R. and D. Lab., Natick, Massachusetts, Sept. 1952.

[245] Iampietro, P. F., and Adams, T., Thermal Balance during Exercise and Environmental Stress, in *Exercise Physiology* (Falls, H. B., ed.), Academic Press, New York, 1968, pp. 188-196.

[246] Iampietro, P. F., Bass, D. E., Vaughan, J. A., and Buskirk, E. R., Heat Exchanges of Men in the Cold: Effect of Humidity, Temperature, and Windspeed, Tech. Rept. EP-99, Environ. Prot. Res. Div., Quartermaster R. and Eng. Center, Natick, Massachusetts, Sept. 1958. PB 137 856.

[247] Iampietro, P. F., Buskirk, E. R., and Vaughan, J. A., Effects of

High and Low Humidity on Heat Exchanges of Lightly Clothed Men, Tech. Rept. EP-131, Environ. Prot. Res. Div., Quartermaster R. and Eng. Center, Natick, Massachusetts, Apr. 1960. PB 146 904.

[248] Ibrahim, S. M., Mechanics of Form-Persuasive Garments Based on Spandex Fibers, *Textile Res. J.,* **38**, 950-963 (1968).

[249] Jackman, A. H., Handbook of Yuma Environment, Rept. No. 200, Environ. Prot. Br., Quartermaster R. and D. Div., Dept. of the Army, Washington, D.C., Feb. 1953. PB 146 815.

[250] Jacquez, J. A., Kuppenheim, H., Dimitroff, J. M., Huss, J., and McKeehan, W., The Spectral Reflectance of Human Skin in the Region 235-700 mu, Rept. No. 193, Project 6-64-12-028, Army Med. Res. Lab., Fort Knox, Kentucky, Apr. 1955.

[251] Johnson, R. P., and Robb, J. S., Heart Rates: Part I. Man, in *Biology Data Book* (Altman, P. L., and Dittmer, D. S., eds.), Federation Am. Soc. Experimental Biol., Bethesda, Maryland, 1964.

[252] Kaswell, E. R., Electrical Resistance of Textile Fibers, in *Wellington Sears Handbook of Industrial Textiles,* Wellington Sears Co., Inc., New York, 1963, p. 402.

[253] *Ibid.,* Fig. 186, p. 574.

[254] *Ibid.,* Electrical Resistivity, p. 620.

[255] Keggin, J. F., Morris, G., and Yuill, A. M., Static Electrification in the Processing of Fibres: Variation with Moisture Regain during Carding, *J. Textile Inst.,* **40**, T702-T714 (1949).

[256] Kennedy, S. J., The Importance of Conservation to the Textile Industry and the American Public, TMEL Rept. No. 52, Textile, Clothing and Footwear Div., Quartermaster R. and D. Center, Natick, Massachusetts, Feb. 1951.

[257] Kennedy, S. J., McQuade, A. J., Darby, M. E., Thomas, G. R., Bailey, T. L., Spano, L., Rizzo, F. J., Ewing, G. J., and Feldman, D., Chemical and Biological Protection for the Soldier, Clothing and Org. Mat. Div., Quartermaster R. and Eng. Center, Natick, Massachusetts, Mar. 1962.

[258] Kennedy, S. J., Weiner, L. I., and Bailey, T. L., Textile Materials Systems and the Soldier, Textile, Clothing and Footwear Div., Quartermaster R. and Eng. Center, Natick, Massachusetts, Aug. 1959.

[259] Kenshalo, D. R., and Nafe, J. P., The Peripheral Basis of Temperature Sensitivity in Man, in *Temperature, Its Measurement and Control in Science and Industry,* Vol. 3 (C. M. Herzfeld, ed.), Reinhold, New York, 1963, pp. 231-238.

[260] Kerslake, D. McK., A Heated Manikin for Studies of Ventilated
      Clothing, Minutes Quadripartite Quartermaster Standing Working
      Group No. 4, Joint Meeting, Sept.-Oct. 1963.
[261] Kerslake, D. McK., and Clifford, J. M., A Comparison of the Per-
      formance of Five Air-Ventilated Suits as Heat Exchangers,
      Measured on a Heated Manikin, N67-10546, Flying Personnel
      Res. Comm., Air Force Dept., Ministry of Def., Great Britain,
      Apr. 1965.
[262] King, G., Permeability of Keratin Membranes to Water Vapour,
      Trans. Faraday Soc., **41**, 479-487 (1945).
[263] Kissen, A. T., and Hall, J. F., Jr., Physiologic Response to Transient
      Heat Stress in Reflective Versus Non-Reflective Clothing, *Aerospace
      Med.,* **34**, 730-735 (1963). AD 419 121.
[264] Koch, W., and Kaplan, D., A Simple Method of Estimating the
      Ventilation of Footwear, *Ann. Trop. Med. Parasitol,* **50**, 113-120
      (1956).
[265] König, W., Physiological Properties of Clothing Made from Foam-
      Backed Fabrics, *Z. Ges. Textilind.,* **65**, 612-617 (1963).
[266] Krasny, J. F., Watson, B. S., and Tovey, H., Some Characteristics
      of Experimental, Warm, Lofty Cotton Fabrics, *Am. Dyestuff
      Reptr.,* **54**, 573-578 (1965).
[267] Kuno, Y., Human Perspiration, Thomas, Springfield, Illinois, 1956.
[268] *Ibid.,* Chap. 8, Chemistry of Sweat, pp. 223-250.
[269] Kyame, G. J., Harper, R. J., Lofton, J. T., and Ruppenicker, G. F., Jr.,
      Improved Durable Press through Fabric Structure and Polymer Treat-
      ment, *Am. Dyestuff Reptr.,* **57**, P662-P667 (1968).
[270] Laby, T. H., and Nelson, E. A., in *International Critical Tables,*
      Vol. V, McGraw-Hill, New York, 1929, p. 214.
[271] Langmuir, I., The Convection and Conduction of Heat in Gases,
      Trans. Am. Inst. Elec. Engrs., **31**, 1229-1240 (1912).
[272] Larose, P., Observations on the Compressibility of Pile Fabrics,
      Textile Res. J., **23**, 730-735 (1953).
[273] Larose, P., Thermal Resistance of Clothing with Special Reference
      to the Protection Given by Coverall Fabrics of Various Permeabilities,
      Can. J. Res., Sect. A, **25**, 169-190 (1947).
[274] Leach, L. L., Fibers, Fabrics and Body Comfort, *Can. Textile J.,*
      74, 59-65 (1957).
[275] Lee, D. H. K., Katin, J. G., Woodcock, A. H., Goddard, W. L., and
      Woodbury, R. L., Studies on Clothing for Hot Environments, Death
      Valley, 1950: Part I. Experiments and Results, Rept. No. 178,

Environ. Prot. Sec., R. and D. Br., Washington, D.C., June 1951. PB 163 075.

[276] Lee, D. H. K., and Lemons, H., Clothing for Global Man, *Geograph. Rev.,* **34**, 181-213 (1949).

[277] Lennox-Kerr, P., Spotlight on Fibers, *Textile Ind.,* **132**, 175-177 (1968).

[278] Libet, E., Estimation of the Thermal Insulation of Clothing by Measuring Increases in the Girth of the Wearer, Mem. Rept. TSEAL-5H-5-241, Army Air Forces Air Tech. Service Command, Personal Equipment Lab., Wright-Patterson AFB, Dayton, Ohio, May 1945. PB 5108.

[279] Liddell, F. D. K., Estimation of Energy Expenditure from Expired Air, *J. Appl. Physiol.,* **18**, 25-29 (1963).

[280] Lind, A. R., Tolerable Limits for Prolonged and Intermittent Exposure to Heat, in *Temperature, Its Measurement and Control in Science and Industry,* Vol. 3, Part 3 (Hardy, J. D., ed.), Reinhold, New York, 1963, pp. 337-345.

[281] Lindberg, J., Relationship between Various Surface Properties of Wool Fibers: Part II. Frictional Properties, *Textile Res. J.,* **23**, 225-236 (1953).

[282] Lindberg, J., Behre, B., and Dahlberg, B., Mechanical Properties of Textile Fabrics: Part III. Shearing and Buckling of Various Commercial Fabrics, *Textile Res. J.,* **31**, 99-122 (1961).

[283] McAdams, W. H., *Heat Transmission,* McGraw-Hill, New York, 1942, p. 222.

[284] McLaren, A. D., and Rowen, J. W., Sorption of Water Vapor by Proteins and Polymers: A Review, *J. Polymer Sci.,* **7**, 289-324 (1951).

[285] McMahon, G. B., and Downes, J. G., Propagation of Temperature and Moisture Changes during Forced Convective Flow of Air Through a Mass of Hygroscopic Fibres, *Intern. J. Heat Mass Transfer,* **5**, 689-696 (1962).

[286] MacPhee, C. W., ed., *American Society of Heating, Refrigeration and Air-Conditioning Engineers Guide and Data Book,* Chap. 6, ASHAE Comfort Chart for Still Air, ASHAE, New York, 1965-1966.

[289] McQuade, A. J., and Kennedy, S. J., Protection Afforded by Clothing against High Intensity Thermal Radiation, Textile Conference of Gordon Res. Conf., Sponsored by AAAS, New London, New Hampshire, July 1955.

[290] McQuain, R. H., Meterological Program, in *Space Applications 1966,* NASA SP-156, 1967, pp. 29-81.

[291] Maggio, R. C., and Gilhooly, T. B., Heat-Reflecting Textiles as Protective Barriers against Intense Thermal Radiation, Final Rept., Lab. Project 5046-3, Part 77, Optics and Nucleonics Br., Naval Mat. Lab., New York Naval Shipyard, Brooklyn, New York, Mar. 1955. AD 270 665.

[292] Mansberg, H. P., and Hendler, E., A Precision Multichannel Body Temperature Measurement System, in *Temperature, Its Measurement and Control in Science and Industry,* Vol. 3 (Charles M. Herzfeld, ed.), Reinhold, New York, 1963, pp. 13-19.

[293] Mark, H. F., Gaylord, N. G., and Bikales, N. M., eds., *Encyclopedia of Polymer Science and Technology,* Vol. 2, Antistatic Agents, Wiley-Interscience, New York, 1965, pp. 202-228.

[294] Mark, M., and Derecho, C. T., Jr., Packing Coefficient and Thermal Conductivity of Textiles, *Bull. Lowell Technol. Inst.,* Ser. **62,** No. 3, 3-13 (1959).

[295] Markham, S. F., *Climate and the Energy of Nations,* Oxford Univ. Press, London and New York, 1944.

[295b] Mathai, T., Personal Computer Power, *Sci. and Technol.,* **93,** 40 (1969).

[295c] May, J. M., Water Repellent Finishes, *Am. Dyestuff Reptr.,* **58,** No. 20, 15-45 (1969).

[296] Mecheels, J. H., Physiological Properties of Knit Goods, *Hosiery Times,* **38,** 43-50, 84 (1965).

[297] Mecheels, J. H., Physiological Wearing Properties of Knitted Fabrics, *Knitted Outerwear Times,* **34,** 25, 73-83 (1965).

[298] Mecheels, J. H., Demeler, R. M., and Kachel, E., Moisture Transfer through Chemically Treated Cotton Fabrics, *Textile Res. J.,* **36,** 375-384 (1966).

[299] Mecheels, O., Concerning Physiological Characteristics of Wool Textiles, *Melliand Textilber.,* **38,** 645-648 (1957).

[300] Mehrtens, D. G., and McAlister, K. C., Fiber Properties Responsible for Garment Comfort, *Textile Res. J.,* **32,** 658-665 (1962).

[301] Mereness, H. A., The Measurement of the Drag of Cotton Fibers, *Textile Res. J.,* **25,** 363-372 (1955).

[302] Miles, T. D., and Delasanta, A. C., Durable Non-Reactive Flame-Retardant Finishes for Cotton, *Textile Res. J.,* **38,** 273-279 (1968).

[303] Mills, C. J., Manmade Yarns and Fibers—Their Invasion of Traditional Cotton Markets, *Mod. Textiles Mag.,* **49(8),** 28-30 (1968).

[304] Minor, F. W., Schwartz, A. M., Wulkow, E. A., and Buckles, L. C., The Migration of Liquids in Textile Assemblies: Part II. The Wicking of Liquids in Yarns, *Textile Res. J.,* **29,** 931-949 (1959).

[305] Minor, F. W., Schwartz, A. M., Buckles, L. C., Wulkow, E. A., and Marks, M. P., The Migration of Liquids in Textile Assemblies: Part IV. Penetration of Fabrics by Liquids, *Textile Res. J.,* **31**, 525-539 (1961).

[306] Minor, F. W., Sookne, A. M., Simpson, J. E., and Harris, M., The Use of Water-Permeability Measurements on Swelling-Type Fabrics, *Textile Res. J.,* **16**, 539-544 (1946).

[307] Monego, C. J., Golub, S. J., Baker, C. A., Gesmer, B. S., Kaswell, E. R., Kobayashi, F. F., Monroe, E. F., and Panto, J. S., Insulating Values of Fabrics, Foams and Laminates, *Am. Dyestuff Reptr.,* **52**, P6-P17 (1963).

[308] Monego, C. J., and Kennedy, S. J., Evaluation of New Fiber Blends in Army Summer Uniform Fabrics, Textile Ser. Tech. Rept. TS108, Quartermaster R. and Eng. Center, Natick, Massachusetts, May 1960. PB 161 331.

[309] Monego, C. J., and Wing, P., Optimum Spacing of Hot Weather Clothing for Convective Cooling, TELR No. 186, Textile, Clothing and Footwear Div., Quartermaster R. and D. Center, Natick, Massachusetts, May 1957.

[310] Moreira, M., Johnson, R. E., Belding, H. S., Wood, R., and Stachelek, J., A Comparison of Performances of Men Marching with Three Types of Raincoat and a Poncho, Rept. No. 20, Harvard Fatigue Lab., Cambridge, Massachusetts, Dec. 1943. PB 99 292.

[311] Mörner, B., and Eëg-Olofsson, T., Measurement of the Shearing Properties of Fabrics, *Textile Res. J.,* **27**, 611-615 (1957).

[312] Morris, G. J., Thermal Properties of Textile Materials, *J. Textile Inst.,* **44**, T449-T476 (1953).

[313] Morris, M. A., Thermal Insulation of Single and Multiple Layers of Fabrics, *Textile Res. J.,* **25**, 766-773 (1955).

[314] Morris, R. O., The Development of the Testing Techniques and Procedures Utilized at the Climatic Research Laboratory, Quartermaster Clim. Res. Lab., Lawrence, Massachusetts, May 1946.

[315] National Research Council, *International Critical Tables,* V, McGraw-Hill, New York, 1929, p. 214.

[316] Nelbach, J. H., and Herrington, L. P., A Note on the Hygroscopic Properties of Clothing in Relation to Human Heat Loss, *Science,* **95**, 387-388 (1942).

[317] Nelms, J. D., An Apparatus for the Measurement of Clothing Insulation, FPRC/Memo 206, RAF Inst. of Aviation Med., Ministry of Def. (Air Force Dept.), Farnborough, Hants, England, June 1964.

[318] Nelms, J. D., and Goodall, J. F., An Apparatus for the Measurement of Clothing Insulation, FPRC/Memo 206 N66-19722, Flying Personnel Res. Comm., RAF Inst. of Aviation Med., June 1964.

[319] Nelson, N. A., Shelley, W. B., Horvath, S. M., Eichna, L. W., and Hatch, T. F., The Influence of Clothing, Work, and Air Movement on the Thermal Exchanges of Acclimatized Men in Various Hot Environments, *J. Clin. Invest.*, **27**, 209-216 (1948).

[320] Newburgh, L. H., ed., *Physiology of Heat Regulation and the Science of Clothing*, Saunders, Philadelphia, 1949; Stechert-Haffner, New York, 1968.

[321] Nilsen, I. U., Onions, W. J., and Whewell, C. S., Pilling of Wool/ Terylene Blended Fabrics, *J. Textile Inst.*, **48**, T374 (1957).

[322] Niven, C. D., The Heat Transmission of Fabrics in Wind, *Textile Res. J.*, **27**, 808-811 (1957).

[323] Niven, C. D., The Heat Transmission of Fabrics in Wind: Part II, *Textile Res. J.*, **29**, 826-833 (1959).

[324] Niven, C. D., Measurements on the "Cooling-Time" Hot Plate in Wind, *Textile Res. J.*, **32**, 958-959 (1962).

[325] O'Brien, S. J., Cyanamide-Based Durable Flame-Retardant Finish for Cotton, *Textile Res. J.*, **38**, 256-266 (1968).

[326] Ogden, L. W., and Rees, W. H., Measurement of Temperature and Relative Humidity on the Skin and Clothing of a Human Subject, *J. Textile Inst.*, **38**, T371-T386 (1947).

[327] Pankhurst, R. C., and Holder, D. W., *Wind-Tunnel Technique*, Pitman, London, 1952.

[328] *Ibid.*, p. 623.

[329] Peirce, F. T., The "Handle" of Cloth as a Measurable Quantity, *J. Textile Inst.*, **21**, T377-T416 (1930).

[330] Peirce, F. T., and Rees, W. H., The Transmission of Heat through Textile Fabrics: Part II, *J. Textile Inst.*, **37**, T181-T204 (1946).

[331] Penoyer, J. A., and Hollies, N. R. S., The Measurement of Moisture at a Fabric Surface, Appendix to Final Rept., Contr. 12-14-100-7183(72), U.S. Dept. of Agriculture, New Orleans, Louisiana, Apr. 1967.

[332] Press, J. J., Some Wool-Like Properties of Fibers and Fabrics, *Rayon and Syn. Textiles*, Aug., 39-44 (1950).

[333] Preston, J. M., and Chen, J. C., Some Aspects of the Drying and Heating of Textiles: Part I. The Moisture in Fabrics, *J. Soc. Dyers Colourists*, **62**, 361-364 (1946).

[334] Preston, J. M., Nimkar, M. V., and Gundavda, S. P., Capillary and

Imbibed Water in Assemblies of Moist Fibers, *J. Textile Inst.*, **42**, T79-T90 (1951).

[335] Price, B. P., The Diffusion of Water Vapor through Textile Fabrics at Varying Environmental Conditions, M. Sc. Thesis, Univ. of Illinois, Urbana, Illinois, 1960.

[336] Rader, C. A., and Schwartz, A. M., The Migration of Liquids in Textile Assemblies: Part V. Two-Component and Two-Phase Liquid Systems, *Textile Res. J.*, **32**, 140-153 (1962).

[337] Ramanthan, N. L., A New Weighting System for Mean Surface Temperature of the Human Body, *J. Appl. Physiol.*, **19**, 531-533 (1964).

[338] Randolph, C. P., The Thermal Resistivity of Insulating Materials, *Trans. Am. Electrochem. Soc.*, **21**, 545-557 (1912).

[339] Rasero, L. J., Anti-Friction Fabric, U.S. Patent 2,862,283 (Dec. 2, 1958).

[340] Rees, W. H., The Protective Value of Clothing, *J. Textile Inst.*, **37**, P132-P153 (1946).

[341] Rees, W. H., The Transmission of Heat through Textile Fabrics, *J. Textile Inst.*, **32**, T149-T165 (1941).

[342] Rees, W. H., and Ogden, L. W., Some Observations upon the Effect of Color on the Absorption and Emission of Radiation by a Textile Fabric, *Shirley Inst. Mem.*, **14**, 59-65 (1944-45).

[343] Rees, W. H., and Peirce, F. T., The Transmission of Heat through Textile Fabrics: Part II, *J. Textile Inst.*, **37**, T181-T204 (1946).

[344] Renbourn, E. T., The Body and Clothing in Retrospect, *Ciba Rev.*, **4**, 2-11 (1964).

[345] Renbourn, E. T., Clothes Make the Man—The Psychology of Dress, *Ciba Rev.*, **4**, 12-16 (1964).

[346] Renbourn, E. T., Human Factors Problems in Tropical Climates, Particularly of Jungle Warfare, 8th Commonwealth Defense Conf. Clothing and General Stores, Australia, 1965.

[347] Renbourn, E. T., Life and Death of the Solar Topi: Protection of the Head from the Sun—A Chapter in the History of Sunstroke, Seventh Commonwealth Defense Conf. Clothing and General Stores, Ministry of Supply, London, 1961.

[348] Renbourn, E. T., The Natural History of Insensible Perspiration: A Forgotten Doctrine of Health and Disease, *Med. History*, **4**, 135-150 (1960).

[349] Renbourn, E. T., The Physiology and Hygiene of Clothing, *Ciba Rev.*, **4**, 26-36 (1964).

[350] Renbourn, E. T., The Physiology of Textiles and Clothing: A Historic Note—December 1952, Rept. No. 20, Directorate of Physiol. and Biol. Res., Ministry of Supply, London, June 1953.

[351] Renbourn, E. T., and Stockbridge, H. C. W., War Office Clothing and Equipment Physiol. Res. Establishment, *Ergonomics,* **4,** 73-79 (1961).

[352] Richards, H. R., Methods for Evaluating the Flammability-Hazard of Fabrics, Eighth Commonwealth Defense Conf. Clothing and General Stores, Australia, 1965.

[353] Rinecker, F. G., Thermal Characteristics of Multilayer Combinations of Aluminum Foil and Nylon and Cotton Fabric in Clothing, Mem. Rept. MCREXD-666-23H, Eng. Div., Aero Med. Lab., Wright-Patterson AFB, Dayton, Ohio, Aug. 1950. PB 102 423.

[354] Rizzo, F. J., Influence of Colorant Systems on Thermal Protection, Textile Series Rept. No. 97, Textile, Clothing and Footwear Div., Quartermaster R. and D. Center, Natick, Massachusetts, May 1957. PB 129 544.

[355] Robinson, H. E., and Watson, T. W., Interlaboratory Comparison of Thermal Conductivity Determinations with Guarded Hot Plates, in *Symp. Thermal Insulating Materials,* Am. Soc. Test. Mat. Spec. Tech. Publ. No. 119, Philadelphia, 1952, pp. 36-44.

[356] Robinson, S., Laboratory and Field Studies: Tropics, in *Physiology of Heat Regulation and the Science of Clothing* (Newburgh, L. H., ed.), Saunders, Philadelphia, 1949, p. 349.

[357] Robinson, S., Physiological Adjustments to Heat, in *Physiology of Heat Regulation and the Science of Clothing* (Newburgh, L. H., ed.), Saunders, Philadelphia, 1949, p. 213.

[358] Robinson, S., and Gerking, S. D., Physiological Comparisons of Water-Repellent and Water-Absorbent Clothing, Interim Rept. No. 24, OSRD Contr. No. OEM-cmr-351, Comm. Med. Res., Office Sci. R. and D., Washington, D.C., Apr. 1945. PB 77 304.

[359] Robinson, S., Turrell, E. S., and Horvath, S. M., The Effectiveness of U.S. Army Inner Helmets as Protection from Radiant Heat, Rept. No. 11, OSRD Contr. No. OEM-cmr-54, Harvard Fatigue Lab., Cambridge, Massachusetts, July, 1943.

[360] Robinson, W. C., Hessen, W. C., and Hogue, D. W., Handbook of Fort Lee Environment, Rept. No. 231, Environ. Prot. Div., Quartermaster R. and D. Center, Natick, Massachusetts, June 1954.

[361] Rodwell, E. C., The Physiological Effect of the Heat of Absorption in Clothing, Quadripartite Quartermaster Standing Working Group No. 4 Meeting, Paper for Military Ergonomics Seminar, 1965.

[362] Rodwell, E. C., Renbourn, E. T., Greeland, J., and Kenching-ton, K. W. L., Physiological Value of 'Sorption Heat' in Clothing Systems, Eighth Commonwealth Defense Conf. Clothing and General Stores, Australia, 1965.

[363] Roller, W. L., and Goldman, R. F., Prediction of Solar Heat Load on Man, *J. Appl. Physiol.*, **24**, 717-721 (1968).

[364] Ross, J. H., High-Temperature Fiber Research, *Textile Res. J.*, **32**, 768-777 (1962).

[365] Rubenstein, C., Review on the Factors Influencing the Friction of Fibers, Yarns and Fabrics, *Wear*, **2**, 296-309 (1959).

[366] Rubner, M., Influence of Moisture on the Ability of Clothing Material to Conduct Heat, *Arch. Hyg. Bakteriol.*, **25**, 29-69 (1896).

[367] Ruskin, R. E., ed., *Humidity and Moisture*, Vol. I, Section III, Electric Hygrometry, Reinhold, New York, 1965, pp. 219-310.

[368] Rust, L. W., Larson, R. E., and Spano, L. A., Heat and Mass Transfer Processes in a Clothing-Airspace-Skin System: Part I, Theoretical Studies, Contr. Nos. DA-19-129-AMC-183(N) and DA-19-129-AMC-683(N), U.S. Army Natick Lab., Natick, Massachusetts, Oct. 1965.

[369] Rydzewska, D., Measurement of the Relative Coefficient of Light Reflection by Colored Fabrics in the Region of Visible and In-frared Rays, *Prace Inst. Wlokiennictwa*, **9**, No. 2(31), 17-37 (1959).

[370] Samueloff, S., Sohar, E., and Givoni, B., Man and Heat, Abstr., Proc. Intern. Union Physiol. Sci., 7, 24th Intern. Congress, Wash-ington, D.C., 1968, p. 486.

[371] Schiefer, H. F., Advantages of a Blanket-and-Sheet Combination for Outdoor Use, *J. Res. Natl. Bur. Std.*, **30**, 209-214 (1943).

[372] Schiefer, H. F., The Compressometer, an Instrument for Evalu-ating the Thickness, Compressibility, and Compressional Resilience of Textiles and Similar Materials, *J. Res. Natl. Bur. Std.*, **10**, 705-713 (1933).

[373] Schiefer, H. F., The Flexometer, an Instrument for Evaluating the Flexural Properties of Cloth and Similar Materials, *J. Res. Natl. Bur. Std.*, **10**, 647-657 (1933).

[374] Schiefer, H. F., Thickness and Compressibility of Fabrics, *ASTM Bull.*, **192**, 48 (1953).

[375] Schiefer, H. F., and Boyland, P. M., Improved Instrument for Measuring the Air Permeability of Fabrics, *J. Res. Natl. Bur. Std.*, **28**, 637-642 (1942).

[376] Schiefer, H. F., Stevens, H. T., Mack, P. B., and Boyland, P. M.,

A Study of the Properties of Household Blankets, *J. Res. Natl. Bur. Std.,* **32,** 261-284 (1944).

[377] Schneider, W. G., Compressibility of Gases at High Temperatures: I. Methods of Measurement and Apparatus, *Can. J. Res. B.,* **27,** 339-352 (1949).

[378] Schrager, H., and Monego, C. J., An Optical Method for Thermal Insulation Studies (unedited report), Textile Eng. Br., Quartermaster R. and Eng. Center, Natick, Massachusetts, Nov. 1957.

[379] Schwartz, A. M., and Minor, F. W., A Simplified Thermodynamic Approach to Capillarity: Part I. Application to Flow in Capillary Channels, *J. Colloid Sci.,* **14,** 572-583 (1959).

[380] Schwartz, S. A., Laboratory Evaluation of Impermeable Protective Clothing, Rept. No. 45, Clothing and Textile Div., U.S. Naval Supply R. and D. Facility, Bayonne, New Jersey, Nov. 1959. PB 150 778.

[381] Seery, T. J., Clothing for Radiation Protection, *Mod. Textiles Mag.,* **45,** 42 (Feb. 1964).

[382] Segall, G. H., A Theory of Water-Resistant Fabrics, *Textile Res. J.,* **22,** 736-741 (1952).

[383] Sendroy, J., Jr., Body Surface Area for Known Weight and Height: Man, in *Biology Data Book* (Altman, P. L. and Dittmer, D. S., eds.), Federation Am. Soc. Experimental Biol., Bethesda, Maryland, 1964.

[384] Shapiro, E. S., Feasibility and Potential Effectiveness of Partial-Body Shielding for Personnel Protection against Ionizing Radiation, U.S. Radiological Defense Lab., San Francisco, California, Apr. 1967. AD 653 459.

[385] Sheldon, W. H., *Atlas of Men,* Gramercy, New York, 1954.

[386] Siple, P. A., Charts for Correlation of Climate Clothing and Men, Climatol. and Environ. Prot. Sec., Quartermaster R. and D. Br., Lawrence, Massachusetts, Dec. 1944.

[387] Siple, P. A., Clothing and Climate, in *Physiology of Heat Regulation and the Science of Clothing,* Chap. 12 (Newburgh, L. H., ed.), Saunders, Philadelphia, 1949, pp. 389-442.

[388] *Ibid.,* p. 433.

[389] Siple, P. A., *90° South,* Putnam, New York, 1959.

[390] Sissenwine, N., and Court, A., Climatic Extremes for Military Equipment, Rept. No. 146, Environ. Prot. Br., R. and D. Div., OQMG, Washington, D.C., Nov. 1951. PB 121 741.

[391] Smuts, J. C., *Holism and Evolution,* Macmillan, New York, 1926, p. 104.

[392] Sookne, A. M., Minor, F. W., and Harris, M., Comparative Rain Resistance of Various Wool Fabrics, *Am. Dyestuff Reptr.*, **39**, 548-554 (1950).

[393] Spain, R. G., and Sanger, A. V., Development of a Fabric to Provide Personal Protection from Toxic Materials, Tech. Rept. WADD 60-198, Wright-Patterson AFB, Dayton, Ohio, June 1960. PB 171 058.

[394] Spano, L. A., Universal Protective Clothing System (Thermalibrium Concept), Vol. I, Chem. and Plast. Div., Quartermaster R. and Eng. Center, Natick, Massachusetts, June 1960.

[395] Spano, L. A., Universal Protective Clothing System (Thermalibrium Concept), Vol. II, Chem. and Plast. Div., Quartermaster R. and Eng. Center, Natick, Massachusetts, June 1960.

[396] Spano, L. A., Universal Protective Clothing System (Thermalibrium Concept), Vol. III, Chem. and Plast. Div., Quartermaster R. and Eng. Center, Natick, Massachusetts, June 1960.

[397] Speakman, J. B., and Chamberlain, N. H., The Thermal Conductivity of Textile Materials and Fabrics, *J. Textile Inst.*, **21**, T29-T56 (1930).

[398] Speakman, J. B., and Cooper, C. A., The Influence of Temperature on the Affinity of Wool for Water, *J. Textile Inst.*, **27**, T191-T196 (1936).

[399] Spealman, C. R., Pace, N., and White, W. A., Jr., Heat Exchange by Way of the Respiratory Tract: I. Theoretical Considerations; II. Relative Efficacy for Conserving Heat Loss of the (1) Salathiel Breath Heat Exchanger, (2) A-14 Rubber Mask, (3) Wool Scarf, Res. Project X-163, Naval Med. Res. Inst., Bethesda, Maryland, Apr. 1944.

[400] Spector, W. S., ed., *Handbook of Biological Data*, Table 147, Stature, Weight, and Surface Area: Man, Various Nationalities and Types, Saunders, Philadelphia, 1956, p. 176.

[401] *Ibid.*, Table 315, Energy Cost, Work: Man; Table 316, Energy Cost, Progression: Man, pp. 347-349.

[402] *Ibid.*, Table 318, Physical Training, Effects on Man, p. 352.

[403] Sprague, M. E., and Ross, C. W., World Guide for Field Clothing, Tech. Rept. EP 1105, Quartermaster R. and D. Command, Natick, Massachusetts, July 1959. PB 143 719.

[404] Steele, R., Factors Affecting the Drying of Apparel Fabrics: Part I. Drying Behavior, *Textile Res. J.*, **28**, 136-144 (1958).

[405] Steele, R., Factors Affecting the Drying of Apparel Fabrics:

Part II. Capillary Size Distribution, *Textile Res. J.,* **28**, 144-147 (1958).

[406] Steele, R., Factors Affecting the Drying of Apparel Fabrics: Part III. Finishing Agents, *Textile Res. J.,* **29**, 960-966 (1959).

[407] Stevens, J. C., and Stevens, S. S., The Dynamics of Subjective Warmth and Cold, in *Temperature, Its Measurement and Control in Science and Industry,* Vol. 3, Part 3 (Hardy, J. D., ed.), Reinhold, New York, 1963, pp. 239-243.

[408] Stevens, S. S., To Honor Fechner and Repeal His Law, *Science,* **133**, 80-86 (1961).

[409] Stimson, H. F., International Practical Temperature Scale of 1948, Text Revision of 1960, *Natl. Bur. Std.* Monograph 37 (Sept. 1961).

[410] Stoll, A. M., and Hardy, J. D., Direct Experimental Comparison of Several Surface Temperature Measuring Devices, *Rev. Sci. Instr.,* **20**, 678-686 (1949).

[411] Stoll, R. G., Functional Characteristics of Wool Fabrics for Military Uses, Textile Eng. Div., Quartermaster R. and D. Lab., Natick, Massachusetts, Feb. 1951.

[412] Stoll, R. G., Potential Constructions and Processes to Conserve Wool in Quartermaster Textiles, TMEL Rept. No. 42, Textile, Clothing and Footwear Sec., Military Planning Div., OQMG, Natick, Massachusetts, Nov. 1950.

[413] Sunderland, W. F., and Boerner, F., *Normal Values in Clinical Medicine,* Saunders, Philadelphia, 1950.

[414] Tallant, J. D., and Worner, R. K., Apparatus for Evaluating Warmth of Textile Fabrics, *Textile Res. J.,* **21**, 591-596 (1951).

[415] Teichner, W. H., Assessment of Mean Body Surface Temperature, *J. Appl. Physiol.,* **12**, 169-176 (1958).

[416] Tesoro, G. C., Sello, S. B., and Willard, J. J., Flame-Retardant Properties of Phosphonate Derivatives of Cotton Cellulose, *Textile Res. J.,* **38**, 245-256 (1968).

[417] Tesoro, G. C., Flame Retardant Fabrics: Are Researchers on the Right Track?, *Textile Chemist and Colorist,* **1**, 307-310 (1969).

[418] Textile Institute, Annual Conference, Fibre Blends and Mixtures-Developments since 1952, *J. Textile Inst.,* **49**, P351-P434 (1958).

[419] Thurstone, L. L., *The Measurement of Values,* Univ. of Chicago Press, Chicago, Illinois, 1959.

[420] Townend, P. P., and Marsden-Smedley, A. B., Some Properties of Wool/Nylon Staple Mixture Yarns and Cloths, *J. Textile Inst.,* **41**, T178-T191 (1950).

[421] Turl, L. H., The Protection of Man against the Cold/Salt/Wet Environment, Sixth Commonwealth Defense Conf. Clothing and General Stores, Australia, 1959.

[422] Turl, L. H., and Kennedy, J. E., The Measurement of the Resistance of Materials to Water Vapor Diffusion by the Control Dish Method, Seventh Commonwealth Defense Conf. Clothing and General Stores, United Kingdom, 1961.

[423] Turl, L. H., and Kennedy, J. E., A Study of the Micro-Climate in Military Footwear, Eighth Commonwealth Conf. Clothing and General Stores, Australia, 1965.

[424] Turrell, E. S., Robinson, S., and Gerking, S. D., Studies of Nylon and Cotton Clothing for Men Working in Humid Heat, Interim Rept. No. 6, OSRD Contr. No. OEM-cmr-351, Comm. Med. Res., Office of Sci. R. and D., Washington, D.C., Feb. 1944.

[425] Urquhart, A. R., and Williams, A. M., The Moisture Relations of Cotton: The Effect of Temperature on the Absorption of Water by Soda-Boiled Cotton, *J. Textile Inst.*, **15**, T559-T572 (1924).

[426] Valko, E. I., Antistatic Agents, in *Encyclopedia of Polymer Science and Technology*, Vol. 2, Wiley-Interscience, New York, 1965, pp. 204-228.

[427] Valko, E. I., Tesoro, G. C., and Ginilewicz, W., Elimination of Static Electricity from Textiles by Chemical Finishing, *Am. Dyestuff Reptr.*, **47**, P403-P409 (1958).

[428] Van Dilla, M., Day, R., and Siple, P. A., Special Problem of Hands, in *Physiology of Heat Regulation and the Science of Clothing* (Newburgh, L. H., ed.), Saunders, Philadelphia, 1949, pp. 374-386.

[429] Van Dilla, M., Malakos, D., and Fitzgerald, J. E., Jr., Measurement of Moisture in Textiles, Rept. No. 186-B, Quartermaster Clim. Res. Lab., Lawrence, Massachusetts, Nov. 1945.

[430] Van Wyk, C. M., Note on the Compressibility of Wool, *J. Textile Inst.*, **37**, T285-T292 (1946).

[431] Vaughan, J. A., MacLeod, A. R., and Iampietro, P. F., Some Physiological Responses of Men Wearing Body Armor in the Desert, Tech. Rept. EP-44, Environ. Prot. Div., Quartermaster R. and D. Center, Natick, Massachusetts, Mar. 1957.

[432] Veblen, T., *The Theory of the Leisure Class*, Macmillan, New York, 1899; New American Library, New York, 1952.

[433] Veghte, J. H., and Webb, P., Clothing and Tolerance to Heat, WADC Tech. Rept. 57-759, Wright Air Dev. Center, Wright-Patterson AFB, Dayton, Ohio, Dec. 1957. AD 142 248.

[434] Waldron, E. T., The Effect of Sample Weight on the Heat Transfer and Ignition Characteristics of a Series of 60/40 Cotton/Nylon Blends, TFFR No. 196, Clothing and Org. Mat. Div., Quartermaster R. and Eng. Center, Natick, Massachusetts, Nov. 1961. PB 160 948.

[435] Waldron, E. T., Textiles for Thermal Radiation Protection, Tech. Rept. TS-132, Clothing and Org. Mat. Div., U.S. Army Natick Lab., Natick, Massachusetts, Apr. 1965. AD 617 707.

[436] Waldron, E. T., The Effect of Textile Finishes on Thermal Protection, *Textile Chemist and Colorist,* **1**, 130-134 (1969).

[437] Walsh, J. W. T., *Photometry,* 3rd ed., Constable, London, 1958, pp. 35-36.

[438] Washburn, E. W., The Dynamics of Capillary Flow, *Phys. Rev.,* **17**, 273-283 (1921).

[439] Webb, P., and Annis, J. A., Bio-Thermal Responses to Varied Work Programs in Men Kept Thermally Neutral by Water-Cooled Clothing, Contr. Rept. CR-739, Contr. No. NASW-1306, National Aeronautics and Space Administration, Washington, D.C., Apr. 1967.

[440] Weiner, Louis I., Some Principles of Construction of Water-Resistant Fabrics, presented at meeting of Am. Assoc. Textile Technol., Feb. 1951.

[441] Werden, J. E., Fahnestock, M. K., and Galbraith, R. L., Thermal Comfort of Clothing of Varying Fiber Content, *Textile Res. J.,* **29**, 640-651 (1959).

[442] Wexler, A. and Hasegawa, S., Relative Humidity—Temperature Relationships of Some Saturated Salt Solutions in the Temperature Range 0°C to 50°C, *J. Res. Natl. Bur. Std.,* **53**, 19-26 (1954).

[443] Weyer, E. W., Advances in Biomedical Computer Applications, *Ann. N.Y. Acad. Sci.,* **128**, 721-1116 (1966).

[444] Whelan, M. E., MacHattie, L. E., Goodings, A. C., and Turl, L. H., The Diffusion of Water Vapor through Laminae with Particular Reference to Textile Fabrics: Part I. Method of Measurement, *Textile Res. J.,* **25**, 197-205 (1955). Correction: *Textile Res. J.,* **27**, 418 (1957).

[445] Whelan, M. E., MacHattie, L. E., Goodings, A. C., and Turl, C. H., The Diffusion of Water Vapor through Laminae with Particular Reference to Textile Fabrics: Part III. The Resistance of Fabrics to the Passage of Water Vapor by Diffusion, *Textile Res. J.,* **25**, 211-223 (1955).

[446] Wilcox, R. T., *The Mode in Costume,* Scribner's, New York, 1958.

[447] *Ibid.,* Chap. 23, pp. 141-148.

[448] Wiley, S. C., Dodd, A. V., and Chambers, J. V., Handbook of Fort Sherman and Fort Gulick, Panama Canal Zone, Tech. Rept. EP17, Environ. Prot. Div., Quartermaster R. and D. Center, Natick, Massachusetts, July 1955. PB 118 437.

[449] Williams, C. G., and Wyndham, C. H., Heat Reactions of U.S. Students during a Multi-Temperature Test, *J. Appl. Physiol.,* **24,** 800-808 (1968).

[450] Willis, C. A., and Long, C. W., Evaluation of Experimental Wool Synthetic Blends in Air Force 18-oz. Blue Serge, WADC Tech. Rept. 54-52, Mat. Lab., USAF Air R. and D. Command, Wright-Patterson AFB, Dayton, Ohio, Nov. 1954. PB 111 676.

[451] Wing, P., and Monego, C. J., A Comparison of Cenco-Fitch and Guarded Hot Plate Methods by Measuring Thermal Insulation, TELR No. 184, Textile, Clothing and Footwear Div., Quartermaster R. and D. Center, Natick, Massachusetts, Apr. 1957.

[452] Wing, P., and Monego, C. J., Optimum Spacing of Hot-Weather Clothing for Convective Cooling, TELR No. 186, Textile, Clothing and Footwear Div., Quartermaster R. and D. Center, Natick, Massachusetts, May 1957.

[453] Winn, L. J., and Schwarz, E. R., Textile Finishing Treatments: IV. A Comparison of Certain Methods of Measuring Stiffness in Fabrics, *Am. Dyestuff Reptr.,* **29,** 469-476 (1940).

[454] Winslow, C. E. A., and Gagge, A. P., Influence of Physical Work on Physiological Reactions to the Thermal Environment, *Am. J. Physiol.,* **134,** 664-681 (1941).

[455] Winslow, C. E. A., Gagge, A. P., and Herrington, L. P., The Influence of Air Movement upon Heat Losses from the Clothed Human Body, *Am. J. Physiol.,* **127,** 505-518 (1939).

[456] Winslow, C. E. A., Herrington, L. P., and Gagge, A. P., A New Method of Partitional Calorimetry, *Am. J. Physiol.,* **116,** 641-655 (1936).

[457] Winslow, C. E. A., Herrington, L. P., and Gagge, A. P., Physiological Reactions of the Human Body to Varying Environmental Temperatures, *Am. J. Physiol.,* **120,** 1-22 (1937).

[458] Winslow, C. E. A., Herrington, L. P., and Gagge, A. P., Physiological Reactions and Sensations of Pleasantness under Varying Atmospheric Conditions, *Am. Soc. Heating and Ventilating Eng. Trans.,* **44,** 179-194 (1939).

[459] Winslow, C. E. A., Herrington, L. P., and Gagge, A. P., Relations between Atmospheric Conditions, Physiological Reactions and Sensations of Pleasantness, *Am. J. Hyg.,* **26**, 103-115 (1937).

[460] Winston, G., and Kennedy, S. J., Sizing and Fitting of Cold Climate Functional Clothing, Rept. No. A 386, Quartermaster R. and D. Div., Natick Lab., Natick, Massachusetts, May 1953.

[461] Woodcock, A. H., Moisture Permeability Index—A New Index for Describing Evaporative Heat Transfer through Fabric Systems, Tech. Rept. EP-149, Environ. Prot. Res. Div., Quartermaster R. and Eng. Center, Natick, Massachusetts, June 1961. AD 265 286.

[462] Woodcock, A. H., Moisture Transfer in Textile Systems: Part I, *Textile Res. J.,* **32**, 628-633 (1962).

[463] Woodcock, A. H., Moisture Transfer in Textile Systems: Part II, *Textile Res. J.,* **32**, 719-723 (1962).

[464] Woodcock, A. H., Wet-Cold: II. A Theoretical Interpretation of the Sensation of Damp Cold Experienced by Clothed Man, Rept. No. 199, Environ. Prot. Br., Quartermaster Clim. Res. Lab., Lawrence, Massachusetts, Feb. 1953.

[465] Woodcock, A. H., Breckenridge, J. R., Pratt, R. L., and Powers, J. J., Factors in Heat Stress, *Mech. Eng.,* **79**, 1029 (1957).

[466] Woodcock, A. H., and Dee, T. E., Jr., Wet-Cold: I. Effect of Moisture on Transfer of Heat Through Insulating Materials, Rept. No. 170, Environ. Prot. Sec., R. and D. Br., Quartermaster Clim. Res. Lab., Lawrence, Massachusetts, Dec. 1950. PB 111 639.

[467] Woodcock, A. H., and Goldman, R. F., A Technique for Measuring Clothing Insulation under Dynamic Conditions, Tech. Rept. EP-137, Environ. Prot. Sec., Quartermaster R. and Eng. Center, Natick, Massachusetts, July 1960. PB 150 748.

[468] Woodcock, A. H., Powers, J. J., Jr., and Breckenridge, J. R., Man's Thermal Balance in Warm Environments, Tech. Rept. EP-30, Environ. Prot. Res. Div., Quartermaster R. and D. Center, Natick, Massachusetts, July 1956. PB 124 637.

[469] Woodcock, A. H., Pratt, R. L., and Breckenridge, J. R., A Theoretical Method for Assessing Heat Exchange between Man and a Hot Environment, Rept. No. 183, Environ. Prot. Br., Quartermaster Clim. Res. Lab., Lawrence, Massachusetts, Jan. 1952.

[470] Woodcock, A. H., Pratt, R. L., and Breckenridge, J. R., Theory of the Globe Thermometer, Res. Study Rept. BP-7, Biophysics Br., Environ. Prot. Res. Div., Quartermaster R. and Eng. Center, Natick, Massachusetts, Sept. 1957.

[471] Wulsin, F. R., Adaptations to Climate among Non-European Peoples, in *Physiology of Heat Regulation and the Science of Clothing,* Chap. I, (Newburgh, L. H., ed.), Saunders, Philadelphia, 1949, pp. 3-69.

[472] Yaglou, C. P., Thermometry, in *Physiology of Heat Regulation and the Science of Clothing,* Chap. II (Newburgh, L. H., ed.), Saunders, Philadelphia, 1949, p. 75.

[473] Yaglou, C. P., and Rao, M. N., Loose versus Close-Fitting Clothing for Work in "Tropical Heat," *J. Ind. Hyg. Toxicol.,* **29**, 140-142 (1947).

[474] Yoshimura, T., Four Japan Firms Develop Antistatic Synthetics, Tokyo Bureau, McGraw-Hill World News, News Release, New York (Nov. 22, 1968).

[475] Zagieboylo, W., and Frederick, E. B., Measurement of the Needle Heat Generated during the Sewing of Wool and Wool-Nylon Fabrics, TMEL Rept. No. 124, Textile and Leather Div., Quartermaster R. and D. Lab., Natick, Massachusetts, Dec. 1953.

[476] Zisman, W. A., Relation of the Equilibrium Angle to Liquid and Solid Construction, in *Contact Angle, Wettability and Adhesion; Advances in Chemistry, Series 43* (Gould, R., ed.), Am. Chem. Soc., Washington, D.C., 1964, pp. 1-51.

[477] Zoch, R. T., The Climatic Handbook for Washington, D.C., Weather Bureau Tech. Paper No. 8, Div. Climatol. and Hydrol. Services, U.S. Dept. of Commerce, Washington, D.C., 1949.

AUTHOR INDEX

Numbers in parentheses are reference numbers and indicate that an author's work is referred to although his name is not cited in the text. Numbers in italics show the page on which the complete reference is listed.

SUBJECT INDEX

A

Acceptability, 7, 79, 92, 106
Acclimatization, 23, 111
Activities, metabolic cost, 20, 22,
    105, 108
Activity, see body motion
Air
    film, 33, 40, 71
    fractional volume in fabric, 31
    insulation of, 34, 39
    layers, 34, 86, 116
    movement, 13, 34, 42, 72, 103,
        152
Arctic uniforms, 36, 78
Area, see surface
Atmospheric pressure, 11
    low, 86

B

Balance, heat, 1
Barometric correction, weighing, 18
Behavioral adjustments (closed-open-
    loose), 6, 44, 45, 54
Belt, 58
Bending properties, 6, 165-168, 182
Body,
    clothing, 57
    motion, 41, 53, 58, 102-104

specific heat of, 108
temperature, calculation, 108
Bulked yarns, 166, 179, 184

C

Calorimetry, 92, 107
    partitional, 65, 77, 107
Cape, 57
Carbon Dioxide, 107
Celsius temperature, 11
Chimney effect, 35, 53, 58, 86, 175
Chromotropic materials, 163
Cleansing, frequency, 114
Climate, 24
Cling, 44, 106
Clo, 8, 15, 17, 48, 60, 201
    minimum perceptible, 48
    per unit thickness, 16, 37
Closures, 6, 46, 103
Clothing
    appearance, 2
    as air, 31
    climatic requirements, 24
    extension of body, 1
    temperature, 1
Cold-dry, 24
Cold, hazards, 110
Cold Stress, 67, 78
Cold-wet, 24, 177